OF A FEATHER

OF A

Harcourt, Inc.

Orlando Austin New York
San Diego London

FEATHER

A BRIEF HISTORY
OF AMERICAN BIRDING

Scott Weidensaul

www.HarcourtBooks.com

E. B. White's "A Listener's Guide to the Birds," is from
Poems and Sketches of E. B. White, copyright 1981 by E. B. White.
Used by permission of HarperCollins, Inc.

Library of Congress Cataloging-in-Publication Data
Weidensaul, Scott.
Of a feather: a brief history of American birding/
Scott Weidensaul.—1st ed.
p. cm.
Includes bibliographical references and index.
1. Ornithology—United States—History. 2. Bird watching—United
States—History. I. Title.
QL682.W45 2007
598—dc22 2007007364
ISBN 978-0-15-101247-3

Text set in Fournier MT
Designed by Lydia D'moch

Printed in the United States of America

First edition
C E G I K J H F D B

To Amy, with love

Contents

1

"Birds . . . more beautiful than in Europe"

IT WAS A COOL, lightly foggy day along the midcoast of Maine, the cries of herring gulls mixing with the throb of lobster boat engines out in Muscongus Bay. A dozen and a half birders were strung out along a beaver pond, spotting scopes perched atop tripods, their binoculars focused on a tangle of blueberry bushes and scraggly, head-high tamaracks that poked up from the boggy mat of sphagnum moss spangled with tiny pink orchids.

Bonnie Bochan, an ornithologist who splits her time between Maine and the Ecuadorian rain forest, stared intently at the thicket, from which a thin, slow trill emerged. "That's a swamp sparrow," Bonnie said quietly. "It sounds a lot like the pine warblers and juncos we've been hearing, but its trill isn't as musical as the junco's, and it's not as fast as the pine warbler's—you can almost count each syllable." As though on cue, the sparrow itself hopped into view, tipped back its head and sang—a dusky bird with bright rufous wings and a dark brown cap, the feathers of its white throat quivering in song.

A little sigh rippled through the group; for most of them, this was a new species, a life bird, and some had come from as far away as California to see it. A few were experienced birders, most of the others complete novices, but all were dressed, as birders are wont to do, with more of an eye toward practicality than fashion— nylon pants tucked into socks, wide-brimmed Gortex hats snugged under chins, outsized vests with pockets big enough for field guides, bug repellent, and water bottles. They wore mismatched rain pants and coats of differing vintage and color, but always muted—nothing so bright that it would scare the birds.

I glanced down at myself: shabby green rain pants, a dark blue raincoat that had seen better days, a scruffy ball cap, and worn boots. Except for the expensive binoculars around my neck, I looked a bit like a hobo. I fit in perfectly.

Every summer, I help teach a course in field ornithology on this surpassingly lovely part of the Maine coast, at an Audubon camp on Hog Island, a 330-acre sanctuary near the town of Damariscotta. For more than seventy years, birders have been coming to this spruce-clad island, including some of the greatest names in birding and bird science. When the island was donated to the National Audubon Society in 1936, NAS director John Baker dispatched a young grad student named Olin Sewall Pettingill Jr. to inspect the place, with an eye toward turning it into an educational camp for adults. Pettingill—who later became the director of the famed Cornell Lab of Ornithology—gave it an enthusiastic thumbs-up, so Baker turned to the question of staffing. He had just the fellow to teach about birds—a chap named Roger Tory Peterson, who had published a revolutionary field guide two years earlier, and had just been placed in charge of Audubon's education program. Peterson—in his twenties, single and good-looking—competed for birds (and for the attention of the young women campers) with Allan Cruickshank, another Audubon staffer who would go on to fame as a writer and bird photographer.

The list goes on and on, from John James Audubon, who passed through the area in 1832–33, to Rachel Carson, who lived just down the coast and wrote about the old ship's chandlery on Hog Island. Kenn Kaufman, who has lifted Peterson's mantle as one of the great popularizers of birding, is an instructor. Audubon scientist Steve Kress worked in the camp kitchen one summer as a college kid, in his spare time reading accounts of the old seabird colonies in the Gulf of Maine and wondering if the birds could somehow be brought back to places like lonely Eastern Egg Rock, nine miles offshore. Today, he is a pioneer in seabird restoration, and thanks to him, puffins again nest on Eastern Egg and many other Maine islands.

Kids keep coming to Hog Island, and dreaming. Along with the thirty-five adults, we had more than a dozen eager teen birders in camp that week, including Eve, whose bleached, bobbed hair had been dyed pink and orange, and Raymond, intense, focused, and mature beyond his seventeen years. Two years earlier, I'd taught Raymond's best friend Ryan, and I was shocked when, the following summer, Ryan had been killed in a car crash while the two boys were on a birding trip. The wreck had almost killed Raymond, too, but he'd survived, and was following through on plans he and Ryan had made, continuing with a sophisticated research project they'd begun together to study the rosy-finches of the New Mexico mountains.

Birding and ornithology; sport and science; amateur and professional. The gulf between the two seems pretty wide today, but in fact it's a fairly recent phenomenon. For most of the history of bird study, there was no such division; the ornithologists were all gifted amateurs, and the science of studying birds was enmeshed with the joy of watching them. Even today, as Raymond's project shows, the threads that link hobby and profession are thick and entangling. "Citizen-science" is the buzzword for public participation in all manner of censuses, surveys, and field research projects, but it goes deeper than that. One friend of mine, the man who knows more about ruby-throated hummingbirds than almost anyone in the world, is a retired electrician, and he's hardly alone. Every fall, I oversee an owl migration study, one combining banding, genetics, and radiotelemetry. Among the nearly one hundred people helping out are, not surprisingly, several wildlife biologists donating their time—but my crew also includes a plumber, a math teacher, a retired soft-drink executive, and a former music teacher who repairs pianos.

And it's hard to find an academically trained ornithologist with a string of initials after his or her name who isn't also an avid birder. I don't know many structural engineers who devote their free time to visiting highway overpasses for fun, but there is something about birds that makes even those whose nine-to-five jobs are ornithological pick up their binoculars as soon as the workday is finished. That's because in almost every case, the job followed the passion, not the other way around. Call it all "bird study," and forget the distinctions.

The number of people with that passion keeps growing, too. Just as the birders keep swarming to Hog Island each year, so do they jam the trails at Santa Ana National Wildlife Refuge in south Texas looking for chachalacas and whistling-ducks, or the scrubby thickets of Cape May, New Jersey, when the warblers are dropping from the sky and the merlins and peregrines are hurtling past the dunes. They come to Point Reyes on the northern California coast, to Point Pelee in Lake Erie, and Whitefish Point in Michigan; they know that the rocky man-made islands of the Chesapeake Bay Bridge-Tunnel attract the damndest rarities, like western rock wrens and Asian black-tailed gulls, and they made an obscure roadside rest stop near Patagonia, Arizona, so celebrated for the exotic Mexican birds that turn up there that the phrase "Patagonia picnictable effect" entered the lexicon.

Birders stalk Central Park in Manhattan, the Mount Auburn cemetery near Boston, and Rock Creek Park in Washington, DC; they haunt the man-made Bellona Marsh in Los Angeles, Agua Caliente Park in Tucson, and Sauvie Island near Portland. They have made famous, at least within their circles, places that would make the general public blanch: the landfill at Brownsville, Texas, where you can usually find Chihuahuan ravens and an occasional Tamaulipan crow (and proximity to which is an actual selling point for nearby RV parks that cater to birders); or sewage treatment lagoons like Mitchell Lake in San Antonio, which is so birdy it has its own Audubon center. Among the hundreds of sites along the Nebraska Birding Trail are stops at sewage lagoons in Oshkosh and North Platte, but sadly, not everyone sees the attraction; the committee creating a Washington State birding trail specifically nixed including such lagoons on its list of hot spots, saying, "There may be birds, but sewage lagoons are not tourist attractions." Which tells me the people creating the Washington birding trail weren't *really* birders. Did they miss the article in *Birding* magazine a few years back, "North America's Topflight Sewage Ponds"? There's nothing like a good whiff of primary effluent to clear the sinuses on a cold morning.

How many of us are there? The latest surveys by the U.S. Fish and Wildlife Service suggest there are 46 million birders in the United States, while another study, also sponsored by the feds but looking at all outdoor recreation, put the figure at 67.8 million— either of which would be impressive, if it were accurate. The USFWS, for instance, counts as a birder anyone who makes an effort to watch or attract birds, which means anyone who hangs a sunflower feeder or plants ornamental sage in the hope of luring hummingbirds is a "birder," whether or not they ever crack open a field guide or join a Christmas Bird Count. (Of those 46 million, the USFWS admitted only 6 million could identify more than twenty species of birds.) But these and other studies agree that birding is one of (if not the) fastest-growing outdoor hobbies in the country. In the 1980s and 1990s, the last period for which numbers are available, it grew at more than 155 percent, more than twice the rate for the next-closest sport, hiking.

It was not always so, of course. Birding as a popular hobby in America was a phenomenon of the twentieth century, especially the decades after World War II, fueled by greater leisure time, affordable optics, and good field guides that made sense of the pleasantly confusing welter of species that fill the forests and marshes. But bird study itself, the foundation on which modern American birding rests, goes back much further than that—back through the nineteenth century, when frontier ornithologists risked an arrow between the ribs to collect new birds, back through the eighteenth and even the seventeenth centuries, back to the dawn of colonization, when the avian wonders of a new continent were unfolding before amazed Caucasian eyes, and exciting the interest of scientists in the Old World. The history of bird study on this continent is bound up with tales of liars, drunks, slave-runners and scoundrels of every unfortunate stripe. They were, in a few luminous cases, also brilliant naturalists in the bargain—and they were, not incidentally, the men who discovered America for Europe.

THE FIRST AMERICAN field ornithologists were the Indians, of course, whose knowledge of birdlife was based on deep association, long observation, and at times lifesaving necessity. Birds featured prominently in the social, religious, medical, and (naturally) gastronomic life of North America's myriad Native tribes, but tragically, much of this traditional ornithology was lost to warfare, disease, and assimilation once the Europeans arrived. A lot of what's left comes to us through the decidedly unreliable lens of accounts written by non-Indians.

Birds populated many Native stories and myths. The raven—often depicted as a morally ambiguous trickster deity—figures prominently in many cultures, particularly in the Arctic and Pacific Northwest. Birds played a role in many creation stories, like the crow who nags the Creator in Lakota mythology into creating dry land from an eternity of water. Other stories spoke of the origin of the birds themselves. According to one tradition among the Chiricahua Apache, the hero Child of the Water killed a buffalo, filled its intestines with blood, and wrapped himself in them, waiting for a hungry golden eagle to carry him back to its aerie. There, he killed both adults with his stone ax, and all of the eaglets save one, which he forced to carry him back down from the high cliff. Then Child of the Water killed that eagle, too, and, pulling out the feathers from the dead raptors, scattered them to the winds, saying, "Let these become all varieties of birds!" In this way, the Apache said, Child of the Water created the birds of the Southwest.

The serendipitously named George Bird Grinnell, a pioneering ornithologist who later founded the first Audubon Society, spent years with the Plains tribes, beginning in the 1870s, recording their stories. In one Blackfoot tale from Montana that Grinnell learned, the trickster figure Old Man fools a bunch of ducks into dancing with their eyes closed while he knocks them on the head, one by one, for his meal; at last, the smallest duck peeks, sees what's happening, and sounds the alarm. This bird became "the red-eyed duck," the Blackfoot elders said, the wary horned grebe that is always the first to spot danger.

Native mythology often used birds to tell moral tales, like fables the world over. In other cases, however, Indians passed on to ethnographers what they considered the mundane details of the natural world—and it sometimes took western science a long time to catch up. The Hopi knew the poorwill, a western relative of the whip-poor-will and common nighthawk, as *hölchoko*, "the sleeping one," believing it passed the winter in a deathlike trance. What ignorant balderdash, white ornithologists scoffed—until in the 1940s several hibernating poorwills were found in the California desert. (Sadly, I don't know the Hopi term for "We told you so.")

So while almost every history of American ornithology begins in early nineteenth-century Philadelphia with Alexander Wilson and John James Audubon casting the mold of this branch of science (and the modern boom of recreational birding that grew from it, and repeatedly merged with it), they were hardly the first to give serious thought to the New World's birdlife. In fact, they weren't even the first Europeans to do so. The young Englishman Mark Catesby spent the better part of two decades, beginning in 1712, describing, collecting, and painting the plants and animals of the

Southeast, and his work was built on that of earlier explorers dating back as much as a century and a half.

From almost the very first moment that European ships dropped anchor in the waters of North America, the visitors made awed note of the continent's teeming skies and waterways, alive with birds. And if these early accounts lacked the scientific rigor that others later brought to the endeavor, they do offer a priceless glimpse of an aboriginal land and its wildlife.

The Vikings, so far as we know, were the first Europeans to find themselves in North America, exploring and briefly settling Newfoundland and the Canadian Maritimes around A.D. 1000. Their oral histories, finally written down in the thirteenth century as the *Graenlendinga Saga,* give scant notice to birds, except to comment on unusually rich seabird colonies in the North Atlantic, or when the presence of birds signaled the approach of land.

The Spaniards, focused with tunnel vision on gold, slaves, and converts, glossed over much mention of birds; the memoirs of Cabeza de Vaca—who fought his way through Florida, then was shipwrecked near Galveston in 1528 and spent eight years in the Southwest, trying to get back to Mexico—makes only passing mention of birds, and then only in terms of food. Later conquistadors did little better, and the first significant attention by Europeans to the western hemisphere's birds came from the French and English. In 1562, a French expedition to the coasts of Florida, Georgia, and South Carolina reported (in the contemporary English translation) "faire meadows . . . full of Hernes, Curlues, Bitters, Mallards, Egrepths, Woodcocks, and all other kinds of small birds." Jacques Le Moyne, an artist who in 1564 spent a year with the French garrison near present-day Beaufort, South Carolina, drew wild turkey gobblers in full display, along with alligators, manatees, and deer.

But the story of early American ornithology is largely an English one, beginning with John White. A man of somewhat mysterious origins, White left a limited but remarkable visual record of sixteenth-century wildlife near the colony of Roanoke, on the North Carolina coast. Little is known about him, and any discussion of him is peppered with uncertainties; he may have had a background in engineering, and he almost certainly had formal training as an artist. White may also have seen quite a bit of North America before he even arrived in Roanoke; historians believe he may have been part of the 1577 Frobisher expedition to the Arctic (his painting of a battle with the Inuit, they argue, could only have been made by an eyewitness), and it's also suspected that he was part of the 1584 Amadas and Barlowe expedition along the East Coast.

The Englishmen who visited North America in the sixteenth century were staggered by the natural wealth they saw—the forests, the prosperous Indian villages with their lush gardens, the game and wild birds. "Having discharged our harquebuz-shot," captains Amadas and Barlowe wrote, "such a flocke of Cranes (the most part white) arose under us, with such a cry redoubled by many ecchoes, as if an armie of men had showted all together." That is the kind of spectacle that greeted White in 1585 when he returned to America as the staff artist for Roanoke.

White's orders were to "drawe to lief one of each kinde of thing that is strange to us in England." And it was *all* strange and wondrous to an English eye, so White's paintbrush flew across the page. Even though some of his paintings were eventually lost, what remain are of immense historical value. White is best known for his many watercolors of Indian life and culture—robust societies before the decimation of European epidemics—but he also painted a variety of animals, including an alligator, a catfish, and a sea turtle, and more than thirty species of birds, among them brown pelican, bald eagle, eastern towhee, and Baltimore oriole.

White eventually rose to become governor of Roanoke, and his daughter and son-in-law became the parents of the first English child born in America, Virginia Dare. She and the rest of the colonists had, however, disappeared without a trace by 1590, when White returned from England with supply ships. Obscurity was also the fate of White's bird paintings; while the Indian watercolors were published, as engravings, in 1590, his animal art languished for more than a century before coming to light again in England.

Such attention as White's to the specifics of the New World's birdlife was rare, however. The Spaniards, gold-hungry to the last, left almost no record of what birds they encountered in Florida or the Southwest. The English, on the other hand, weren't looking as single-mindedly for treasure; many of the gentlemen adventurers who wrote about America were essentially land speculators, eager to convert royal land-grants into income by selling their version of paradise to potential colonists back in England. Birds thus became one more item in a laundry list of enticements, to be dangled before an eager audience.

"Squirels, Conies, Black Birds with crimson wings, and divers other Fowles and Birds of divers and sundrie collours of crimson, Watchet, Yellow, Greene, Murry, and of divers other hewes naturally without any art using," wrote George Percy in 1606, tallying what he'd seen in his visit to Virginia. "We found store of Turkie nests and many Egges, if it had not beene disliked, because the ship could not ride neere the shoare, we had setled there to all the Collonies contentment."

"The Turkyes of that Countrie are great, and fat, and exceeding in plentie," agreed the Council for Virginia, in 1610. "The rivers from August, or September, till February, are covered with flocks of Wildfoule: as swannes, geese, ducke, mallard, teal, wigeons, hearons, bitters, curlewes, godwights, plovers, snights, dottrels, cormerants . . . in such abundance as are not in all the world to be equalled."

The fact that the council's report was titled *A True Declaration of the estate of the Colonie in Virginia, With a confutation of such scandalous reports as have tended to the disgrace of so worthy an enterprise* might have given a suspicious reader pause. But by all accounts (even those not trying to spin a financial angle) the New World was bursting at the seams with birds. "Turkyes" were mentioned at every opportunity, with some observers claiming with straight faces that the wild gobblers exceeded sixty pounds. "Fowls of the air are plentiful here, and of all sorts as we have in England as far as I can learn, and a great many of strange fowls which we know not," wrote the Reverend Francis Higginson about Massachusetts, in 1629. "Here are likewise [an] abundance of turkeys often killed in the woods, far greater than our English turkeys, and exceeding fat, sweet and fleshy."*

Another species that came in for frequent, and unsurprising,

---

*The fact that the wild turkey was the one North American bird that every European could identify is ironic, since it's unlikely any of them, including Rev. Higginson, realized the species was a New World native to start with. Domesticated by Mexican tribes, turkeys were brought to Europe by the Spanish in the first years of the sixteenth century and given a name that had been previously applied to peafowl and guineafowl. Domestic turkeys spread so rapidly across the continent that by 1541, Thomas Cranmer, the Archbishop of Canterbury, issued an edict that no more than one could be served at any state dinner.

mention were the immense flocks of passenger pigeons that migrated through eastern forests. William Penn gushed about them, and Higginson said he'd seen the hordes and eaten them, finding them good. Then he made an astute observation. "They are of all colours as ours are, but their wings and tails are far longer, and therefore it is likely they fly swifter to escape the terrible hawks in this country." "Turkie cockes and Turkie hennes: Stockdoves [another name for passenger pigeons], Partridges, Cranes, Hernes & in winter great store of Swannes & Geese," reported Thomas Hariot (or Harriot), the scientist who accompanied White to Roanoke. "There are also Parats, Faulcons & Marlin haukes."

A modern birder may search in vain through a field guide for many of the species mentioned in these old accounts. *Parats? Marlin haukes?* And what on earth is a *snight?* In fairness, these Englishmen were doing the best they could with make-it-up-as-you-go spelling and often a casual familiarity (at best) with birds—and one usually gained, at that, over the barrel of a gun back in England. For the most part, they did fairly well. *Marlin haukes* were merlins, the same species of sleek, speedy falcon found in the Old World, while *snights* were in all likelihood snipe. As for *parats,* that one is easy, if bittersweet; it seems certain Hariot was describing Carolina parakeets, eastern North America's only native parrot, a green-and-orange dazzler that ranged as far north as Illinois and New York in large, screeching, spectacular flocks.

Among the most interesting accounts, and one often lost in Catesby's shadow (as Catesby is often lost in Audubon's), are the writings of John Lawson, who in 1709 published *A New Voyage to Carolina,* a report of his two-month journey from the coast of South Carolina up into the hill country and back to the coast of North Carolina. Lawson was a surveyor and land speculator, and he must have had an impetuous streak; he had prepared to travel to Rome, when a casual acquaintance mentioned how fine the land was in Carolina—and with that, Lawson canceled his passage to Rome, hopped a different ship, and spent the next eight years in the New World.

As his book makes clear, he was not one of those "Persons of the meaner Sort, and generally of a very slender Education; who, at their Return, [are] uncapable of giving any reasonable Account of what they met." Lawson was a fine naturalist and a keen observer, whether it was of Indian customs or the quality of the soil. Wildlife, particularly birds, come up frequently in his narrative; in fact, he went so far as to declaim, "Birds in America [are] more beautiful than in Europe."

While Lawson shared the usual habit of exaggerating the size of wild turkeys ("I never weigh'd any myself, but have been inform'd of one that weigh'd near sixty Pound Weight"), he was precise in many of his other descriptions, as of this first encounter with the male wood duck, or "scarlet ey'd duck," as he called it. "We all set out for Sapona, killing, in these Creeks, several Ducks of a strange Kind, having a red Circle about their Eyes, like some Pigeons that I have seen, a Top-knot reaching from the Crown of their Heads, almost to the middle of their Backs, and abundance of Feathers of pretty Shades and Colours."

Lawson's report includes a detailed appendix—a modern birder would call it an annotated checklist—on the wildlife of the Carolinas, including at least 136 species of birds, though he acknowledged that others may have "slipt" his memory. Lawson correctly noted the presence of two species of swans in winter—"trompeters" and "hoopers," the former larger and found in freshwater, the other restricted to coastal areas; we know them as trumpeter and tundra swans today, though trumpeters have been long extirpated from the region. He correctly noted that many species of waterfowl and some shorebirds were similar to those in England (a fact that some observers as late as Thomas Jefferson disputed), and for the most part, the natural history information he relayed was accurate.

Of the "Mocking-Bird," he said, "they sing with the greatest Diversity of Notes, that is possible for a Bird to change to . . . They often sit upon our Chimneys in Summer, there being then no Fire in them, and sing the whole Evening and most part of the Night." Lawson also noted what he called "the Ground-Mocking-Bird. She is the same bigness, and of a Cinnamon Colour. This Bird sings excellently well, but is not so common amongst us as the former"— not a bad description of a brown thrasher.

While the names may seem archaic and at times altogether incomprehensible, Lawson's descriptions are usually good enough to determine what he meant. The *Old Wife,* which he said "makes a dismal Noise, as he flies, and ever and anon dips his Bill in the Salt-Water," was the black skimmer. *Sand-Birds* appear to be sanderlings, "about the Bigness of a Lark, [they] frequent our Sand-Beaches; they are a dainty Food, if you will bestow Time and Ammunition to kill them."

He, too, remarked on both *Parrakeetos* "of a green Colour, and Orange-Colour'd half way their Head," and wild pigeons, "which were so numerous in these Parts, that you might see many Millions in a Flock; they sometimes split off the Limbs of stout Oaks, and other Trees, upon which they roost o' Nights . . . At this time of the Year, the Flocks, as they pass by, in great measure, obstruct the Light of the day." But Lawson's greatest enthusiasm—like that of many early English explorers—was reserved for the ruby-throated hummingbird, which was such a marvel that the first reports were dismissed as moonshine by the learned folk back home.

> The Humming-Bird is the Miracle of all our wing'd Animals; He is feather'd as a Bird, and gets his Living as the Bees, by sucking the Honey from each Flower. In some of the larger sort of Flowers, he will bury himself, by diving to suck the bottom of it, so that he is quite cover'd, and oftentimes Children catch them in those Flowers, and keep them alive for five or six days. They are of different Colours, the Cock differing from the Hen. The Cock is of a green, red, Aurora, and other Colours mixt. He is much less than a Wren, and very nimble. His Nest is one of the greatest Pieces of Workmanship the whole Tribe of wing'd Animals can shew, it commonly hanging on a single Bryar, most artificially woven, a small Hole being left to go in and out at. The Eggs are the Bigness of Pease.

Lawson was, for his day, unusually sympathetic to the Indians; writing of the Tuscaroras, he admitted, "They are really better to us, than we are to them; they always give us Victuals at their Quarters, and take care we are arm'd against Hunger and Thirst: We do not so by them (generally speaking) but let them walk by our Doors Hungry, and do not often relieve them."

Among the many customs Lawson described among the local tribes was a particularly gruesome form of torture, in which the victim was impaled with hundreds of pitch pine slivers, then set afire. In this he may have been morbidly prophetic. In 1711, not long after writing to his sponsor in England that he was undertaking a comprehensive natural history of North Carolina, Lawson set out for the lands of the Tuscarora, even though tensions were running high over encroachments by the English for which Lawson, as surveyor-general, was in some measure responsible. Lawson and his companions were seized, and while the rest of the party was eventually released, Lawson was executed—by being set afire, according to some reports, though at other times the Tuscarora said he'd been hanged, or his throat slashed. Regardless, it was the opening act of the two-year Tuscarora War, which ended as disastrously for the tribe as for its first victim.

In April 1712, however, a young Englishman arrived in the colonies, hungry for their natural wonders, who picked up Lawson's mantle (and, it must be said, appropriated some of his and John White's work along the way). At first, however, there was little to distinguish Mark Catesby as a rising star of natural history. In his early thirties, he came from a landed, rather genteel family with excellent connections in Virginia, where an older sister had married a wealthy doctor serving as the colony's secretary of state.

What little we know about Catesby suggests he was then a bit of a dilettante; not especially well-educated, though he seems to have picked up an interest in botany from relatives back in England, where he despaired of living in the country, "too remote from *London* the Center of all Science"; and with no real art background beyond the general introduction a young gentleman would likely receive. Catesby himself left no diary and relatively few letters, so the man who would become pivotal in the development of American ornithology remains something of a cipher.

He spent the next seven years wandering around the countryside, west as far as the Appalachians, and with one sea voyage to Jamaica, but by his own admission, he did little with the opportunity. "In the Seven Years I resided in that Country, (I am ashamed to own it) I chiefly gratified my Inclination in observing and admiring the various Productions of those Countries," he lamented.

Something changed, however, once Catesby returned to England, in 1719. He had not been completely idle in America—he'd shipped botanical specimens and live plants to Chelsea Gardens in England, among others—and his experiences gained him entrée with influential men, some of whom had been correspondents of Lawson's. Now they encouraged him to take up the project his predecessor's death had cut short. Catesby assembled a cadre of important sponsors, including the incoming governor of South Carolina, who agreed to underwrite his further explorations. This was almost derailed by an opportunity to join an expedition to Africa, but that never materialized, and in the spring of 1722, Catesby embarked for the New World once again, landing three months later in Charlestown, South Carolina.

The once-dilettante now had a mission—to create an exhaustive natural history of the American Southeast. It's hard to say what changed—maturity, the recognition of an opportunity to further science, or simple economics, since what modest means Catesby had once enjoyed were now largely gone and he was relying on what his "curious friends" would pay for the specimens he regularly shipped home to England. In any event, he buckled down over the next four years, traipsing around the Carolinas and Georgia, from the coast up into the mountains, "which afforded not only a Succession of new vegetable Appearances, but [the] most delightful Prospects imaginable, besides the Diversion of Hunting Buffello's, Bears, Panthers, and other wild Beasts," into Florida and out to the Bahamas.

Plans to visit Mexico apparently fell through, but Catesby was now in a frenzy of activity, collecting, preserving, and painting plants, birds, mammals, fish, invertebrates, and reptiles. He drew the "Largest White-bill Wood-pecker," the first-ever depiction of the ivory-billed woodpecker; he took note of the ferocious territoriality of the eastern kingbird, which he called "the tyrant," writing later that he saw one batten on to the back of an eagle, forcing the larger bird to eventually land. Confounded in his attempts to collect a yellow-breasted chat, he finally hired an Indian to shoot one. He took painted bunting chicks from the nest, keeping them as pets, though ruefully noting that "when they are brought into this cold Climate, they lose much of their Lustre."

Some of the paintings he shipped back to his sponsors, along with specimens, though not all of the latter survived the ocean crossing; Catesby frequently preserved whole animals in spirits, and sailors—who would hardly let an embalmed rattlesnake stand in the way of a drink—had a habit of tippling away the contents. Birds were crudely stuffed, then safeguarded from insects by dousing the skins with powdered tobacco.

Back to England he sailed in 1726, ready to convert his observations, collections, notes, and paintings into a book—and instead found himself hard against a financial wall. Many of the sponsorships he'd been relying upon in America dried up, since he was no longer sending back specimens, and Catesby was forced to seek a loan from a friend, the Quaker botanist Peter Collinson, and to work as a nurseryman—no doubt growing many of the very North American plants he'd helped introduce to England. For three years he worked as best he could on the first volume of his book, learning to do the engraving and hand-coloring of the plates himself to save money.

The Natural History of Carolina, Florida, and the Bahama Islands came out piecemeal beginning in 1729—issued in installments of

twenty plates and accompanying text over the next three years—
and the reception could hardly have been more gratifying. Besides
brisk sales in England and abroad, the book brought Catesby scientific acclaim, including election as a Fellow of the Royal Society. It
eased his financial situation, and he was able to afford professional
engraving and coloring on the plates for volume 2, which began appearing in 1734 and were completed nine years later.

Catesby's book is generally credited with being the first true
ornithological text dealing with American birds, but it owed heavily to the work of Lawson and White—some of which Catesby
credited, and some of which he did not. When writing of Indians,
he gave ample credit to Lawson's "curious sketch of the natural
dispositions, customs, etc. of these savages," saying that his observations confirmed what Lawson had written, and suggesting that
there was no need for him to reinvent the wheel.

But as ornithologist Alan Feduccia and others have noted, the
overall structure of Catesby's text was strikingly similar to Lawson's, right down to some of the descriptions, such as that of the
white-tailed deer. Such borrowing was common in those days, and
even egregious plagiarism did not carry the same stigma it does
today. In fact, this was not even the worst case of intellectual theft
regarding poor Lawson's work; the 1737 *Natural History of North-
Carolina*, written by (and one uses the term loosely) John Brickell,
is essentially a verbatim copy of Lawson's book. But to his dis-
credit, Catesby also directly cribbed seven of John White's 1588
engravings of fish, an iguana, and a swallow-tailed butterfly, for
volume 2, tracing them so that his own depictions were reversed,
and not crediting his source.

In the end, none of this really diminishes the importance of
Catesby's work, which finally lit the spark of widespread interest in

English naturalist Mark Catesby painted a heath hen—the now-extinct eastern race of the greater prairie-chicken—along with the flowers of a shooting-star, for his book *The Natural History of Carolina, Florida, and the Bahamas,* which began appearing in installments in 1729. *Courtesy of the Academy of Natural Sciences, Ewell Sale Stewart Library*

American ornithology. There were 220 reasons for this—the handsome plates engraved from his watercolors. Catesby was a self-taught artist and made no bones about it: "As I was not bred a Painter I hope some faults in Perspective, and other Niceties, may be more readily excused," he wrote in his preface. But in his day, the critics were few.

While Catesby's work may seem stiff to us today, it was groundbreaking for its time. He first had the idea, later brilliantly developed by Audubon, of placing the bird with an element of its environment, like the bough of a tree or shrub—not some generic bit of floral stage-dressing, but a specific, closely rendered specimen that added another layer of scientific value to the illustration. He also claimed to have painted all but a few of his birds from life, rather than specimens, though in most cases it's likely Catesby used both.

He painted more birds than anything else, and made the rather bold claim that he'd left almost no species unpainted: "I was induced chiefly (so far as I could) to compleat an Account of them . . . by which Method I believe very few Birds have escaped my Knowledge, except some Water Fowl and some of those which frequent the Sea." In fact, his book listed 116 birds, which when duplicates are taken into account (like the "brown bittern" and "crested bittern," which were the adult and immature forms of the yellow-crowned night-heron) comes to 109 species, fewer even than the 136 Lawson tallied. That's about what a modern birder could expect to find in a good weekend during migration—a slim list, it may seem, for many years' work in the field.

But consider how many birds pass through the Carolinas in a matter of a few weeks in migration, and stay in the forest canopy— small, fast-flitting warblers and vireos, the kind that birders depend on sharp hearing, knowledge of birdsong, and good binoculars to pick out; it's really no wonder Catesby missed so many of them. Though he did include some of the more obvious and common forest songbirds, like the hooded warbler and the American redstart, it is puzzling why Catesby missed some of the most conspicuous species of the region, like any of the large buteos; several of the biggest egrets and herons, including the great blue; and the great horned owl (a bird Lawson included, "big as a middling goose"), and all but half a dozen species of waterfowl, including mallards, both species of swans, and the snow geese that Lawson said were plentiful along the North Carolina coast.

Each plate was accompanied by a brief description and an account of the life histories of the species he portrayed. In this, Catesby did a fine job, though sprinkled among his own observations was a dash of folklore, which he credulously passed on to his readers, and inaccurate bits and pieces of Lawson's earlier work, such as the claim that turkey vultures often kill snakes.

Catesby was the first to state that the guts of Carolina parakeets are "certain and speedy poison to Cats," a claim Alexander Wilson tried to confirm a century later. Wilson—rather cold-bloodedly—used his own cats, which survived, and Audubon tried much the same experiment on his dog, with similar results. But as Wilson himself noted, the captive parakeets he used had been feeding on corn, not their usual diet of cockleburs—a plant known to be toxic to livestock, and whose chemicals might linger in the birds' digestive tracts. Researchers today wonder if Catesby was on to something besides folklore; if the parakeets enjoyed a kind of secondary toxic defense from their food, as do monarch butterfly caterpillars feeding on milkweed, or poison-dart frogs feeding on toxic ants, it might explain why large flocks of parakeets were able to roost in hollow trees, where one would expect them to be at risk from climbing predators, like raccoons.

Catesby was also the first to record the piracy of bald eagles stealing fish from ospreys, and he correctly credited the turkey vulture with "a wonderful sagacity in smelling." Audubon later tested—and thought he had conclusively refuted—this idea by covering a fetid carcass with a tarp; vultures ignored it. Only recently have ornithologists shown that not only do turkey vultures possess a highly developed sense of smell, they also exhibit more refined tastes than anyone gave them credit for. It turns out they prefer their meat fairly fresh, and simply turned up their beaks at what Audubon was offering.

The annual arrival and departure of "Birds of Passage" was of particular interest to Catesby, and it is here that we see most clearly the sharp mind of an observant naturalist at work. He rejected the idea, still prevalent in the eighteenth century, that migratory birds hibernated in caves or hollow trees, or in the depths of the ocean— "Notions so ill attested and absurd in themselves, that they deserve no farther Notice," he said. "If the Immenseness of the Globe be considered, and the vast Tracts of land remaining unknown but to its barbarous Natives, 'tis no Wonder we are yet unacquainted with the Retreats of these itinerant Birds."

Catesby was aware of the nocturnal, oceanic migration of the bobolink, having heard their distinctive flight notes as flocks passed over his ship in the Bahamas. He incorrectly assumed the "rice-birds" were flying from Cuba north to the Carolinas, when in fact, the birds would have been on their way from North America to the grasslands of South America. But his experiences led him to make a significant deduction about such birds.

"The Place to which they retire," he argued, "is probably in the same Latitude of the southern Hemisphere, or where they may enjoy the like Temperature of Air, as in the Country from whence they came: By this Change they live in perpetual Summer, which seems absolutely necessary for their Preservation, because all Summer Birds of Passage subsist on Insects only, and have tender Bills adapted to it, and consequently are unable to subsist in a cold Country, particularly Swallows, Martins, and a few others that feed only on the Wing."

One such bird was "the American swallow," his name for the chimney swift, which he guessed passed the winter in "most probably Brazil . . . where, the seasons reverting, they may, by this alternate change, enjoy the year round an agreeable equality of climate." This may at first seem like a tidy bit of prescience on Catesby's part; chimney swifts do winter deep in the Amazon forest, but ornithologists didn't discover that until the 1940s. In reality, Catesby's deduction was correct but was based on a false assumption. Recognizing the similarity between the swifts he had observed and a species described from Brazil, he leaped to the conclusion that they were one and the same, having no way of knowing that there are almost a dozen generally similar species of swifts in Central and South America.

But there is another and far more surprising case of Catesby getting a jump on the rest of science—coming to an incorrect conclusion, but basing it on reasoning that stunningly foreshadowed one of the twentieth century's major insights.

Catesby was intrigued by the presence of a few European species of birds in Carolina (not realizing, as later ornithologists did, that some of them are different though closely related species, like the European goldcrest and the North American golden-crowned kinglet). These, he surmised, had colonized the New World from the Old, "admitting the World to have been universally replenished with all Animals from Noah's Ark after the general Deluge."

Although land birds were sometimes blown from the mainland to Bermuda, Catesby said, the distance was far greater between Europe and America; therefore, any birds that made the crossing must have done so at some then-unknown point, probably near the Arctic Circle, where the continents might meet. Catesby bolstered his argument by pointing out that the birds shared by both lands are species adapted to colder climates.

All well and good; Catesby makes a pretty sound case, though we know today from radar studies that even tiny land birds like warblers can make overwater journeys that would have left the good naturalist gob-smacked, like blackpoll warblers flying non-stop from Cape Cod to the coast of Venezuela. For gulls, waterfowl, and raptors, a hopscotching dispersal route around the North Atlantic via Iceland and Greenland (or across the Bering Strait from Asia) isn't that big a stretch.

But having constructed a strong rationale for natural dispersion, Catesby offers up a mind-blowing alternative: "To account therefore for this extraordinary Circumstance there seems to remain but one more Reason for their being found on both Continents, which is the nearness of the two Parts of the Earth to each other heretofore, where now flows the vast Atlantick Ocean."

Read that again; your eyes are not playing tricks on you. It wasn't until 1912 that the theory of continental drift was first proposed, and not until the 1960s that enough evidence had emerged to convince skeptical scientists of its accuracy. Yet here is Mark

Catesby—a man who just a few sentences earlier was affirming his belief in the Biblical Flood—suggesting that moving continents may have, in effect, rafted birds to America. What other thoughts he might have had on the subject are a mystery; this single, hesitant reference is the only time he mentioned it in print. Doubtless he'd be gratified to learn that even today, the *vast Atlantick*—which did indeed split a formerly unified landmass some 230 million years ago—continues to widen, at about the rate your fingernails grow.

HIS *NATURAL HISTORY* A SUCCESS, Catesby gave up the traveling life, hardly stirring from England again. Even a friend described him in those years as "tall, meagre, hard-favoured and sullen look[ing]," and his later life is murky; he married late, though when and to whom, exactly, is clouded in confusion. Experts have even debated his death and resting place, some saying he died at home in December 1749, others noting evidence that he went to sea on an East India Company ship in the autumn of that year, contracted a fever, and was consigned to the deep in April 1750.

As celebrated as he was during his lifetime, Catesby's work eventually fell into obscurity, and even today he remains little-known. Perhaps his most lasting contribution to American ornithology was the names he gave to the birds he described, many of which have come down to us today unchanged, or with a few grammatical tweaks: *blew jay*, *red-headed* and *hairy wood-peckers*, *blew gross-beak*, and *hooping crane*, as well as Canada goose, blue-winged teal, laughing gull, and purple finch.

Catesby also created Latin names for the plants and animals he painted, and in the fashion of the day, these tended to be long and descriptive, following no real rules except the namer's whim. They might be two words long, or six, or twelve. Thus, the ivory-billed woodpecker was *Picus Maximus rostro albo,* "the large woodpecker with the white beak," while the brown noddy, a chocolate-colored tern with a white cap, was *Hirundo Marina Minor Capite Albo,* "the small sea-swallow with the white head." The "crested titmouse" (our tufted titmouse) was just *Parus cristatus,* which means pretty much the same thing as its English name.

Anyone could name any organism anything, and the result was nomenclatural chaos. At times, Catesby wasn't even consistent in what *he* called a bird; his name for the blue grosbeak was *Coccothraustes caerulea* in the text of his book, but *caeruleus* on the illustration plate. Science needed order, and the great Swedish botanist Carl von Linné imposed it, creating a concise, workable system in which every living thing was given a Latinized genus name (shared by closely related species) and its own specific name. The two-part combination would be unique to each organism. This binomial approach had been pioneered two centuries earlier by a pair of Swiss brothers named Bauhin, but Linné—better known by his own Latinized name, Carolus Linnaeus—took the ball and ran with it. His *Systema Naturae,* published in 1758, remains the gold standard today.

Linnaeus swept up all the available information on plants and animals around the world, reclassifying many species that had already been given names by other scientists, including Catesby, condensing and restructuring them to fit his new format, sometimes keeping elements of the original names, sometimes junking them completely. Thus, the American robin went from Catesby's *Turdus pilarais migratorius* to just *Turdus migratorius* under Linnaeus, and the ivory-billed woodpecker from *Picus Maximus rostro albo* to the far more manageable *Picus principalis.* (The genus of largest New

World woodpeckers has since been changed to *Campephilus,* "caterpillar-lover," a reference to their diet of beetle grubs.)

In all, Linnaeus's book covered more than twelve thousand plants and animals, including seventy-five birds Catesby had originally described and named from North America. While Linnaeus noted where he drew on the work of others, one aspect of his system was a notation giving credit to the person who first described the species for science under his new framework, and the year of its publication. Linneaus started the clock, so to speak, with his own work, and so we have *Picus principalis* (Linnaeus 1758) and *Turdus migratorius* (Linnaeus 1758). Because Linnaeus's system was so universally embraced, Catesby's contribution disappeared, and the credit he should have received for his pioneering work was, for centuries, largely overlooked.

But Linnaeus's binomial system did eventually produce one lasting memorial to Mark Catesby. In 1802, the English naturalist George Shaw officially named a species Catesby had illustrated in *Natural History of Carolina*—not one of the New World's gloriously plumaged birds, but the bullfrog, forever hence to be known as *Rana catesbieana.*

LINNAEUS WAS ONLY PART of an explosion in European natural science, much of it focused on ornithology. Through the sixteenth and seventeenth centuries, most scientists still deferred to the ancient Greeks like Pliny and Aristotle as the authorities on the natural world—men who argued that worms were born of horsehair soaked in mud puddles and that birds passed the winter under lakes or the ocean. By the eighteenth century that was changing, however, and fresh perspectives were emerging, driven by great minds like Mathurin-Jacques Brisson and Georges-Louis Leclerc de Buffon in France, who published treatises on ornithology in the mid-1700s. In south England, a vicar named Gilbert White, in the country parish of Selborne, was carefully noting the migratory movements and breeding behavior of the neighborhood birds, and corresponding with eminent colleagues in London; his letters would eventually be published as *The Natural History and Antiquities of Selborne.*

Among those London naturalists was a Quaker wool merchant named Peter Collinson, a friend of Catesby's, to whom the artist had turned for an interest-free loan when he was strapped for cash after his second American sojourn. An ardent scientist with a passion for botany, Collinson counted among his friends Linnaeus and, later, Benjamin Franklin, whose work on electricity he shepherded into print.

In 1732, Collinson began a correspondence with a fellow Quaker in Philadelphia named John Bartram. Several years earlier, after one of the epidemics that swept the city with morbid regularity had carried off his wife, Bartram turned to the serious study of botany; the story (perhaps apocryphal) goes that while plowing one day, Bartram saw a daisy between his feet and was struck by the fact that he'd destroyed such beautiful plants all his life without knowing anything about them. Although he was a farmer with no formal training, and relatively little education of any sort, Bartram applied himself with great effect, and by the time he and Collinson came into contact, he was traveling widely through the East, bringing back plants to his five-acre farm, the first botanical garden in the New World.

Collinson, eager for whatever Bartram could send him in the way of new and unique species, quickly became his sponsor, financing his expeditions and serving as a conduit for the seeds, cuttings, and specimens Bartram shipped regularly to England. It was a relationship of mutual benefit—intellectually, scientifically, and financially—that the men would maintain for the next thirty-six years, though without ever actually meeting. Through Collinson's efforts, the Quaker farmer from Philadelphia gained acclaim across Europe—Linnaeus is said to have called him the greatest natural botanist in the world—and in 1765, he was appointed royal botanist to King George III.

Bartram remarried shortly after his first wife's death, and he fathered eleven children in all. The seventh was a son, William, who took after his father; "Billy, my little botanist," John called him. Unlike his father, William had the benefit of an excellent education, with some of the finest minds in Philadelphia tutoring him—when they could drag Billy away from botanizing and drawing,

William Bartram, painted late in life by Charles Willson Peale, was the first American-born naturalist to write extensively about the continent's bird life, especially the many species he encountered on his rambling expeditions through the Southeast. *Courtesy of the Independence National Historical Park*

that is. When he was only in his teens, William began accompanying his father on collecting trips, and bid fair to follow in his botanical and scientific footsteps. But with parental concern, the elder Bartram felt his son needed a trade. "I want to put him to some business by which he may, with careful industry, get a temperate, reasonable living," John confided to Collinson.

More easily said than done. Benjamin Franklin, a family friend, offered to take on the young man as a printing apprentice; William declined. Surveying, engraving, and medicine were similarly rejected. Billy failed at attempts at business in Philadelphia, and in coastal North Carolina, where he opened a store with the help of an uncle. John Bartram—now nearly seventy, bearing the title of Royal Botanist and traveling on King George III's shilling—was glad for Billy's company on his last major expedition, a year-long tramp through South Carolina, Georgia, and Florida, starting in 1765. When it was over, William decided to remain in Florida, trying his hand at indigo and rice farming along the Saint Johns River. Perhaps predictably, that went belly up as well. "No colouring can do justice to the forlorn state of poor Billy Bartram," a family friend wrote reprovingly in a letter to John. Billy returned to Philadelphia, dogged by debt, and became enmeshed in yet another bad business deal before heading back to North Carolina once more. One can only imagine the sleepless nights he gave his father, who had decided to turn the family gardens over to William's younger (and more business-savvy) brother.

But while he was making a shambles of his business ventures, Billy Bartram was smitten with the plants, animals, and landscapes he saw in the South. Collinson, who had praised his drawings when the lad was still a teenager, now circulated the young man's more mature work among his circle of influential friends. It was almost the last service the old wool dealer performed for the family before his death, in 1768, but it proved crucial. One of the men impressed by William's drawings was John Fothergill, a physician with a keen interest in botany.

Something changed in Billy Bartram as he entered his early thirties. Like Catesby before him, something stiffened in the once aimless man, some nascent resolve. Who knows when he got the itch for an epic adventure, but finally, in 1772, he wrote to London with a proposal: Would Dr. Fothergill sponsor an expedition to Florida? Although Fothergill's botanical interests lay with more boreal species, he agreed, paying Bartram fifty pounds per year in return for specimens, drawings, and an account of his journey.

Bartram set out from Philadelphia in 1773 on what proved to be a five-year, 2,400-mile trek that took him throughout the Southeast—through the cypress swamps and coastal lowlands of the Carolinas and Georgia, into the azalea-spangled southern Appalachian highlands controlled by the Cherokee, overland to Mobile Bay and Baton Rouge, then back east and down south into Seminole country in Florida. Although his later narrative suggests one long continuous expedition, Bartram alternated forays in the field with time spent in cities, like Savannah and Mobile. Along the way he met Indian chiefs, battled alligators, was blinded by disease, and discovered a wealth of new plants and animals, from Mississippi kites, Florida sandhill cranes and limpkins to gopher tortoises, flame azaleas, and oakleaf hydrangeas.

Bartram's ramblings were the first comprehensive exploration of an entire region of America by a trained scientist, who was, to boot, an eloquent writer and a skilled artist. His primary focus was plants—the Seminole called him *puc-puggy,* or flower hunter— but his ranging eye lit on curiosities everywhere he looked, from wildlife to the manner and customs of the Indians. Those Indians, it's worth remembering, lived, farmed, and hunted the land in such numbers that it was wilderness only in the view of a visiting white like Bartram. Yet he nevertheless saw a land vastly different, and vastly wilder, from what it is today, and Bartram's is one of the clearest pictures we have of the eastern frontier in its now-lost splendor—of flocks of whooping cranes and waterfowl on the Mississippi, stands of enormous old-growth hardwoods and cypresses that left him awestruck, and forests alive with wolves, panthers, and bears.

Birds are a recurrent theme in Bartram's account of his journey; leaving Charlestown, he noted "the gay mock-bird, vocal and joyous, [that] mounts aloft on silvered wings, rolls over and over, then gently descends and presides in the choir of the tuneful tribes." Tired of pushing against the current on Georgia's Altamaha River, he rests his paddle and watches the scenery slip by:

> My progress was rendered delightful by the sylvan elegance of the groves, chearful meadows, and high distant forests, which in grand order presented themselves to view . . . The air was filled with the loud and shrill whooping of the wary sharp-sighted crane. Behold, on yon decayed, defoliated Cypress tree, the solitary wood-pelican [wood stork], dejectedly perched upon its utmost elevated spire; he there, like an ancient venerable sage, sets himself up as a mark of derision, for the safety of his kindred tribes. The crying-bird [limpkin], another faithful guardian, screaming in the gloomy thickets, warns the feathered tribes of approaching peril; and the plumage of the swift sailing squadrons of

Spanish curlews [white ibis] (white as the immaculate robe of innocence) gleam in the cerulean skies.

Bartram described "the laughing coots with wings half spread," the "young broods of the painted summer teal [wood ducks], skimming the still surface of the waters" of the upper Saint Johns River, and the "snake bird," or anhinga. On the Saint Johns, too, he gave one of his most evocative (and imaginative) descriptions of alligators: "Behold him rushing forth from the flags and reeds. His enormous body swells. His plaited tail brandished high, floats upon the lake. The waters like a cataract descend from his opening jaws. Clouds of smoke issue from his dilated nostrils. The earth trembles with his thunder . . . The shores and forests resound his dreadful roar."

Bartram apparently had a rough time with alligators, recounting many close encounters and fearful near-brushes with them, including a battle on the Saint Johns in which he said he held off several attacking gators with an improvised club. "I was attacked on all sides, several endeavouring to overset the canoe. My situation now became precarious to the last degree: two very large ones attacked me closely, at the same instant, rushing up with their heads and part of their bodies above the water, roaring terribly and belching floods of water over me. They struck their jaws together so close to my ears, as almost to stun me, and I expected every moment to be dragged out of the boat and instantly devoured." The next night, he said, he shot one enormous gator that climbed into his boat, and narrowly missed the grab of another.

Not everyone found this credible; alligators do not spew smoke like medieval dragons, after all, and they usually don't mount frontal assaults on canoeists. His claim to have seen twenty-footers, and to have heard of some twenty-three feet long, met with raised eyebrows. Bartram stood by his stories, though in later years, the devout Quaker was said to be highly sensitive to any suggestion that he embellished them, especially the account of his epic fight. Clearly, the great reptiles made a deep impression on him; his friend and biographer George Ord said that Bartram had recurrent alligator nightmares all his life.

The book Bartram eventually published about his explorations, *Travels Through North and South Carolina, Georgia, East and West Florida*,* devotes a long passage to birds, in which its author says humbly that he noted few species that Catesby and others had not already described—a false modesty, though he also took the opportunity to politely amend mistakes he'd found in his predecessors' works. He accurately surmised that "blue linets" (indigo buntings) were not, as many assumed, simply young painted buntings that had yet to acquire their spectacular color, and he corrected Catesby's disparaging characterization of the catbird's song, "a mistake very injurious" to that bird, though he forgave Catesby for making a similar error about hermit thrushes, since they don't sing their lyrical, flutelike songs on the wintering grounds where Catesby knew them. Bartram reported on the belief that Carolina parakeets might hibernate inside hollow trees, but said he'd seen no evidence for this in his travels—and lamented that the colorful parrots never came so far north as Pennsylvania, where "we abound with all the fruits which they delight in."

---

*Or to give it its full, take-a-deep-breath name, *Travels Through North and South Carolina, Georgia, East and West Florida, the Cherokee Country, the Extensive Territories of the Muscogulges or Creek Confederacy and the Country of the Choctaws; containing an account of the Soil and Natural Productions of these regions, together with observations on the Manners of the Indians.*

He also made some shrewd observations on migration, a phenomenon he'd observed all his life with keen interest. "In the spring of the year the small birds of passage appear very suddenly in Pennsylvania, which is not a little surprising, and no less pleasing: at once the woods, the groves, and meads, are filled with their melody, as if they dropped down from the skies. The reason or probable cause is their setting off with high and fair winds from the southward; for a strong south and south-west wind about the beginning of April never fails bringing millions of these welcome visitors."

Bartram seems to have had something of an inferiority complex, the colonial hayseed in the shadow of European scholarship. After he returned to his family's farm in 1777, instead of publishing his findings on his own say-so, Bartram shipped his specimens to Fothergill, in London, where the Swiss botanist Daniel Solander was supposed to "officially" classify them. Only Solander didn't; British expeditions were returning with crates of natural wonders from the far corners of the world, far more exotic than Bartram's, which languished until Solander died, in 1782, two years after Fothergill's death.

It must have been a rough time for Bartram. His father died just nine months after he ended his trip, and the Revolutionary War was raging around them, with the British occupying Philadelphia, and major battles just a short day's ride away. Bartram began assembling his chaotic notes and journals (some dating back to his earliest southern travels with his father) into a book soon after he returned home, but it was slow going. His original route across the South meandered and curlicued, doubling back and repeating itself over the years, but William merged his various trips and experiences into a single narrative, whose dates and places do not always jibe—something that has given fits to the many people who in later centuries tried to retrace his movements.

It was almost a decade before a publisher in Philadelphia began an abortive attempt to advertise Bartram's book, and not until 1791 did it finally appear. It proved modestly popular in Europe (though mostly through pirated editions), but the book landed with a thud in America, and even European scientists sniffed that it was, well, just a shade too *enthusiastic,* too lyrical and poetic.* One reviewer dismissed it as "disgustingly pompous," but in fact, it is a mix of rhapsodic, almost purple prose and straightforward scientific description.

More crushing to Bartram than the poor sales and biting reviews was the very permanent legacy of his long delay—the loss of scientific recognition for his many discoveries. All but a handful of the new species of plants and animals he discovered were trumped by other scientists, some using his own specimens in England, men who got their own descriptions into print first, bumping Bartram into the shadows. It is believed he discovered more than two hundred species, yet only a dozen or so carry his name today. Bartram, writing to a friend in 1788, said he sought "no other gratuity than the bare mention of my being the discoverer, a reward due for traveling several thousand miles mostly amongst Indian Nations which is not only difficult but Dangerous, besides suffering sickness cold & hunger."

In the end, what distinguishes Bartram's *Travels* from everything that came before isn't its significant improvement in scientific

---

*Which made it an ideal inspiration, however, for the new Romantic poets in England, like Wordsworth and Coleridge, the latter of whom drew repeatedly on Bartram's imagery. In *Kubla Khan*, for example, the River Alph, flowing past Xanadu through "caverns measureless to man," was based on Bartram's description of the Great Sink (Alachua Sink) in Florida.

merit, or a tally of newly discovered species, important as they may be. What marked this book as a turning point is the same thing that has drawn readers like me back to it repeatedly over the years—the way Bartram reveled in the beauty of the primal American landscape.

For the first time, we encounter not an immigrant, but an American naturalist on his home turf, a man exulting in the wilderness he explores. True, Bartram tended to see it through the lens of his religious and political beliefs—the natural world as a reflection of the mind of God, and the frontier settlements and farms along its edges, a manifestation of the young republic's strength and vigor. Most of Bartram's contemporaries—and many of his successors for generations thereafter—saw wilderness as the barbaric haunt of savages and snarling beasts. He celebrated it as a sublimely (and divinely) ordered realm of beauty and majesty.

The youthful wanderlust seems to have burned itself out in Bartram, and in his later years, he stuck close to the family farm, run by his younger brother John. William had lost the vision in one eye from an illness that had first struck him on Mobile Bay, but he remained active, classifying his collections, corresponding with scientists in Europe and America, illustrating plates for a groundbreaking textbook called *Elements of Botany,* by Benjamin Barton, accumulating scientific honors, and entertaining visitors as august as Jefferson, Madison, and Washington. (In 1804, Jefferson offered Bartram a place on a federal expedition into the new Louisiana Purchase, either up the Red River into what is now Arkansas, or Zebulon Pike's 1805 excursion up the Mississippi to Minnesota; historians aren't sure which, and in any event, Bartram declined, citing his health.)

Not every visitor was a Revolutionary luminary. In 1803, a young man with a Scottish brogue showed up at the door, introducing himself as a schoolteacher from Gray's Ferry, a mile away along the Schuylkill River, who shared a passion for nature. Within a few months, the slender, intense fellow was taking art lessons from William's niece Nancy, and poring over her uncle's extensive library. There's some evidence to suggest he'd also taken a romantic shine to Nancy.

Her father, John, held a low opinion of the would-be suitor; the young man was a poor schoolteacher with a checkered past, a poet, and a political rabble-rouser back in Scotland; he may even have known that the fellow had been imprisoned for blackmail. Any suggestion of a match was out of the question. William, though, likely saw something of himself in the Scot, a man who had drifted through life, from place to place and occupation to occupation, before finding an anchor in natural history.

He was also impressed with his erstwhile pupil's determination. The fellow was ravenous when it came to reading and questioning; he was taking additional art lessons from a well-known engraver in the city, and was with each passing week becoming more and more entranced with America's birds—and with the idea of a book. A book like Catesby's, but complete and comprehensive, a thorough, illustrated review of the continent's birdlife in its glorious entirety.

This may have struck Bartram as an amusingly conceited goal for a newcomer with little field experience and of then-limited artistic ability. But if so, he'd underestimated his pupil—for the eager young Scotsman was Alexander Wilson, known today as the Father of American Ornithology.

2

"Except three or four,
I do not know them"

FOR A QUIET, sensitive boy who loved birds and the outdoors, the Scottish Lowlands of the mid-eighteenth century were a lovely place to be born, except for one flaw. Lovely, because Paisley—the small town west of Glasgow, where Alexander Wilson's family lived—sat beside a picturesque waterfall known as Laigh Linn, or the Hammills, on the White Cart River; in fact, the home in which he was born was just three doors down from the falls. Outside of town was moorland and pastures; wagtails nested on the stone bridges that arched the little streams, corncrakes made their rasping cries at night from the boggy meadows, and every fall, the great flocks of waders, greylag geese, and other waterfowl came through the valley of the Clyde, into which the Cart flowed.

But Paisley was a company town, and therein lay the flaw. By the late seventeenth century, weavers were already its largest trade group, and their importance grew in the first half of the eighteenth century, as the fame of their silks and muslins spread. (Paisley would later lend its name to the famous shawl designs woven there, a nineteenth-century knockoff of vastly more expensive Kashmiri fabrics bearing tiny, interlocking patterns.) In Paisley, the future for a working-class child lay indoors, with the weaver's hand loom, which dominated local life to the exclusion of almost all else; there were only forty-five families in Paisley, but sixty-six looms.

Alexander Wilson was born on July 6, 1766, to one of those weaving families. His father, Alexander Senior (or Saunders, as he was known), had given up smuggling—another local specialty—when he'd married a respectable girl, and did rather well as a weaver, supplementing his income with a hidden still in the backyard of their home, in the neighborhood known as the Seedhills. It was not an overly comfortable life, but young Sandy, as the family called the

A penniless convicted blackmailer, Alexander Wilson left Scotland in 1794 for America, where he fell in love with his new country's birds. In a rush of enthusiasm, he decided to create a book illustrating all of them—even though he could only identify a handful himself. *Courtesy of the American Philosophical Society*

boy, was smart, and looked to have good prospects—perhaps in the ministry, always an option for a bright young Presbyterian.

But revolution in America bludgeoned the economy, and life for Sandy and his two older sisters became harder still after their mother died, when he was ten years old. His father quickly remarried, a woman with children of her own, and the large (and still-growing) family struggled, even though Saunders resumed smuggling, later moving his family out of town and into the ruined castle tower of Auchinbathie, some miles away.

Young Sandy had a bit of school and, according to some accounts, may have spent a summer herding livestock, but at age thirteen, his future closed in on him and he was apprenticed as a weaver, ending his formal education. He wove for the next seven years, three as an apprentice to his brother-in-law William Duncan, and four as a journeyman in various shops earning a shilling a day, reading the classics when he could, poaching grouse on the moors when he had free hours. He went back to his brother-in-law's business, now in Edinburgh, but Duncan's weaving trade was foundering, and Sandy spent much of his time on the road, peddling their wares across Scotland.

No doubt this fed the young man's thirst for the outdoors, and gave him a chance to stretch his poetic legs as well (he'd been writing verse since an early age). But life as a "packman," as peddlers were known, was usually hard and frequently miserable; his letters from this period speak of rough quarters and the regular hunger he faced. On one occasion, he walked through mud and cold rain until, exhausted, he fell to the ground in a stupor, barely rousing himself in time to avoid being run over by a stagecoach.

He kept writing poems, though—and in the process, followed another Paisley tradition. Scotland is known for its working-class poets who, like Wilson's hero Robert Burns, wrote in the tongue-twisting vernacular, but Paisley seems to have had more than its share. Locals still talk about the time someone proposed a toast, "To Paisley poets!" and every man in the pub stood to accept the accolade.

Wilson published a small volume of poetry in 1790, which he peddled himself to no great success; and little wonder, because it's not especially good, though he did have flashes of brilliance. Amid peddling far and wide, his work on the book, financial woes, and a socially awkward love affair with a woman well above his station, Wilson's health began to crack—a problem that would revisit him throughout his life.

In 1792 he authored an anonymous poem, "Watty and Meg: A Wife Reformed," about a drunkard who silences his complaining wife by threatening to leave her, which was enormously popular (and initially ascribed to Burns). But Wilson's pen also got him into trouble. He was becoming a political radical, agitating on behalf of the weavers against mill owners, who were mechanizing their operations. He wrote another anonymous work, this one a satire called "The Shark, or Lang Mills Detected," about a mill owner who is cheating his workers.

Not only did the poem bring a charge of libel from its thinly disguised target, William Sharp, but Wilson apparently tried to blackmail Sharp in the bargain. "The enclosed poem, by particular circumstances, has fallen into my hands," said a letter to Sharp signed "A.B." "If you know any person who will advance *five guineas,* the manuscript from which I copied the enclosed, shall, with the utmost regard to justice and secrecy, be immediately destroyed." Confronted by the authorities, Wilson confessed to writing the poem and the letter and was ordered by the court to publicly burn the offending article in the town square, but he could not pay the fine and was imprisoned, on and off, over the course of the next eighteen months.

As pointed out by Wilson's biographer Robert Cantwell (on whose work I have heavily depended), something doesn't quite add up here. The charges against Wilson were civil, and quickly admitted to, yet he was held on criminal charges. The reason seems to have been the growing political roil across Scotland against English rule; "the police and British agents were kept busy jotting down the names of people who were heard giving the new toast— 'To George the Third and last!'" The weavers whom Wilson's poems celebrated were at the heart of this anti-English movement, and he was among their champions.

Wilson was finally released, a humiliated man whose hopes of a literary career were ruined, and he went back to work as a weaver just long enough to earn his passage to America. Accompanied by his nephew, he sailed in May 1794 and landed that July, all but penniless, in Delaware. Wilson shouldered his pack, picked up his gun, and walked the thirty miles to Philadelphia. He shot the first bird he saw (by most accounts a red-headed woodpecker, a species he did not recognize), and in the days to come, he was struck by how much more colorful the birds of this new country appeared to be. His ornithological path, like the wagon road to Philadelphia, lay open before him, even if Wilson didn't know it yet.

Alexander Wilson was twenty-eight years old when he arrived in America. A portrait made years later shows a lean and spindly man with deep-set eyes and dark hair framing a high, square forehead. Charles Robert Leslie, an artist who later assisted Wilson, described him as resembling his subjects:

> He looked like a bird; his eyes were piercing, dark, and luminous, and his nose shaped like a beak. He was of a spare bony form, very erect in his carriage, inclining to be tall, and with a light elastic step. He seemed perfectly qualified by nature for his extraordinary pedestrian achievements.

Initially, though, Wilson fared not much better in the New World. Philadelphia was recovering from an horrific yellow-fever epidemic and looked more like a ghost town than a thriving city. Work was hard to come by, and Wilson drifted from printing to day labor to weaving to peddling, bouncing from place to place before finally finding steady employment as a schoolteacher. His first appointment came in 1796, near Philadelphia, but after that ended in 1801 (caused, it is thought, by a scandalous affair with a married woman, which sent him temporarily to New York), Wilson took a job teaching at Gray's Ferry, also near Philadelphia and an easy stroll from the Bartram estate.

William Bartram appears to have been generous with his time and advice, even lending original paintings to Wilson so that the younger man might copy and learn from them.* Wilson also combed through Bartram's library, where he found and was entranced by Catesby's volumes. Another inspiration appears to have

---

*One such painting, which appears to show an immature field sparrow, turned up in 1991 in school workbooks from students at Gray's Ferry around the time of Wilson's tenure. Originally thought to be the early work of Wilson himself, it has since been determined (based on composition and execution) to more likely have been Bartram's—one of many take-home examples generously loaned or given to Wilson to help along his studies. If true, then it probably represents the type specimen of field sparrow, a species first named by Wilson, but whose discovery he credited to Bartram.

been George Edwards, a protégé of Catesby's, whose four-volume *A Natural History of Uncommon Birds* launched British ornithology and included several American species. The realization that Edwards drew his own illustrations and etched his own plates, as had Catesby, seems to have given Wilson the idea that he could do the same—create a book documenting all of his adopted land's birds, a dream he shared in a letter in 1803 to a friend back home in Scotland.

But there remained one serious—one would think insurmountable—obstacle to writing the definitive work on New World ornithology: Although he had collected many of them, and kept a number (ranging from hawks to hummingbirds) as pets, Alexander Wilson still didn't know very much about American birds, even how to identify the majority of them. A letter he wrote to Bartram in March 1804 shows just how far behind the curve Wilson was when he finally discovered his life's calling. The letter accompanied several bird paintings for the older man's critique, and Wilson was self-deprecating regarding his abilities—he hoped Bartram's "good nature will excuse their deficiencies." He needed not only his mentor's artistic advice, but some ID help as well.

"I have now got my collection of native birds considerably enlarged; and shall endeavor, if possible, to obtain all the smaller ones this summer," Wilson wrote. "Be pleased to mark on the drawings, with a pencil, the names of each kind, as, except three or four, I do not know them." And this was almost a year *after* Wilson first confided his dream for a complete American ornithology. Whatever the Scots-Gaelic term for chutzpah might be, Wilson had it in spades.

Call it determination or arrogance, it served him well. Wilson was by then working with Alexander Lawson, a Philadelphia engraver born near Paisley, learning how to etch his own copper-plates—a tricky process, and one that Wilson, not surprisingly, at first bungled. But he quickly got the hang of it. By the beginning of 1806, Wilson had successfully etched the first plate of his "Birds of the United States," and had triumphantly sent it to Bartram for his "amusement and correction." (He had earlier sent some of his drawings to President Thomas Jefferson, who eagerly sought Wilson's help in identifying a bird—it proved to be a wood thrush—that Jefferson did not know. But Wilson, who had made public orations in support of Jefferson's policies, was stung when his request to accompany the Pike Expedition that year was ignored.)

Meanwhile, Wilson was finally able to leave teaching, taking on the job of revising a twenty-two-volume encyclopedia—a position that not only gave him more free time and a steadier salary, but, more importantly, the ear of one of Philadelphia's better publishers, Samuel Bradford, whose sons Wilson was tutoring. When Wilson pitched his idea for a multivolume set he titled *American Ornithology*, Bradford agreed, though Wilson was required to solicit subscriptions to pay for it.

Wilson threw himself into the work with a vengeance, converting into copperplate etchings the paintings he'd been accumulating. Fervent American nationalists, he and his publisher made a point of using only American-cast printing type, and American paper made from American-discarded linen rags. Only the colors used to hand tint the plates were, by necessity, imported from Europe, though Wilson stressed that "some beautiful native ochres . . . and one of the richest yellows" came from the United States. Throughout the years of production, Wilson always shot fresh birds for his colorists, "so there should be no chance of the fading or changing of the brilliant tints of life."

With lessons in drawing and bird identification from William Bartram, Wilson turned next to learning how to engrave his own plates for *American Ornithology,* many of which he also hand-colored. *Courtesy of the Academy of Natural Sciences, Ewell Sale Stewart Library*

The first volume appeared in 1808, with Wilson hitting the road in the autumn of that year, examples in his trunk, to peddle orders from New Jersey to Maine and Vermont, then south to the Carolinas and Georgia. He was on the road until the following March, through sometimes severe winter storms, chatting up the luminaries in every major town for subscriptions and combing the woods and marshes for new birds. The reception was uneven; he sold a subscription to the president of Dartmouth College in New Hampshire, and President Jefferson (who had already subscribed) received him warmly, but the governor of New York glanced at the book, then told Wilson, "I would not give you one hundred dollars for all the birds you intend to describe, even had I them alive."

Wilson wandered constantly—even before the book, he'd careened all over the place, including a 1,200-mile walking trip to Niagara Falls in 1804 that resulted in an epic poem titled *The Foresters*. Once he got rolling on *Ornithology*, though, he was unstoppable. Scholars have put the accumulated distance he covered at something like ten thousand miles, and it was rough travel much of the way. Wilson slept in Indian villages, in bug-ridden frontier taverns, in open boats, and in the saddle. He fell deathly ill more than once, and on the worst nights, he must have felt little better off than the Scottish packman of his youth. Melancholy overtook him at times. But generally he was doing what he loved—taking copious notes, shooting and stuffing birds, and grilling locals about what they knew of their region's birdlife.

He was amazingly thorough; by one modern estimate, Wilson described 268 of the almost 350 species he could have seen east of the Mississippi, including twenty-six that were entirely new to science. (Wilson thought he had named fifty-one new species, but some were simply new plumages of previously described species. In other cases he'd been beaten to the punch by competing scientists; for example, in September 1808, he described the "yellow-throated flycatcher"—now the yellow-throated vireo—not knowing a French author had published a description of the same bird a month earlier.)

Wilson took what was probably the first stab at calculating regional bird populations, estimating that one hundred million birds entered Pennsylvania each spring, with about four hundred pairs remaining to nest in each square mile of land (ornithologists now consider both figures grossly low). He also used some shrewd, back-of-the-envelope figures to estimate the size of a passenger pigeon flock he witnessed in Kentucky; the flock was a mile wide and passed by for four hours at a rate of one mile a minute, he said, so assuming that each square yard of space "comprehended" three pigeons, that "would give two thousand two hundred and thirty millions, two hundred and seventy-two thousand Pigeons!"

Wilson accomplished so much by working himself nearly to death. Over the six years he worked on *Ornithology*, he spent nineteen months in the field, eventually visiting fifteen of the eighteen United States as well as four federal territories. Typical was a journey that he began in January 1810 (he had invited Bartram to accompany him, but the elderly botanist, just weeks away from his seventy-first birthday, wisely declined the winter tramp). With his second volume fresh from the printer, Wilson set out overland to the Ohio River—two hundred and fifty miles of bad road, in freezing weather. From Pittsburgh he floated more than seven hundred miles down the Ohio in a small boat on whose stern he had grandly painted the name *The Ornithologist*, going with the current and in the motley, ever-changing company of keelboat crews, pioneer families, Indians, scalawags, and thieves, all using the Ohio as their highway to the frontier. Then he traveled by horse and by foot a thousand miles to New Orleans, with a Carolina parakeet that he'd winged, then nursed back to health, riding on his shoulder or wrapped in a handkerchief in his pocket the whole way.*

The pickings were better in some places than others; Pittsburgh surprised him with the strong reception his project received from its leading citizens, and he was met with acclaim in New Orleans, while he made no attempt to hide his contempt for Louisville: no culture, no intelligence—and no subscriptions. He was there in March, and Wilson did come close to making a sale; he'd walked into a store and struck up a conversation with the shopkeeper, a fellow speaking eccentric, French-accented English, who seemed dazzled by Wilson's plates. But then the man's partner muttered something to him in French, and the climate in the room chilled distinctly; no, the would-be subscriber said, pushing back the volumes he'd been admiring; thank you, but no. Wilson's eyes hardened, and not long after, he shook the unfriendly dust of Louisville from his clothes and headed south again. "Science and literature has not one friend in this place," he grumped to his journal.

IT WAS ONLY by a stroke of luck that the man with the French accent was even working that day in 1810, because John James Audubon did everything in his power to avoid being trapped behind the counter of the Louisville store he owned with his friend

---

*In this, he had better luck than with another wounded bird, an ivory-billed woodpecker that he'd shot in North Carolina. Telling the suspicious innkeeper that the madly squalling bundle in his arms was a baby, Wilson hurried it to his room, then left to find it some food. In his absence, the huge bird proceeded to demolish the bed, a table, and much of one wall.

Ferdinand Rozier. He spent most of his time shooting, riding, teaching art, or painting the birds that he obsessively collected and which his network of local hunters brought him, piling up thick stacks of watercolors. Anything but business. "My days were happy beyond human conception," he later wrote. "I seldom passed a day without drawing a bird, or noting something respecting its habits, Rozier meantime attending the counter."

It's unclear how Rozier felt about this, but it's easy to guess; he had a twenty-five-year-old slacker for a business partner, and most of the work fell to him. Rozier was eight years Audubon's senior, a friend from their days in France, but friendship goes only so far, and their partnership had but a few more months to run. Audubon's single enthusiastic contributions to the business were the long overland trips to Philadelphia or New York for more goods, which took him for weeks at a time "through the beautiful, the darling forests of Ohio, Kentucky and Pennsylvania," where he'd let the pack animals wander while he went chasing a new bird.*

Audubon, with his young wife Lucy and his friend Rozier, had arrived in Louisville two years earlier, from Pennsylvania. The illegitimate son of a French sea-captain and a chambermaid, who died shortly after his birth, Audubon had already seen a lot of the world; he'd been born, in 1785, in what is now Haiti, where he was known as Jean Rabine. His father, accurately predicting violence

---

*Reader, be warned: Maria Audubon and her cousin Eliza badly bowdlerized their grandfather's journals before destroying most of the originals, leaving us with a much sanitized, maddeningly tidy view of this messy, brilliant, fascinating, ambiguous man. With a few exceptions, Audubon's journals, including his account of the meeting with Wilson, ought to be viewed more as a paraphrasing than an accurate representation of what he wrote. (And it's clear that Audubon himself fudged the facts on many important points, such as how far along he was with his bird painting when he and Wilson crossed paths.) Even his *Ornithological Biography,* published by Audubon himself, is not entirely reliable—the avian material is, for the most part, solid, but the entertaining "Episodes" about his own experiences, which he sprinkled through these five volumes, are often exaggerations or fabrications.

between white plantation owners and their slaves, had Jean, still not four, sent to France for his safety, and gave the boy his own family name. Jean learned the things a young gentleman needed—some schooling, some art and music, some military training—but his father's antennae were twitching again. Eighteen-year-old Jean—his name now anglicized to John James Audubon—was packed off to America, in 1803, to avoid possible conscription into Napoleon's army.

Audubon père's idea was that John would profit from learning to manage his father's estate of Mill Grove, just above the confluence of Perkiomen Creek and the Schuylkill River, less than twenty miles north of Philadelphia. In fact, the young man had little aptitude for and even less interest in the farm and its small lead mine, and devoted himself to riding, shooting, dancing, and music. He was a dandy, going out in shooting parties dressed in black breeches, silk stockings, and ruffled shirts. After he made the acquaintance of pretty Lucy Bakewell, whose father owned a neighboring property, he paid even less mind to his responsibilities.

One thing Audubon did apply himself to with fierce determination, however, was the study of birds, something that had fascinated him all his life. In France, he'd drawn the stuffed birds in his father's home, in a flat, stiff style that Catesby would have recognized. Audubon found Mill Grove a paradise for this work—not only did the area abound with game birds, like ducks, geese, grouse, and woodcock, which the local hunters all sought, but there were also all manner of smaller species he'd never seen before, and which most of his neighbors ignored.

Charging his fowling piece with bird shot, he'd set out in the first damp light of day, looking for specimens to bring back to the house. At first, he drew them as they hung before him, tethered by the feet, like the still-life paintings of game so popular in those days. Several of these early, long-lost paintings have recently turned up in France, and one can understand why Audubon was unhappy with them—he wanted to capture the vitality and movement of the live bird, like a pair of phoebes whose "graceful attitudes" he watched and sketched endlessly, and in rising frustration.

He tinkered with threads to hold up the wings or heads of his freshly shot birds, to no avail. He tried to make an articulated mannequin of cork and wire in the shape of a bird, hoping to use it as a model, but the result was a "grotesque figure," and when a friend laughed at it, Audubon kicked apart the mannequin in a fit of pique. He failed again and again, until at last he struck upon the idea of a clever armature that allowed him to impale the warm, limp carcass on slender wires, holding it in a natural pose. In great excitement, he rode to town for supplies, assembled the framework, and then raced to the creek, where he shot the first thing with feathers that he saw, a belted kingfisher. Audubon pinned it into position, and—*mon dieu!*—it was as though the bird were patiently sitting for its portrait.

There are still kingfishers along Perkiomen Creek, where the old Audubon home—a handsome stone farmhouse with a large barn and outbuildings—sits on 175 acres owned by Montgomery County and managed by the National Audubon Society. Ivy cloaks the rear of the house, which is now a museum, while the porch (which was added years after Audubon left) looks across a lawn falling away to the placid millpond on the creek. Valley Forge, where Washington's forces spent the winter of 1777–78, is just a mile away. You can squint and imagine it in 1803, especially if, as I did, you try it on a spring day when the old maples and sycamores are full of migrants. Small waves of birds rippled through the treetops—a black-throated green warbler singing brightly, a couple of red-eyed vireos, a black-and-white warbler hitching like a nuthatch in spirals around the branch of a large oak. But leaving the present, even briefly, can be a tough job. The Philadelphia suburbs have engulfed this area, leaving Mill Grove marooned among homes, businesses, and industry; almost everywhere on the property, you can hear the growl of traffic noise from a commuter expressway just across the creek.

But in Audubon's day it was paradise for someone as bird crazy as he was. Every time I visit Mill Grove during the warm months, I look for eastern phoebes, which in Audubon's era nested in the eaves of the farm buildings and the steep, rocky banks of the creek. Curious if the same birds returned every year, he tied what he described as "silver thread" to the legs of a nesting pair and, with delight, noted their reappearance the following year—the first case of bird banding (after a fashion) in the New World.

It's ironic that he and Wilson met on the distant Kentucky frontier instead of here along the Schuylkill, where they lived for several years within an easy morning's ride of each other and had several mutual acquaintances. But when the meeting came at last, it was pivotal, for it seems likely that it shocked Audubon into finally thinking of completing his own collection of American bird paintings and may have been his first inspiration to create a published work of his own.

Of course, we only have Audubon's word for what transpired that spring day in 1810; Wilson's original journals from that period are lost, and the varying accounts published after his death (apparently based on those missing journals, and edited by Audubon's enemies) raise more questions than they answer. It appears the men did meet, and went hunting two days later, but beyond that, we're left with Audubon's version, which casts the tale in a predictably flattering light. Wilson, he said, came into the counting room of the store, two volumes of *Ornithology* under his arm, looking decidedly out of place—dressed too formally for a frontier town, with a long nose, keen eyes, and prominent cheekbones that "stamped his countenance with a peculiar character."

Audubon said he'd known nothing of Wilson's project until that moment and was so struck by what he saw that he had a pen in hand, ready to subscribe, when Rozier, looking over his shoulder, asked in French, "My dear Audubon, what induces you to subscribe to this work? Your drawings are certainly far better, and again, you must know as much about the habits of American birds as this gentleman." Audubon changed his mind, and Wilson's attitude grew frosty. With that, Audubon took down his portfolio, which he claimed was stuffed with almost two hundred paintings. Wilson, he said, was amazed; did Mr. Audubon intend to publish them? One is meant to imagine Wilson's relief when Audubon replied that no, he hadn't given it a thought.

Audubon claimed he loaned Wilson several paintings,* and even took him hunting, showing him new birds, and receiving from Wilson an agreement that any work of Audubon's that appeared in future volumes would be credited. That there is lingering doubt about the veracity of these statements is an indication of what a damnably awkward challenge Audubon still poses, almost two centuries after his pinnacle.

---

*This may have been a clever attempt to reverse the inevitable charge of plagiarism, since several of Audubon's birds, including the Mississippi kite, are clearly direct copies of Wilson's earlier plates, and almost forty of them show a distinct similarity to Wilson's. Likewise, Audubon probably borrowed freely from Wilson's published estimates of passenger pigeon numbers for his own, now more famous, description of the great flocks.

Much has been written about the complex, often paradoxical layers to John James Audubon. It's hard to read much about him without feeling the twin urges to lionize and strangle him. He was a genius, pure and simple; no one had ever brought such vitality, such raw emotion and surging power, to the painting of birds. Audubon smashed centuries of artistic convention, packing his pages with action and movement, setting fluid, believably living birds among lovely vignettes or fully realized landscapes: a pair of white-crowned pigeons gently billing among the orange blossoms of a geiger tree; a lesser yellowlegs in a moss-draped swamp near Charleston; two warbling vireos feeding among the huge, creamy flowers of a magnolia; a pair of great crested flycatchers in a violent dustup, their tail feathers scattered to the wind. (Many of the botanical and landscape elements of Audubon's later paintings were added by his assistants, whom he trained and whose work he often repainted and refined.)

Yes, his work could be melodramatic—two peregrine falcons, their beaks dripping gore, hunch over ducks; four brown thrashers battle a black snake, one bird snared in the coils; a young red-shouldered hawk, its talons flared, slams into a covey of quail. But these were birds as individuals, birds that flew and breathed and sometimes died on his sheets of linen rag paper, in watercolor, pastels, pencil, and ink. And they were always drawn lifesized, which meant that Audubon had to find compositionally creative ways to mold the largest species to the page, like the whooping crane twisting down to catch a baby alligator. They were not generic, pasteboard silhouettes, although Audubon drew a few of those, too, especially the ones he lifted from Wilson. These, however, were the anomaly. The break between past and future was clean; there was bird painting before Audubon and after—and after him, nothing was ever the same. Wilson may be lauded as the Father of American Ornithology, but Audubon's very name has become synonymous with birds.

Unfortunately, no one held a higher opinion of Audubon than Audubon himself. He was self-aggrandizement personified, a master at the calculated effect; whereas at Mill Grove he had tried to hide his humble origins and project an air of nobility, when he eventually traveled to England and Scotland in the 1820s to promote his *Birds of America,* he made sure to look every inch the "American Woodsman" he proclaimed himself to be—the long, flowing hair, a hunting shirt and wolfskin jacket, a fur cap with bushy tail. It was a shrewd affectation that fit perfectly with the Romantic view of the wilderness then in vogue, and it would have worked equally well in our celebrity-conscious century. Yet lurking beneath this bluster was a murky current of self-doubt, manifested in the way he hid his illegitimacy, lied about where he was born (Louisiana, he often said), his assertion that his father had been a French admiral, or his extravagantly unnecessary claims to have studied art under Jacques-Louis David, painter to the French court. Most people would have considered it a triumph for a self-taught artist to reach such heights; Audubon seems perennially embarrassed by that fact.

And finally, what must Wilson have thought, that day in Louisville, leafing through Audubon's portfolio? Audubon was still years away from the peak of his powers, but Wilson must have sensed the potential there. Was he excited, unsettled, amused? Except for Audubon's claim (filtered through his meddling granddaughter) that Wilson's "surprise appeared to be great," we don't know. But Rozier was right: My dear Audubon, you are clearly the superior artist.

Wilson ended his western trip in New Orleans, sailing back to New York by way of Florida and the Carolinas, where he collected fourteen "stormy petrels," a species that would later bear his name. He arrived in Philadelphia in August 1810, almost eight months after he'd left. Over the next two years, he completed volumes 3 through 6 of *American Ornithology,* living part of the time at the Bartram estate and making short trips into the Appalachian ridges and Pocono plateau to the north, or south and east to the New Jersey coast, for more specimens.

The copperplate etchings were simply black-and-white line prints, each of which needed to be hand-tinted with watercolors— a laborious process that rendered each reproduction, in effect, an original work of art. In Europe, large publishing houses maintained staffs of trained colorists, but Wilson struggled throughout the period to find artists able to maintain the quality of the finished plates. Making a smooth, even wash with ink or watercolor across a sheet of linen paper is hard, nerve-wracking work; if the brush hesitates for a second, or overlaps a previous wash, the image is indelibly marred with a line. The pace and stress were tearing at Wilson's body and making this naturally quiet and reserved man crankier than normal, so that he had a hard time retaining colorists and had to do much of the work himself.

Biographer Robert Cantwell has noted the herculean task Wilson set himself. *American Ornithology,* by normal reckoning, took seven years, but Wilson was at first teaching school, and then for five years serving as editor of the encyclopedia, which actually paid his bills. "Nearly a full year was given to his three great trips, through New England in 1808, the Southern states to Savannah in 1809, and the West to New Orleans in 1810. Really, only five years were spent on the *Ornithology* itself, and between thirty-six and forty-eight months of uninterrupted labor." Travel, writing, collecting, painting, engraving, coloring, hustling subscribers—it's a wonder the man found time to eat.

Wilson, caught in a financial squeeze, made one last major trip into New England in 1812, trying to secure subscription payments on which the book hinged, though he found most people more gripped by concern over the war with England than with matters ornithological; in Haverhill, New Hampshire, he was briefly detained on suspicion that he was a spy.

Still, in some circles *American Ornithology* was making Alexander Wilson a celebrated figure in his adopted country. Men of importance elbowed to become his friends, which was not an altogether comfortable position for the convicted felon, whose personal background was a source of pain and embarrassment. One newfound admirer was George Ord, a wealthy Philadelphian whose money came from the family rope-making business, but who, like many gentlemen of the day, spent most of his time pursuing science. Ord became one of Wilson's contributors, sending him descriptions of bird behavior and, on at least one trip to the New Jersey coast in 1812, throwing himself into collecting specimens for Wilson, whose energy was visibly flagging. (Among the birds Ord collected was the first Cape May warbler ever described, by Wilson, for science.)

Ord, no specialist himself, became a sort of zealously involved hanger-on, moving into scientific circles largely on the weight of his association with Wilson, though he later made significant contributions of his own. He was described by contemporaries in a barrage of unflattering terms—*quarrelsome, picky, intolerant,* and *abrasive* among them. With Ord, Cantwell wrote, "there was no distinction between someone with whom he disagreed, and an enemy." Malvina Lawson, whose father was Wilson's engraver and a close acquaintance of Ord's, recalled in later years that Ord was "very much respected but not very much loved," a man whose temper brought him to the brink of more than one duel before her father stepped in as peacemaker. Ord's generalized hostility would eventually find a particular target in John James Audubon, in whom Ord saw a challenge to Wilson's—and his own—primacy in ornithology.

By April 1813, Wilson wrote to Bartram, "I have been extremely busy these several months, my colorists having all left me; so I have been obliged to do extra duty this past winter." He was pushing himself relentlessly, and his health, which had never been robust, was failing. He had chronic problems with the "flux," or dysentery, a common problem in those days of contaminated water and poor sewerage disposal. Hard enough on a healthy man, dysentery can be deadly to a compromised system.

In August, Wilson came down with flux once more; the story was told by Ord, and others, that this followed a cold he caught after swimming a chilly creek to retrieve a bird, but there is little evidence to support this. Wilson, realizing the end was at hand, drew up his will, naming Ord as coexecutor, and died a few days later, on August 23, 1813. He was forty-seven.

Ord, who was traveling when Wilson died, stepped in as the official protector of his friend's reputation and legacy, a task he completed in a spectacularly uneven fashion. Ord wrote an incomplete and only sporadically accurate biography of Wilson, unable even to supply his birth date, but he also brought out the eighth volume of *Ornithology*, in 1814, and gathered the material to publish the ninth and last volume a few months later. In it, Ord named a newly described plover for Wilson, and in the years to come, a warbler, a phalarope, and the storm-petrel would follow, honors bestowed by other admiring naturalists. Ord, meanwhile, moved to the pinnacle of Philadelphia's scientific establishment, eventually becoming president of the Academy of Natural Sciences. He made it his mission to preserve Wilson's reputation—by destroying Audubon's, if necessary.

So WHAT WAS IT about America's frontier that kept turning rudderless dreamers, ne'er-do-wells, and idlers into maniacally focused naturalists? It happened with Catesby and with William Bartram; it happened with Wilson and—most famously—with Audubon, he of the silk breeches and ruffled shirts, more interested in impressing the ladies with his fashionable dance steps than doing anything concrete with his life. Audubon's interest in drawing and in birds was there from the start, but he floundered for years, even when he had a family to support and a business to mind. Then something clicked, and the happy-go-lucky layabout became ferociously dedicated to studying birds.

For Audubon, at least part of that "something" was meeting Wilson in Louisville, which all but certainly started Audubon thinking about publishing his own great ornithological book. But there must have been something about the birds themselves—the sheer numbers and vivacity of North America's birds that grabbed these men. Imagine spring as Audubon saw it—not just the sight of things now gone, the magnificent torrents of passenger pigeons blotting the sun and raining their droppings thick as snow, the heath hens strutting and booming by the thousands in the meadows, the whooping cranes and trumpeter swans heading north, or the screeching flocks of parakeets. Simply imagine the raw spectacle of a healthy, undiminished continent's worth of songbirds overwashing the winter-gray land with movement and color, the incalculable hundreds of millions of warblers, vireos, thrushes, orioles, tanagers, flycatchers, and more. Even today, after centuries of erosion, the great aerial ballet of spring migration is a staggering thing to see. In those days, it must truly have been breathtaking. The question isn't why were these men ensnared by America's birds; the question is why wasn't *everyone* struck dumb by them?

Rozier and Audubon moved their business downriver to Henderson, Kentucky, in the summer of 1810, but soon thereafter they went their separate ways—Rozier to great commercial success in Missouri; Audubon to continue to muddle along as a storekeeper, this time in partnership with his brother-in-law, using the proceeds from the sale of Mill Grove. Things looked brighter for a while, but by 1819, when an economic panic swept the country, the business was in ruins and the Audubons were bankrupt. John James was taken up for unpaid debts in Louisville and briefly imprisoned. For the second time in as many years, an infant daughter died.

The only thing left to him was his art, and even that, fortune tried to steal. Rats had gotten into the trunk in which he stored his drawings, shredding all but a few and forcing him to start afresh. But from this lowest ebb, Audubon scratched his way back. He and Lucy, with their two surviving sons, moved to Cincinnati, where he got a short-lived job doing taxidermy work for the museum; by this time, he had clearly set his sights on completing a Wilsonesque collection of all North American birds—in fact, one reason for seeking the museum job was access to Wilson's volumes in the college library. He taught art, and made money on the side by drawing commissioned portraits in charcoal and pencil.

From Cincinnati, Audubon rode a barge south along the Mississippi, and again his family followed, fetching up in New Orleans and Natchez, where Lucy and the boys would spend the next nine years. Audubon was teaching, painting portraits, and collecting birds and drawing them at a feverish pace. The rats back in Kentucky had done him an enormous favor; his newer compositions were far more complex and challenging, their execution infinitely better than those early works. Lucy, now settled in New Orleans, was supporting the family by working as a governess; John James had hired an assistant, Joseph Mason, to add the floral and landscape elements of his paintings.

By 1824, Audubon was ready to begin marketing his grand publication, which he called *Birds of America*, and he set out to find a publisher. He visited Philadelphia and was invited by Charles Lucien Bonaparte (a nephew of Napoléon's and a talented ornithologist who was completing a four-volume extension to Wilson's books) to speak at the Academy of Natural Sciences. It was a disaster. Audubon may have foolishly begun by criticizing Wilson's work, as one story claims, but regardless, he earned the immediate and lasting enmity of George Ord, Alexander Lawson, and other Wilson partisans.

They recognized a rival when they saw one, and thereafter missed no opportunity to attack Audubon's paintings, scholarship, and credentials. They pointed out, with perfect validity, the places where Audubon had cribbed Wilson's drawings and then awkwardly fibbed to hide that fact. Ord further complained that Audubon had shockingly mixed botany and zoology by setting his birds among flowers and plants (even though Wilson had done the same) and charged that Audubon's dramatic poses were "attitudes never seen in nature." When Audubon's former assistant, Joseph Mason, stepped forth to say he'd been unfairly denied credit for his botanical paintings, Ord added artistic theft to his litany of charges.

It was a drumbeat of criticism that Ord and his friends would maintain for the next twenty-five years. In the long run, of course, the sheer force of Audubon's gift won out, which is why Wilson is a footnote today and Audubon's name is shorthand for *birds*. In the near term, however, Ord and his compatriots were effective; Audubon had no hope of publishing in America and was forced to look to Europe. In 1826, he sailed to London with his now extraordinary collection of paintings, spending the next three years shepherding it into engraving and publication. He exulted over the reception he received. What America had denied him—recognition of his genius—Europe was happy to supply. An exhibition of his paintings at the Royal Institution in Edinburgh brought wide acclaim; he was wined by the highest circles of London society and given honorary memberships in lofty societies and academies of science. In Paris, Baron Georges Cuvier, perhaps the greatest biologist of his day, told the members of the French Royal Academy of Sciences that *Birds of America* was "the most magnificent monument which has yet been raised to ornithology."

But Audubon was also chronically short of funds, painting copies of his larger works to sell for cash; he made multiple oils of his *Otter in a Trap* and *Eagle and Lamb*, scenes of hunting dogs, fighting cats, and variants on his huge wild turkey, which became something of his trademark. The same chase after subscribers that wore down Wilson had a similar effect on Audubon, who found

A family of pileated woodpeckers feeding in a grape-tangled snag—a work Audubon completed along the upper Lehigh River in Pennsylvania in 1829— is typical of his later, complex compositions, many painted with help from his assistant, George Lehman. *Courtesy of the New-York Historical Society, accession number 1863.17.111*

himself beset by black depressions. "The same sad heart to-day, and but little work and much company," he despaired in his journal while in Scotland. "The papers give such accounts of my drawings and myself that I am quite ashamed to walk the streets; but I am dispirited and melancholy." He missed Lucy terribly, but she—busy keeping the family afloat back in Louisiana and no doubt resenting his squiring around the urban centers of Europe—rarely wrote him.

When Audubon returned to the United States in 1829, he threw himself into traveling, collecting, and painting. *Birds of America* was gathering steam, and he needed new specimens, new species, new paintings. He spent months along the New Jersey coast, then traveled to the "Great Pine Swamp" of Pennsylvania, the virgin pine and hemlock forest along the upper Lehigh River, where he stayed in a logger's cabin and ate "juicy venison, excellent Bear flesh, and delightful trout." It was a remarkably productive period for Audubon, who completed drawings of ninety-five birds and sixty eggs, with a new assistant, George Lehman, supplying the floral and background elements. These were some of his most dramatic paintings, including that of the thrasher nest attacked by a black snake, and another of a family of pileated woodpeckers in a grape-tangled snag.

Back to England again, this time with Lucy in tow, one of four transatlantic crossings in the next eight years as Audubon shuttled between the production of the book, in London, and acquisition of new species. *Birds of America* had become a family enterprise; Lucy handled paperwork, Victor came to London to ride herd on the engravers, and John Woodhouse Audubon (himself a talented artist) helped his father with painting and taxidermy. Audubon was in his glory now, traveling south through the Carolinas and Florida to the Dry Tortugas off the Keys, hobnobbing with turtle hunters, egg collectors, and salvagers; north to Labrador, with John Woodhouse, in a chartered schooner, collecting gannets, puffins, three-toed woodpeckers, and Lincoln's sparrow, a new species named for a young man on the expedition.

Ord and the Wilsonians kept interest in *Birds of America* damped down in Philadelphia, but elsewhere the subscriber list grew, despite its steep price—$1,050, the equivalent of about $40,000 in modern currency. The aquatint prints made from the original paintings were huge, printed on enormous sheets of paper, $39\frac{1}{2}$ by $28\frac{1}{2}$ inches, that printers called a "double elephant." Andrew Jackson received the Audubons in the White House, and if money remained a perennial problem (Audubon was briefly detained again for old debts) his reputation grew with the release of each new folio in the series—massive books of one hundred plates each (one hundred thirty-five in the fourth and final volume), which came out in "numbers" of five plates at a time over the course of eleven years.

But enough, for a moment, about the emerging science of birds—what about the pure *pleasure* of watching birds, which by the opening of the twenty-first century would grow to one of the most popular outdoor pastimes? Were there birders—in spirit, if not name—in the early years of America when Audubon was at work?

Of course; our species has been watching and enjoying birds for as long as we've been human. But while history has noted those giants like Catesby, Wilson, and Audubon, who moved the science of ornithology forward, it overlooked those who rested at the plow to watch a flight of teal come twisting down the creek valley, or the farmwives who shared crumbs of scarce family bread for the pleasure of seeing juncos and sparrows scuff in the snow on a cold day. Early Americans, especially those in rural areas, were astute observers of birds, though it was not usually the purely recreational pastime it is today. Birds were guideposts to the seasons, to planting and harvest, forecasts of the changing weather and even changing personal fortune—visible tokens of what was soon to come.

Birds figured in all sorts of old folk wisdom, especially regarding the weather. Some was clear and accurate; Bartram noted that when the "pewit, or black cap flycatcher" (our eastern phoebe) first arrives in southern Pennsylvania in mid-March, "we may plant peas and beans in the open ground . . . and almost every kind of exculent garden seeds, without fear or danger from frosts." Swallows flying close to the ground presaged rain, the old farmers believed, while geese flying high meant fair weather—both beliefs having some basis in truth. Cuckoos were known as "rain crows" for the way they call on humid, storm-brewing summer days, and ruffed grouse were thought to drum most often in fall and winter before a big snowstorm. Wilson wrote that when an osprey circles high while calling, then dives, it means an approaching storm—an observation that time has not borne out.

Nor were the auguries all related to weather. A bird flying into a house meant impending news, while a whip-poor-will or a screech-owl calling outside the window heralded approaching death for a loved one. Most of the odd or unusual birds were the subjects of superstition, and whip-poor-wills, a species Wilson first described, had more than their share. The family to which they belong is still known formally as the goatsuckers, stemming from the ancient belief that they sucked milk from the teats of livestock. Besides being an omen of death, a calling whip-poor-will could bring luck if you wished on the first one of the spring—and if you had backache, turning somersaults in time with the whip's call would cure you.

This folk wisdom came down through the oral tradition, and few of these rural people in the eighteenth and nineteenth centuries wrote down their observations, other than in a handful of journals, diaries, and newspaper accounts. But what they have bequeathed to us is a rich, exuberant, linguistically joyful store of old folk names for American birds—a reflection of the newness of the continent they were settling, and a mirror held to a frontier culture that was, like Adam, putting names to things.

Not surprisingly, these mostly European settlers looked for similarities with the birds they'd known back home, giving them names that recalled (often with bitter poignancy) the lands and birds they'd left behind. Europe has an orange-breasted thrush known as the robin, and the name was pinned to the larger American species with a similarly rusty breast, even though they belong to different subfamilies. Thrashers were called thrushes, wood warblers were known as flycatchers, and kinglets were wrens (even though there are kinglets in Europe, too). It was a nomenclatural mess, and exactly what the relationships were between Old and New World birds set the specialists to scratching their heads.

But even as scientists like Wilson were trying to sort things out, you had new generations across the eastern frontier with no first-hand memory of Old World birds, nor much interest in academic arguments, creating their own regional names for the birds they encountered on their farms and in their forests. Most were descriptive—"hangnest" for a Baltimore oriole, "cutwater" for a black skimmer, "high-hole" or "yellowhammer" for a flicker, "sawbill" for a merganser.

The result was a welter of colloquial English names that grew up in different regions, varying sometimes from valley to valley. One person's "silver tongue" was another's "hedge sparrow" or even "everybody's darling"—all names for what we now call the song sparrow. American bitterns were called "thunder pumpers," "water-belchers," "mire drums," or "bog-bulls" because of their booming calls; their habit of freezing in the cattails, bill pointed skyward, gave them the names "stake-bird," "look-up," "sky-gazer," and "sun-gazer." Flush a bittern or a heron, and it'll usually void a stream of excrement as it takes off; such birds were known as "shitepokes" in polite company, but the middle *e* vanished when the audience was rougher.

One popular reference lists nineteen alternate names for American woodcock, including "bog-borer," "bog-sucker," "Labrador twister," "night-peck," "siphon snipe," and "hookum-pake." Only one, "timberdoodle," is in anything like wide use today, and then mostly as a fond nickname among hunters. In most cases, these old names have vanished entirely, but once, almost every bird had dozens of them. Nineteenth-century hunters along the coast might report shooting checkered snipe, bishop-birds, calico-jackets, chuckatucks, jinnys, creddocks, rock-birds, redlegs, and sea quail, all of which represent fewer than half the more than two dozen vernacular names for ruddy turnstones.

It was a big, confusing country out there, full of far more birds than any of the early naturalists realized. Wilson, Audubon, and their contemporaries tried to make sense of it all, but given the pioneering nature of their work, mistakes were inevitable. Wilson, for instance, described a new songbird he named the "autumn warbler," not realizing it was the blackpoll warbler in nonbreeding

plumage, while Audubon mistook a very large, very dark immature bald eagle for a new species, dubbing it "the Bird of Washington." He also named "Brewer's duck," even though he suspected
(correctly) that it was merely a hybrid between a mallard and a
gadwall.

Interestingly, though, not all the mystery birds in Wilson's and
Audubon's paintings can be dismissed as simple misidentifications.
They include Wilson's "small-headed flycatcher," which he painted
from a specimen said to have been collected in New Jersey, and
which he said he encountered again several times. "Flycatcher"
was the name then commonly used for warblers, and the bird depicted in Wilson's plate—which Audubon copied, claiming to have
found the same species in Kentucky—could be a hybrid warbler,
or perhaps a weird kinglet or *Empidonax* flycatcher. Regardless,
nothing matching the drawings and descriptions has ever been seen
again.

Wilson and Audubon also described the "Blue Mountain
warbler," again possibly a hybrid, and Audubon the "carbonated
swamp-warbler," about which specialists have been arguing ever
since. Some believe the latter represents an immature Cape May
warbler, perhaps inaccurately drawn from memory—Audubon
had lost many of his original paintings from his days in Kentucky.
Others, including Roger Tory Peterson, thought it very likely was
a legitimate species, so rare that it soon vanished entirely, leaving
Audubon's painting of the two males he collected as the only
evidence. Audubon's "Cuvier's wren" may have been an odd golden-
crowned kinglet with an all-red cap, or a hybrid between a golden-
crowned and a ruby-crowned. Townsend's bunting, collected near
Philadelphia in 1833 and named by Audubon for its discoverer, is

thought by some to have been a hybrid, and by others to be a dick-cissel lacking the normal yellow pigment; unlike the other hypothetical species, the specimen skin is still in the Smithsonian.

Actually, though, some of the most fascinating examples of lost species involve those pioneering naturalists Catesby and William Bartram, if only because the birds involved are so spectacular and the idea of them once inhabiting the United States is so exotic. Catesby referred to the "red curlew," or scarlet ibis, as being common in the Bahamas, and Wilson recorded that it was widespread in the Carolinas, Georgia, and Florida. Given that this vividly colored wading bird is today found no closer than Trinidad and the coast of South America, it seems unlikely that their reports were accurate, and both men may have been relying too heavily on what they'd been told by others.

It's much harder to dismiss William Bartram's enigmatic "painted vulture" in Florida: "a beautiful bird . . . white or cream colour, except the quill-feathers of the wings and two or three rows of the coverts, which are of a beautiful dark brown; the tail which is large and white is tipped with this dark brown or black." His description, of which this is a small excerpt, is almost spot-on for the king vulture of the neotropics—a species which, sadly for Bartram's reputation over the years, does not occur any closer to Florida than southern Mexico.

Forget whatever unfortunate mental image the word *vulture* conjures up in your mind, because the king vulture is nothing short of dazzling. The body plumage is gleaming white, the wing feathers and tail a glossy black, and the head—well, the head looks as though Picasso had tried his hand at designing a bird right after he painted *Guernica,* all abstracted oranges and purples, wattles and carbuncles. The first time I saw one, in the Maya Mountains of southern Belize, I was watching a kettle of black vultures and swallow-tailed kites playing on the humid updrafts. From the hazy sky, a single white bird appeared, dwarfing the smaller vultures; then another, and another, until seven kings were swirling in tight circles above me. A few days later, I encountered one early in the morning, perched on a dead snag, and marveled at that kaleidoscopic head.

So this is, you'll understand, an unmistakable bird, and it's hard to see how anyone who reads Bartram's description could think he was talking about any other species. And yet this record has been ignored or dismissed, sometimes in the most disparaging terms, by ornithologists for centuries. Naturalists of the late eighteenth and early nineteenth centuries generally accepted it, perhaps because Florida remained a soggy wilderness where anything was possible. But as ornithologists pushed into every corner of the state without ever finding Bartram's "sacred vulture," doubts began to grow. By the 1850s, authors were expressing reservations, and twenty years later, Bartram's sighting was derided as a "purely mythical species" by one prominent ornithologist, who called the report "a confused mixture of . . . pure fiction and truth, with the former in preponderance."

Bartram had many faults as a writer; his *Travels* were written years after the fact, which led to many mistakes, vague generalities, and misplaced locations, but this would be a degree of falsehood or sloppy fieldwork that seems beyond possibility. More and more ornithologists have come to believe the record is valid; manuscripts by Bartram, uncovered in England in the 1930s, include an account of his finding and shooting a "Croped" (cropped) vulture that matches his later description of the painted vulture, including the distinctive, brightly colored bare crop that protrudes from a king vulture's chest feathers.

Audubon, who on his southern expedition put in along the Saint Johns River almost seventy years after Bartram's first visit, found no painted vultures, but he did paint a subspecies of crested caracara that would come to bear his name. Like the caracara, Florida is still home to many species of birds with disjunct ranges, marooned on the peninsula when climate change or rising sea-levels cut them off from the rest of their kind. It's one of the Sunshine State's big attractions for birders—western species like burrowing owls and scrub-jays (the latter an endemic form), and tropical raptors like the snail kite and short-tailed hawk, both of which are common across Latin America. It seems at least reasonable to think that a disjunct population of king vultures was originally found in Florida as well—so reasonable, in fact, that a few raptor conservationists have called for reintroducing the king vulture to its old Floridian range.

We like to think that Audubon was witnessing the untouched frontier, and when one reads his account of, say, collecting twenty Carolina parakeets and two ivory-billed woodpeckers along the Mississippi, that impression is plaintively reinforced. But the tide of exploration and settlement—and the frontiers of ornithology—had already passed far to the west, and although Audubon burned to go there himself, he was chained to the East and to London by the trials of bringing *Birds of America* to life.

He was also moved by the changes he saw in the land he'd adopted as his own. In October 1836, Audubon was in Philadelphia, negotiating for the purchase of western bird skins brought back by some of the early expeditions. "Passed poor Alexander Wilson's schoolhouse, and heaved a sigh," he wrote in his journal.

> Alas, poor Wilson! would that I could once more speak to thee, and listen to thy voice. When I was a youth, the woods stood unmolested here, looking wild and fresh as if just from the Creator's hands: but now hundreds of streets cross them, and thousands of houses and millions of diverse improvements occupy their places. Bartram's Garden is the only place which is unchanged. I walked in the same silent wood I enjoyed on the same spot when first I visited.

The Philadelphia that they both knew is gone. It was Wilson's hope, as he was dying of the flux, that he would rest where he could always hear birdsong. Wilson's grave lies in the cemetery of Gloria Dei (Old Swedes) Church, which today is wedged between I-95 and Columbus Boulevard in Philadelphia, a small clot of trees amid the mayhem of traffic and the commercial waterfront of the Delaware River. There's little birdsong today, although the Canada geese and ring-billed gulls still move up and down the river. Wealthy admirers had offered to move Wilson's remains to a prominent location in the Laurel Hill cemetery, overlooking the falls of the Schuylkill River, but Ord refused.

Remarkably, Bartram's Garden has managed to withstand the times; like Mill Grove, it remains an oasis in an urban landscape, protected as a monument to its namesake. The old stone house and barn, John Bartram's rock cider press, the historic gardens, all remain much as they were. On a spring morning, the migrant songbirds still come back to the old trees around the homestead, like the giant yellowwood that Bartram planted in the 1790s, which still explodes in white blossoms, and to the thickets of ash and river birch along the Schuylkill. Along the boardwalk that passes through the soggy, riverine forest, there is a flickering of wings, and the song of a warbling vireo, a yellowthroat, a catbird. I suspect that if the shade of Sandy Wilson walks anywhere to hear the birds, it is here.

3

Pushing West

THE YELLOWSTONE RIVER empties into the Missouri on the plains of western North Dakota, just a couple of miles from the Montana border. It's empty country, mostly wheat and beef cattle, a long way between towns like Williston and—well, pretty much anywhere else. Locals call the region MonDak, but it's Big Sky country, regardless of which side of the state line you're on. Little coulees run from the low, crumpled hills full of sagebrush and juniper down to the Missouri, and cottonwoods crowd the meandering old channels that mark where the rivers used to meet—the confluence of two such big, brawling rivers is always a work in progress.

It was a hot, late-summer day, the thermometer topping a hundred for the second week in a row, but there was a breeze blowing with a promise of storms and a break in the weather, and the northwestern horizon was gray with clouds. Out over the Missouri,

Caspian terns were pushing into the wind, long silver wings rowing hard to make headway, while above them a single bald eagle
sailed along like a small plane. A line of white pelicans rose above
the tree line, undulating like a snake, then fell again behind the
screen of cottonwoods, to the water. Somewhere behind me, in the
sage and brown grass, a lark sparrow was singing, its mechanical
trills even slower than usual, an oh-what-the-hell sense to its song
that signaled the end of the breeding season and an ebbing hor-
mone tide. Soon the sparrow would fall silent until next spring.

Lewis and Clark were the first whites to see the mouth of the
Yellowstone, and these military officers quickly recognized that the
bluffs overlooking the confluence would be an ideal place for a fort.
But what struck Lewis most forcefully was the raw beauty and fe-
cundity of the "wide and fertile vallies" that he saw. "The whol
face of the country was covered with herds of Buffaloe, Elk & An-
telopes; deer are also abundant, but keep themselves more concealed in the woodland," he wrote on April 25, 1805. "The buffaloe
Elk and Antelope are so gentle that we pass near them while feeding, without apearing to excite any alarm among them."

It didn't take long for the American Fur Co. to act on Lewis and
Clark's suggestion about fortifying the spot. By 1828, they'd begun
work on Fort Union, which controlled trade with the Assiniboine,
Crow, Blackfoot, and Hidatsa. Indians brought their pelts to the
fort, camping on the wide floodplain around the square stockade. If
times were peaceful, the front gate stood open and everyone came
and went as they pleased, one big, never-ending party fueled by
liquor and the implicit understanding among tribes, many of
whom were mortal enemies, that this was neutral ground. If tensions were running high, the exchanges took place through a small
hatch in the outer wall by the trade room, which was packed with

thousands of items, ranging from iron kettles, Dutch muskets, and packets of vermilion to bolts of cloth and cutlery from Sheffield, England, including the foot-long steel spear points the Assiniboine favored for hunting bison.

Fort Union is one of my favorite places along the Lewis and Clark trail, because the past is close to the surface here. Look south out over the meeting of the waters—the flat landscape dominated by the low swell of the cottonwood forests, the Missouri sliding past in muddy haste just a few hundred yards away—and it's easy to imagine how it looked to the Corps of Discovery in 1805. Look the other way, to the north, and it's even easier to envision the past, because the fort (now a national historic site) has been reconstructed to its 1851 appearance, with high wooden walls enclosing a parade ground over which a huge thirty-eight-star flag snaps in the breeze, and a two-story, red-roofed administrative house; in summer, the grounds outside are dotted with white canvas tepees, from whose lodgepole tips flutter colored streamers. The trade room is even stocked with the same items it originally held, including Sheffield scissors and those wickedly long spear points.

In 1803, a year before the expedition set out, Thomas Jefferson sent Meriwether Lewis—twenty-eight, Jefferson's personal secretary, a bright army officer with an interest in natural history, but little formal education—to Philadelphia for a cram course in the sciences. Bartram's colleague Benjamin Barton taught him the basics of botany and how to prepare herbarium specimens (Lewis eventually brought back more than two hundred sheets of pressed plants); pioneering physician Dr. Benjamin Rush tutored him in medicine, while others instructed him in celestial navigation, taxidermy, ethnology, surveying, and even the rudiments of paleontology, in case they came across signs of the mammoths and other ice age mammals Jefferson thought might still live in the unknown West.

The training paid off; the Corps was the first truly scientific exploration of North America, with Lewis taking copious notes about nearly everything—mammoths were about the only thing to escape his attention. During their time exploring the mouth of the Yellowstone, he noted the quality and features of the soil and the drainage of the land, weather conditions and river flows, tallied the principal species of trees ("Cottonwood, with some small elm, ash and boxalder") and recorded the makeup of the various plant communities from river edge to the hills. He and Clark examined a trumpeter swan one of the men shot; noted the extraordinary number of bald eagles and commented on how often magpies nested in close proximity to the eagles' own nests; tried to collect the first bighorn sheep they'd seen; and killed one of the many grizzly bears that were feeding on drowned buffalo, from which Lewis prepared the first scientific description of the species. (He called it a "furious and formidable anamal," and said "it is asstonishing to see the wounds they will bear before they can be put to death." But he pooh-poohed the stories they'd heard from Indians about the beasts: "In the hands of skillfull riflemen they are by no means as formidable or dangerous as they have been represented." Lewis would quickly come to abandon this last notion.)

By the time the expedition returned to the East in 1806, they had shipped back crates of specimens, including some of the first new birds from the Louisiana Purchase—among them, four live black-billed magpies, sent to Jefferson from their first winter camp. They were the first white men to note the greater sage-grouse, the first Americans to see California condors (the Spanish had recorded them as early as 1602), the first to describe greater white-fronted geese, least terns, common poorwills, and McCown's longspurs, among many other species. Lewis noted the difference between the "old-field lark" back east and a species on the Plains with the same buttery yellow breast but a much more melodious song—the western meadowlark.

Although he never realized his dream of accompanying one of the western expeditions, it was Alexander Wilson who, with great excitement, received the Lewis and Clark bird specimens for publication. There is no indication that Lewis and Wilson met prior to the expedition, but afterwards the two men struck up a firm, but short-lived friendship.* It was Wilson who named "Clark's crow" (now Clark's nutcracker) and Lewis's woodpecker in honor of their discoverers, depicting them with a Louisiana (now western) tanager, also new to science, in the third volume of *American Ornithology*. He also painted a magpie, using as his model one of the live birds the expedition had shipped home.

The Lewis and Clark expedition provided the first of what soon grew to be a flood of new bird discoveries from the western half of the continent, almost all of them a result of military expeditions. In fact—because of continuing hostilities with Indian tribes who took understandable umbrage at the invasion of their lands—the story of ornithology in the West through most of the nineteenth century is largely one involving men on horseback with guns. In particular, the U.S. Army Medical Corps had a remarkable number of ornithologists in its ranks, some of whom in later life rose to the top of the profession (when ornithology finally became

---

*In fact, Wilson went out of his way, during his 1810 trip down the Mississippi, to seek out the spot along the Natchez Trace where Lewis had either been murdered or committed suicide six months earlier. Wilson paid the landowner to have the grave protected, interviewed witnesses, and wrote the most comprehensive account of the circumstances of Lewis's still-mysterious death.

a profession). Women naturalists, scarce even in the East during the nineteenth century, were all but unheard of on the frontier—which makes the one or two exceptions all the more intriguing, as we'll see.

The interlocking arcs of the science of birds and the sport of birding—so clearly differentiated today—are a lot trickier to trace in earlier centuries. After all, most of the early ornithologists were really just fanatical amateurs, some (like Catesby and Bartram) with a decent education, others like Wilson essentially self-taught, or tutored by generous mentors. "Natural philosophy" might be taught as part of a broader education, but there was no formal training program for an ornithologist in the way that tradesmen had apprenticeships, or physicians colleges. The best one could do was apply him or herself by reading the growing canon of published work, and getting into the field to seek out new specimens.

Thomas Say was one such fellow, another Philadelphia Quaker—the Friends' tradition of education and serious inquiry was one reason Philadelphia became an early scientific hub. As a young man, Say brought his insect collections to his great-uncle, William Bartram, and spent an excessive amount of time at the first natural history museum in America, established by the painter Charles Willson Peale. Say eventually became an apothecary, but his interest in nature (and his family's seemingly genetic wanderlust) won out. He did some exploring along the southern coast with George Ord and others, but in 1819, Say, then thirty-two, signed on to the Stephen Long expedition to the West.

Say was accompanied by Peale's nineteen-year-old son, Titian, himself a talented artist and naturalist who the year before had become the youngest elected member of the Academy of Natural Sciences. The Long expedition traveled up the Platte to the front range of the Colorado Rockies, then looped back along the Arkansas and Canadian rivers through the southern Plains. This was not the first military operation in this area; the 1806 Pike expedition, which Wilson longed to join, had passed up the Arkansas and into the Rockies more than a decade earlier. But Pike didn't have a naturalist with him and produced nothing of scientific note.

The Long expedition, by contrast, was a gold mine—the first time trained, professional naturalists got a peek at the interior of western North America. Say described a host of new animals, including such classically Plains species as mule deer, coyotes, and prairie rattlers, as well as such western birds as band-tailed pigeons, sooty (formerly blue) grouse, western kingbirds, lazuli buntings, and lesser goldfinches. Peale's watercolors and drawings are particularly lovely—among them field sketches of prairie dogs and

As naturalists pushed west, they encountered exciting new species of birds like this lark sparrow, sketched by Titian Peale in 1819 when he accompanied the Long expedition across the southern Plains to the Colorado Rockies. *Courtesy of the American Philosophical Society*

horned lizards, families of burrowing owls, with notations on coloration, and the first illustration of bison on the western prairies. In fact, because Say was mostly interested in insects and mollusks, it may have been Peale who did most of the bird collecting.

Another pair of naturalists from Philadelphia figure in a now largely forgotten episode in western exploration, the Wyeth expedition of 1834–35, which crossed the Rockies to Oregon. Thomas Nuttall was a journeyman printer from England who, on his second day in America, stumbled into Benjamin Barton and became his pupil, eventually developing into a superb botanist. In 1811, only five years after Lewis and Clark, he traveled up the Missouri to the Dakotas, then, in 1819, ascended the Arkansas to what is now Oklahoma, eventually publishing a botany manual and becoming curator of Harvard's botanical gardens.

But Nuttall was also interested in birds. In 1832, he published the first volume of a two-volume *Manual of the Ornithology of the United States and Canada,* a groundbreaking work in two regards—it was small enough to carry into the field (though the first volume alone, covering land birds, ran to eight hundred pages), and it was illustrated with woodcuts instead of expensive hand-colored plates. Primitive as it was (and heavily indebted to Wilson, from whom Nuttall borrowed without always giving credit) this was in a sense the first field guide to North American birds, and it remained in print—and in use—into the first years of the twentieth century.

Nuttall might have been happy to settle into the academic life at Harvard had he not, in 1833, received a package that propelled him west once again. Dispatched some months earlier from the upper Snake River (then known as Lewis's River) in Idaho, it was sent by Nathaniel J. Wyeth, a Massachusetts ice merchant and entrepreneur who had trekked to Oregon, in the hope of setting a business on the coast, and was returning home in failure. Very little seems to have daunted Wyeth, though, and as he crossed the Rockies heading back east, he was already planning a return trip, this time to establish a fur-trading post—and conduct a scientific exploration along the way.

Heads of Lewis River, July 4th 1833

Dear Sir: I have sent through my brother Leond of N. York a package of plants collected in the interior and on the western coast of America somewhere about Latt 46 deg. I am afraid they will be of little value to you. The rain has been so constant where I have been gathering them that they have lost their colors in some cases, and they will be liable to further accident on their route home.

I shall remain here one more year. You if in Camb[ridge] may expect to see me in about one year from the time you receive this. I shall then ask you if you will follow another expedition to this country in pursuit of your science. The cost would be less than living at home.

I have several times attempted to preserve birds to send you but have failed from the moisture and warmth. Excuse the shortness of this as I have many letters to write and little time to do it in.

Resply Yr. obt. servt. Nathl. J Wyeth

The gift of plants was a shrewd incentive on Wyeth's part. Nuttall took the bait, resigning his post at Harvard, and in turn he tapped a young acquaintance from yet another studious, professional

Quaker family, this one inclined toward medicine. John K. Townsend was twenty-four, half Nuttall's age, with a freshly minted doctorate and a passion for birds that would complement Nuttall's botanical interest. The year before, he'd collected that odd bunting, which Audubon named for him and which to this day defies identification.

The expedition set off from Independence, Missouri, on April 28, 1834, a company of seventy men, two hundred and fifty horses, the legendary trapper Milton Sublette, and a herd of cattle trailed by missionaries who were tagging along. Soon they were among birds Townsend had never seen before: "I think I never before saw so great a variety of birds within the same space," he later wrote. "All were beautiful, and many of them quite new to me; and after we had spent an hour amongst them, and my game bag was teeming with its precious freight, I was still loath to leave the place, lest I should not have procured specimens of the whole."

Reading Wyeth's journals from his two expeditions, one gets the impression of a blunt, refreshingly candid fellow with an active curiosity about the land through which he traveled—the plants, soils, and wildlife (including the apparently satisfying taste of bald eagle chicks, which they ate when other food was scarce). But whatever his personal feelings about science and the work Nuttall and his colleague were doing, his journal from 1834 is all business, and he only mentions Nuttall and Townsend once in the entire five months it took them to reach the coast.

Townsend's journal is another matter—chatty, literate, often self-deprecatingly funny, full of his excited observations and concerns, admission of an initial homesickness and an eventual enthusiastic embracing of the adventure, from buffalo hunting to stalking grizzlies. The young man, raised in polite urban society, at first had a hard time adjusting to the rough familiarity of the band's trappers and hunters, however much he admired it. "It is noble . . . but for myself, I have not been accustomed to seeing it exercised, and when a rough fellow comes up without warning, and slaps me on the shoulder, with, 'Stranger what for a gun is that you carry?' I start, and am on the point of making an angry reply, but I remember where I am, check the feeling instantly, and submit the weapon to his inspection."

Such prissiness resurfaced when they reached the fur rendezvous on the Green River in Wyoming, where the ill Townsend was "compelled all day to listen to the hiccoughing jargon of drunken traders, the *sacré* and *foutre* of Frenchmen run wild, and the swearing and screaming of our own men, who are scarcely less savage than the rest, being heated by the detestable liquor which circulates freely among them." Likewise, when Wyeth allowed the crew to celebrate the Fourth of July with rum, Townsend tut-tutted "a renewal of the coarse and brutal scenes of the rendezvous." (Wyeth, by contrast, simply confessed to his journal that "I gave the men too much alcohol for peace [and] took a pretty hearty spree myself.")

The birds, however, were a constant source of delight for Townsend. (Nuttall, for the most part, appears to have devoted himself to botany, though his journals from the trip are lost.) Along the way to the Columbia, they found mountain plovers, whooping cranes, white pelicans, chestnut-collared longspurs, lark buntings, and a host of other new or little-known species, including Lewis and Clark's "cock of the plains," the greater sage grouse, a bird they shot with an eye toward a generous meal, only to find its diet of sage rendered it almost inedible. "From this time the cock of the plains was allowed to roam free and unmolested, as he has failed to please our palates, we are content to admire the beauty of his plumage, and the grace and spirit of his attitudes," Townsend wrote.

The expedition contended with bad weather, illness, sparse rations, and the need to discard most of their personal possessions. "Already we have cast away all our useless and superfluous clothing, and have been content to mortify our natural pride, to make room for our specimens," Townsend noted in his journal. "Such things as spare waistcoats, shaving boxes, soap, and stockings, have been ejected from our trunks, and we are content to dress, as we live, in a style of primitive simplicity."

The crew's privations had a direct impact on Townsend's work; an owl he collected was roasted and eaten by Nuttall and another man ("The temptation was too great to be resisted . . . and the bird of wisdom lost the immortality which he might otherwise have acquired"), and Catesby himself would have sympathized with one problem Townsend experienced. Having amassed a nice assortment of snakes and lizards, preserved in a two-gallon jug of whiskey, Townsend found that one of the men—a fellow whose "appetite for ardent spirits was of the most inordinate kind"—had drunk the reptiles dry, ruining them.

Having reached the Pacific, Townsend went into a flurry of collecting, including the warbler that now bears his name, an honor bestowed by Nuttall. Then the two men kept right on going, hopping a ship headed for Hawaii, before returning to the Pacific Northwest and, ultimately, Pennsylvania, their notes and crates of specimens safely in hand. (Taxidermy would later be the death of Townsend, who died in 1851, apparently poisoned by the arsenic that he, like most scientists, used to preserve his skins.)

So many men; were there no women ornithologists? In the strictest sense, no, since few women had careers of any sort in those days, and of the precious few in the sciences, most were in botany. Thomas Say's wife, Lucy, was an extraordinarily talented artist, who illustrated his *American Conchology* and hand-colored the prints for the 1830 publication; she was the first woman elected to the Academy of Natural Sciences, although this was for her donation of her husband's collection rather than her own substantial achievements. Similarly, Alexander Lawson's daughter Helen inherited her engraver father's artistic abilities and turned them to scientific illustration, and John Townsend's sister Mary wrote a book on the lives of insects.

Not until the middle of the nineteenth century, though, did a woman make any significant professional headway in American ornithology. Graceanna Lewis, born in 1821 into still another progressive Philadelphia Quaker family, was urged by her mother to study the natural world. She became the protégé of John Cassin, an irascible crank who served brilliantly as the unpaid curator of birds for the Academy, despite his off-putting personality. (One official history of the institution describes him as "an unhappy, bitter man with a sharp tongue that produced a lonely isolation.")

But he couldn't have been all bad, because with Cassin's help, Lewis blossomed as a scientist, gaining the respect of the leading male ornithologists of her time. Had her mentor not died prematurely (again, probably from arsenic poisoning—a real occupational hazard in those days, and one that Cassin was aware of but unable to avoid) she might have achieved lasting fame, for shortly after the Civil War, she published the first volume of an expected ten-volume series on the natural history of birds. But sexism ran deep, and with her patron's death in 1869, Lewis found many doors closed to her; she was unable to secure a teaching post and is best remembered today for her popular writings on nature, and her illustrations of insects, flowers, and trees by which she made a living. The sole volume of *A Natural History of Birds* shows what she—and other women—could have contributed if they'd been allowed to live up to their potential.

AUDUBON, back from Scotland in 1836, tried to get access to Nuttall and Townsend's specimens but was blocked by Ord; instead, he purchased duplicate specimens directly from the two collectors, and depicted many of these new western birds in the third and fourth volumes of *Birds of America*—along with an account of the two men's journey through the Rockies that is as entertaining as it is largely fictitious. "How grand and impressive the scenery presented to their admiring gaze . . . while on wide-spread wings the Great Vulture [California condor] sailed overhead watching the departure of the travellers." Condors in the Rockies? Nuttall and Townsend recorded no such thing, but Audubon used their sparse notes as a creative springboard.

Audubon had his own dreams of the Great Plains, the western mountains, the Columbia, and the Pacific coast; it must have irked the old wanderer to be unable to ascend the western rivers to the continental divide, where others were making such exciting discoveries. But the workload for *Birds* and *Ornithological Biography* was just too great, and not until their completion in 1839 was he free to begin to think seriously about a trip west of his own. Other matters came first, though, including the purchase of a home on a large, wooded estate along the Hudson in upper Manhattan that he named Minnie's Land ("Minnie" being Lucy's family nickname). It was the first home the family had owned in more than twenty years.

His great project on birds was completed, but ever restless, Audubon had leapt into another enormous challenge, *The Viviparous Quadrupeds of North America,* a work on mammals he was coauthoring with his close friend, the Rev. John Bachman of Charleston, South Carolina, and with artistic help from his sons. (The ties between Audubon and Bachman were deep and tragic, as John Woodhouse and Victor Audubon had married Bachman's daughters Maria and Eliza, who died within a few months of each other, in 1840–41.) Audubon was also bringing out a smaller, more affordable version of his bird volumes, this time in what was known as an octavo edition, about the size of a modern hardcover book, and hoped to include more western species.

With all this, the western expedition didn't come to pass until 1843. Audubon and his four companions set out from Saint Louis in April, in the steamboat *Omega,* which was jammed with fur-company trappers, more than a hundred of them headed up the Missouri for the season. Audubon watched the men—some "drunk, and many in that stupid mood which follows a state of nervousness produced by drinking and over-excitement"—fire a disorganized volley of celebratory gunfire as they left the shore, then queue up in the main cabin to receive their sparse allotment of gear.

In the days ahead, Audubon tried to stick to his task, which was collecting and observing mammals; at a plantation just north of Saint Louis, his host had slaves dig up the extensive burrows and storage chambers of "pouched rats," as Audubon called pocket gophers, several of which he kept in his cabin, where they kept getting loose, chewing holes in his hunting jacket and the leather straps on his trunk.

But if his mind was on mammals, Audubon's heart—and his journal—was full of birds. At first, these were familiar eastern varieties, though here, as always, it is the mention of lost species that grabs the eye of a modern reader. On May 2, near Fort Leavenworth, in Kansas, Audubon noted that taxidermist John Bell had shot two Carolina parakeets. The next day: "Seeing a great number of Parrakeets." A few days later: "Killed a Cat-bird, Waterthrush [and] seventeen Parrakeets." May 6: "I shot a Wild Pigeon and a Whippoorwill." Perhaps, had we shaved things a bit closer to the edge of extinction in the mid-twentieth century, we would have a similar reaction to Audubon's mention of "white-headed eagles" and peregrine falcons in the same stretch of river, but those references haven't the air of impending tragedy carried by his descriptions of parrots, passenger pigeons, and, later in the trip, vast herds of bison and Plains grizzlies.

Audubon was still a good-looking man. In a pencil portrait by Isaac Sprague, a young naturalist-artist who had agreed to come as one of his assistants, Audubon still sports the same long, waving hair and heavy sideburns, the shirt worn open at the neck—still very much the American Woodsman. But he wasn't the young dandy he'd been back in Mill Grove, or even the dashing artist that Europe had embraced. That long hair was now white, he had aches and pains in legions, and Sprague may have taken some license in drawing a firm mouth, since at the time of the portrait, a few months before their departure, Audubon had only one remaining tooth, and his lips must have been sunken. By the time the *Omega* sailed, Audubon was fifty-eight but looked a good decade older, and that last tooth had fallen out.

His health deteriorating, toothless, and his eyesight all but gone, John James Audubon sat for this daguerreotype by Mathew Brady in 1847, four years after his Missouri River expedition. Already, Audubon's sons had taken over much of his work, and the great naturalist had only a few more years to live. *Courtesy of the Smithsonian Institution Archives*

The same day he shot seventeen parakeets, Audubon also collected "a new finch, and very curious," a sparrow he would later name for Edward Harris, one of Audubon's closest friends and patrons, who was along for the jaunt, having previously accompanied Audubon to the Gulf coast, in 1837. (Audubon didn't realize that Nuttall had already collected the same sparrow nine years earlier, when he was ascending the Missouri, but "Harris's sparrow," the name Audubon published in his octavo, is the one we still use.) Sprague collected a new species of pipit, and Bell was on a roll, pointing out—as had Meriwether Lewis—that western meadowlarks are distinct from those in the East, shooting the first LeConte's sparrow, as well as a new vireo, which Audubon named for him.

Sprague's pipit, LeConte's sparrow, Bell's vireo—any birder, flipping through a field guide, wonders aloud, "Who the heck were these people?" This is especially true if one is birding west of the one-hundredth meridian, the line that divides the lush, wooded

East from the central grasslands. Eastern birds, by and large, bear physically descriptive English names, a function of the organic, bottom-up process through which common folk coined the names by which many are still known. Where the name includes a proper noun, it's usually a place name: Philadelphia vireo or Cape May warbler, for instance. Honorific names among eastern birds are fairly rare, and they tend to belong to the species that were rare, cryptic in nature, or had long been confused with look-alike cousins and thus weren't noticed and named by popular consensus.

As ornithology moved west, however, it left that folk name tradition behind. Now, the first whites to see a new species were often scientists, jostling for the opportunity to name it—and the names they chose were often those of friends, colleagues, or patrons. Audubon is credited with discovering thirty-four species and subspecies of birds, twenty-three of which he named for people. He named Henslow's sparrow for the Rev. John S. Henslow, a British botanist who helped secure subscriptions to *The Birds of America,* Bewick's wren for Thomas Bewick, another English supporter, and Harlan's hawk (now considered a subspecies of the redtail) for Dr. Richard Harlan, a Philadelphia doctor who took Audubon's part in the battles with Ord's Wilsonians.

So, the best way to be immortalized is to find a new bird and name it after yourself, right? Actually, no; that violates one of the longstanding prohibitions in the world of nomenclature. There is an Audubon's warbler (now considered a subspecies of the yellow-rumped warbler), but not even John James had the audacity to name it for himself; that honor was bestowed by Townsend. It's fine if a friend, admirer, or associate names a species for you, but it's considered beyond tacky to do so yourself.

Which is why William Gambel may have gone blushing to his early grave. A protégé of Nuttall's when still in his teens, Gambel was born around 1819 (the sources disagree) to a Philadelphia family of modest means, but he became a talented young naturalist. He headed west in 1841, swinging south along the Santa Fe Trail from Kansas down into New Mexico, where he discovered the mountain chickadee. Then he pushed on for California over the Old Spanish Trail through Nevada, where he collected a lovely quail with a curling topknot, chestnut flanks, and a rusty cap. Believing that his mentor Nuttall had already described the quail during the Wyeth expedition some years earlier—and what's more, believing Nuttall had named it for him—he labeled it "Gambel's quail." Then he soldiered on to California, where he spent several years as a naval secretary, devoting all of his spare time to collecting such new species as wrentit, oak titmouse, and a woodpecker he named for Nuttall. No doubt Gambel felt good about returning the favor.

Except that Nuttall hadn't, in fact, collected that unusual quail at all, nor had he named it for his young friend. It was a new species, and Gambel's description of it was the first published; under the rules of priority, in which the first published name becomes official, the name stuck. If Gambel was embarrassed by this, he didn't have long to suffer. On his return to Philadelphia in 1845, he failed to get a job he'd sought with the Academy of Natural Sciences, so he became a physician, anxious to return to California as news of the 1849 Gold Rush spread. He should have waited; the wagon train he joined made a horrifically difficult journey across the Great Basin, crossing the Sierra Nevada in midwinter, and Gambel died of typhoid in a mining camp a few weeks shy of Christmas, his bride-to-be waiting vainly for him in San Francisco.

His grave, along the Feather River, was later washed away by a placer mining operation.*

Most of the time, when Audubon named a bird for someone, he was rewarding powerful supporters, but he had a more personal reason to name Bell's vireo after his companion, since Bell saved his life on the upper Missouri. The *Omega* had arrived at Fort Union in the late afternoon of June 12, 1843, having just spotted a herd of two dozen bighorns—"the finest sight of all," Audubon wrote excitedly in his journal. But despite his hope to continue upriver another four hundred miles to the Rockies, this was the end of the line, and he and his companions spent the next two months as the guests of American Fur Co. chief trader Alexander Culbertson.

The time at the fort turned into one long hunting party—and Audubon, bone-tired and footsore, was left out of much of it. His younger companions chased bison on horseback compulsively, while he watched from a safe distance, fretting about the utter waste of meat and animals' lives. He was far from squeamish when it came to shooting; he'd hunted all his life, but the sheer scale of the slaughter at Fort Union left him deeply troubled. "What a terrible destruction of life, as it were for nothing, or next to it, as the tongues only were brought in, and the flesh of these fine animals was left to beasts and birds of prey, or to rot on the spot where they fell." The sight of Culbertson and his Blackfoot wife feasting on raw buffalo brains, he said, left him physically ill. "Handsome, and

---

*Gambel's final journey has become a minor historical bugaboo, thanks to a mixup of famous names. Not long after leaving Missouri, Gambel joined an ox-team, trading his services as a physician for passage across the Rockies. The team was led by a "Captain Boone of Kentucky," and with time, the assumption that this was none other than Daniel Boone himself crept into the literature—even though Boone had died in 1820 and would have been almost 115 years old by the time Gambel arrived. Despite that, this spurious "fact" has appeared in everything from a 1970s history of ornithology to a host of modern websites.

really courteous and refined in many ways, I cannot reconcile to myself the fact that she partakes of raw animal food with such evident relish."

A month after their arrival, Audubon and his companions were out hunting along the Yellowstone—at least, *they* were hunting, while he caught catfish for the pot. But the day took a dramatic turn when one of the fort's hunters, Owen Mckenzie, went after a solitary old buffalo bull while Bell and Audubon watched. Chasing it down on his winded horse, the hunter fired twice, bringing the bull to a halt; Audubon and Bell, thinking the pursuit was over, ran down to join Mckenzie, but when they came near, the bull—still a long way from dead—charged. The two men fired their pistols "with little or no effect, except to increase his fury with every shot." With the bull only a few feet from goring Audubon, Bell snatched McKenzie's rifle and shot the animal, killing it.

BEFORE AUDUBON had left the East, he had tried to add another member to the expedition—a twenty-year-old from rural Pennsylvania named Spencer Fullerton Baird, who had been corresponding with the old Frenchman for the preceding five years. Baird had sent him specimens that he and his older brother William had collected, including two previously unknown flycatchers, the yellow-bellied and the least. "Precocious" hardly begins to describe Spencer Baird. At age thirteen, he'd entered Dickinson College in Carlisle, where Wilson's *Ornithology* was a revelation. When Baird came across it in the school library, he read it straight through, all nine volumes, blowing off classes in a pleasant haze of birds. His reaction to *Birds of America* and *Ornithological Biography* was much the same, sparking his correspondence with Audubon.

He graduated at seventeen and two years later began studying medicine, while continuing to pursue natural history. His professional reach would eventually encompass not just ornithology, but mammalogy, herpetology, ichthyology, archaeology; a stint as the formative second secretary of the Smithsonian Institution; and a pivotal role in founding the American Ornithologists' Union.

Baird had clearly made an impression on Audubon, who the year before had given the young man the majority of his bird skin collection, including the precious "type specimens," those on which the description of a new species had been based. It was a profoundly generous act, and Audubon wanted Baird to join him on the Missouri. The younger man certainly had the stamina for such a grueling journey; when he was eighteen, Baird set out on foot on a collecting trip through the Pennsylvania mountains, covering four hundred miles in three weeks, including a march of sixty miles the last day alone.* The following year, he logged more than two thousand miles on foot. Oddly, Baird fretted all his life about a supposedly weak heart, and his mother and other relatives, concerned for his health and safety in the West—Indians! Wild animals!—persuaded him not to go, even though Audubon offered to pay Baird's share of the expenses. To their mutual disappointment, Audubon set off without him.

But during the sojourn at Fort Union, the redoubtable Bell shot a pair of sparrows, a yellowish tinge to their heads and a distinctive necklace of dark spots. Audubon named the new species for Baird, drawing it for the five-hundredth (and final) plate of the octavo

---

*Ever the scientist, one evening partway through his long trek, Baird carefully measured himself, having hiked ten miles with a forty-pound pack, then again in the morning after a night's sleep—and found that he'd gained three-quarters of an inch in height by daybreak.

edition. It was an honor with unusual resonance, since Baird's sparrow was the last wholly new species the aging naturalist would describe, although as they headed downriver in September, Bell shot a small goatsucker "that I have no doubt it is the one found in the Rocky Mountains by Nuttall, after whom I have named it," Audubon wrote. He dubbed it Nuttall's whip-poor-will, *Caprimulgus nuttallii*, though today it is known as the common poorwill.

The trip up the Missouri took a lot out of Audubon. Back at Minnie's Land, he sat for a portrait by his son John Woodhouse—the heavy beard he would soon shave, as he did at the end of all his expeditions, a green hunting coat trimmed with fur, his fowling piece cocked and ready in his hands—then set about working on the plates for *Viviparous Quadrupeds*. But he struggled; his eyes were going, and for all the buffalo hunting and fourteen new birds, the expedition had produced little in the way of mammalian discoveries, its intended purpose. Bachman, Audubon's friend and coauthor, gnashed his teeth with frustration. Then, even as the first volume appeared in 1845, Audubon's vision gave out, and his sons had to take over for the final two volumes, with John Woodhouse painting the mammals (many from museum specimens in England) and Victor adding the backgrounds as well as serving as Bachman's editor.

Audubon was fading rapidly, essentially blind and falling into "his little fancies," as the family delicately called his growing dementia. The Audubons, never financially secure, had some serious reversals; during the Gold Rush of 1849, they invested in a California mining cooperative, which John Woodhouse was to oversee, but he almost died crossing the desert, and then the investment went bust. More money was lost on a foundry. Word of their father's condition spread, and not all of the reaction was sympathetic.

Characteristically, Ord draped his concern in condescension and malice: "Had he merely stuck to painting birds he might have jogged on pretty fairly. But when he borrowed the character of an ornithologist, it bore him too high up, then let him fall," he wrote through crocodile tears to a colleague.

For his part, Audubon was beyond the petty squabbles of the past. On January 27, 1851, he died at home, with Lucy and the boys beside him; he was sixty-five. He was buried in Trinity Cemetery along what is now upper Broadway, where he still lies. With his death, the family faced even more hardships. The octavo edition of *Quadrupeds* appeared that year, but five years later, Victor fell from a train and became an invalid; he died in 1860, and John Wood-house two years thereafter. By 1863 money was so tight that Lucy decided to part with both Minnie's Land and the original water-colors of *Birds of America*—although she couldn't find a taker for the paintings, at least at first. Finally, the New-York Historical Society raised four thousand dollars for the set, which it continues to hold today.

Lucy, resourceful to the end, had reverted to teaching in the years after her husband's death, an echo of her days as a governess in Louisiana while John James was overseas. Before she was forced to dispose of all of it, she sold off parcels of Minnie's Land, including one tract to a businessman who had just moved to the neighborhood from Brooklyn and who apparently made the purchase as a kindness to the family. His young son attended Madam Audubon's small school, and for his part, the boy, named George Bird Grinnell, was smitten with this "most kindly, gentle, benignant woman," always wearing mourning black, a white cap, and spectacles.

Although the railroad had run a line right along the edge of the Audubon estate, bringing in a flood of well-to-do commuters, the area of Manhattan north of 155th Street known as Audubon Park (today's Washington Heights) was in those days still a dense forest of white pine and hemlock, with tidal ponds along the river, full of ducks and snipe; the boy was called to the window one day to see a flock of passenger pigeons descending on a fruiting dogwood, and in winter, bald eagles were a common sight on the Hudson's ice floes. The youngster, true to his middle name, absorbed everything he could about birds from "Grandma" Audubon, who encouraged him; one day he used a crab net to catch an odd greenish bird, which the elderly woman identified as a female red crossbill.

George was fascinated by the house. "In the hall were antlers of elk and deer, which supported guns, shot pouches, powder flasks and belts. Pictures that are now famous hung on the walls," he recalled in later years. "The painting of pheasants started by a dog— now in the American Museum [of Natural History]—was in the parlor . . . and the picture of the eagle and the lamb upstairs in Madam Audubon's bedroom. Everywhere were vivid reminders of the former owner of the land."

The eagle painting held a particular fascination for the boy. It was one of two versions in oil that Audubon painted while in London in 1828 or '29, trying to generate cash to keep *Birds* afloat. One was obtained by the Earl of Derby, a noted natural historian, and this one, the original (which some sources indicate he'd hoped to sell to King George IV's mistress), came back to the States with him. A golden eagle, one wing thrown wide and talons outstretched, descends on a lamb against a backdrop of roiling clouds, just the sort of melodrama to hook a boy.

Young George Grinnell made no secret of his love of the painting, and Lucy even once told him that he could have it after her death. "Boylike, I treasured this memory, but the promise was not referred to again." Yet she did not forget, and years later, in 1873—shortly before leaving for Louisville on what would be her last journey—Grandma Audubon sent George a single-page note. Addressed "Dear young friend" (even though George was by now in his mid-twenties), the crabbed writing is hard to decipher, but in it she makes a gift of the painting, "with all the care and esteem for yourself & your parents."

By now, Grinnell was pursuing a career in science, studying under the great Yale paleontologist O. C. Marsh and making annual collecting trips to the West. In 1874, the year Lucy died, a financial panic shuttered his father's business, and George headed west again, this time to the Black Hills as naturalist for Lt. Col. George A. Custer; the next year, he was in Yellowstone, but in 1876 he declined a chance to join Custer once more, thus avoiding the Little Bighorn debacle. In fact, Grinnell developed a great sympathy for the Plains Indians, becoming a noted ethnographer of the Pawnee, Cheyenne, and Blackfoot, and was their impassioned defender against the hardships of reservation life and the chicanery of the federal Indian agents. Out of gratitude, the Blackfoot eventually made him the honorary head chief of the tribe.

The delight at birds that Lucy Audubon planted in him never faltered, however; among his many other achievements was a distinguished career as an ornithologist and conservationist. His editorials in *Forest and Stream* magazine about the beauty and fragility of the West were instrumental in gaining protection for Yellowstone's wildlife and for what became, through his tireless efforts, Glacier National Park, in Montana, much of which he explored and named. When he died, in 1938, the *New York Times* called him "the father of American conservation."

But he is best remembered for founding, in 1886, an association devoted to the protection of wild birds, which he named after his mentor and her husband: the Audubon Society. Grinnell's brainchild was short-lived—it's hard to maintain a national organization with no dues, as he tried to do—and the entity which we know today as the National Audubon Society arose a decade later, thanks to the efforts of wealthy women in Boston. But nevertheless, George Bird Grinnell bridged the three phases of American ornithology—its rough-and-tumble origins at the hands of a few geniuses like Wilson and Audubon, its maturity into a profession populated by scientists like Dr. Grinnell himself, and the explosive growth of birding as a hobby for the masses, propelled in large measure by the various state Audubon associations he helped prod into existence.

It's here that the tidy, fairly linear narrative, which began with the earliest European explorers and flowed west toward the frontier, finally fragments entirely. We'll be coming back to Grinnell and his Audubon society, but not immediately; by the middle of the nineteenth century, the history of American ornithology and birding scatters like a flushed covey of quail, and from here on, tracing its varied movement entails a lot of backtracking and overlap—the rise of recreational birding, the growth of the bird conservation movement, the evolution of field guides, the widening of a sometimes bitter divide between professionals and amateurs a century ago that is now bridged at the hands of millions of "citizenscientists." The cast includes army officers chasing birds with as much zeal as Indians, philandering ornithologists, spiritualists, high-school dropouts, egg collectors, society women, and "operaglass fiends," as the first birders were known.

Although Lucy Audubon was as good as her word, it took some years before *The Eagle and the Lamb* passed to Grinnell as she intended; after her death the enormous painting remained in the family, and it wasn't until 1893 that her granddaughter, Harriet Bachman Audubon, found she had no room for the great canvas and at last gave it to Grinnell. It became, understandably, one of his most prized possessions, and on his death, in turn, Grinnell's widow presented it to the National Audubon Society.* Today, the painting hangs at the Audubon center at Mill Grove, a visible symbol of the links between birding's roots and its future—and still theatrical enough to snatch the eye of passing children and, perhaps, to open for them the splendor and drama of birds.

---

*The story of *The Eagle and The Lamb* has a number of enlightening twists. National Audubon obtained the painting in 1940, but five years later, with permission from Grinnell's widow, attempted to sell the piece. If this seems strange, consider the subject matter, and the fact that Audubon was then trying to convince western ranchers to stop shooting golden eagles for killing sheep; it was felt that *The Eagle and The Lamb* was too inflammatory to be associated with the organization. It sat in several New York City galleries but attracted no purchaser until 1953, when Sarah Moyer, an Audubon member from the Philadelphia suburbs, bought it and loaned it to Mill Grove, at the time a county park. The gift was made permanent in 1985. Recently, when the painting was cleaned, Audubon's signature on the reverse was found, with a date of 1820—which seems unlikely, since that year Audubon was wandering from Kentucky to Cincinnati to Louisiana.

4

Shotgun Ornithology

ON A SPRING MORNING in 1872, Charles Bendire was riding along Rillito Creek, a cottonwood-lined stream that came down from the Santa Rita Mountains north of Tucson, then a dusty town of ramshackle adobe buildings and a few thousand souls.

It was a pretty day to be out, the mesquite green and the cottonwood leaves flickering in the warm breeze, but the early 1870s were, frankly, an otherwise rather miserable time to live on the Arizona frontier. The economy was in the tank, and as a troublesome former Confederate hotbed, Arizona Territory wasn't high on Washington's list of priorities. The scandal-plagued federal government of President Ulysses S. Grant was in turmoil, anyway, the army was stretched thin across the Southwest, and the result was a power vacuum in Arizona, into which stepped vigilantes, outlaws, and scoundrels of all description.

Indian wars had been simmering for decades—Apache against their longtime enemies, the Navajo and Tohono O'odham (Papago); Anglos against the Yumans; Apache and the newly arrived Americans against the Mexicans; and then later, as Anglos began flooding into the territory, Apaches against the Anglos and Hispanics both. By the late 1860s and early 1870s, the raids, counterraids, kidnappings, and murders stoked the fires on both sides as never before. One of the worst atrocities had occurred the year before, in April 1871, when a large band of Anglos, Hispanics, and O'odham crept north of Tucson to Arivaipa Canyon, to attack a sleeping camp of Apache who thought they were under the army's protection. The attackers massacred as many as 150 men, women, and children, and took alive twenty-eight babies to sell into slavery in Mexico. President Grant threatened martial law and ordered a trial for the vigilantes, but all 104 defendants were acquitted within minutes, and one of them was later elected mayor of Tucson.

It was against this messy, murderous backdrop, in April 1872, that Charles Bendire—a cavalry officer posted at nearby Camp Lowell—was riding along Rillito Creek, and it explains why he was keeping a sharp lookout for trouble as he did. But when movement caught his eye down in the creek bed, it was a bird he saw, not an Indian—a large, all-black raptor that flew up through the dappled shade of the cottonwoods. Had it been soaring overhead, it would have been all but indistinguishable from a turkey vulture, for this was a zone-tailed hawk, a rare species of the Mexican borderlands that mimics the shape, color, and lazy, drifting flight of a vulture, to fool its prey.

Bendire pulled up his horse, and when the hawk flew off, Bendire shook his reins and followed it, picking his way excitedly along the stream, which the dry season had shrunk to a few stagnant pools. He managed to keep the hawk in sight until, about five miles from camp, it perched on the dead limb of a massive cotton-wood, close to a bulky nest. For the young officer, just a few days shy of his thirty-fifth birthday, it must have seemed like an early present, because Charles Bendire was mad about birds.

Not that "Charles Bendire" was really his name. Karl Emil Bender had been born in Hesse-Darmstadt, one of the jumble of principalities that made up what is now Germany. He had some home tutoring, and then spent five years in a theological school before being bounced out for a prank in 1853 at age seventeen. Turning his back on Germany, he and his younger brother Wilhelm quickly emigrated to America, though the brother, homesick, turned around and headed back to Europe shortly after their arrival. (Sadly, he never made it, being washed overboard on the return trip.) Karl, on the other hand, embraced his new home, anglicizing his first name to Charles, dropping his middle name and altering his surname. He also answered a recruiting poster for the First U.S. Dragoons, the only mounted unit in the army, which was looking for "able-bodied men between the ages of 18 and 35 years, being above 5 feet 3 inches, of good character, and of respectable standing among their fellow citizens."

His unit may well have sounded a bit like home, since German immigrants had been joining the Dragoons for years; in 1847 more than a quarter of the privates in another company were German, and officers complained about having to command men whose English was all but nonexistent. Whatever the incentive—the promise of three meals a day, the chance to serve with fellow Germans, or the eight dollars a month a private earned—Bendire joined for a five-year stint, and for most of the next thirty-two years, the cavalry would be his home.

Bendire spent his time in New Mexico and Arizona, for the Dragoons were the mobile army units that patrolled the Southwest, broiling in their hot wool uniforms beneath the desert sun, trying to chase Comanche or Apache warriors while riding horses one observer described as little better than carrion, weighted down with a hundred pounds of gear. The work was frustrating, the frontier postings a nightmare of boredom and physical hardship, and the risk of death from hostile fire very real. Yet after his first enlistment ended, Bendire, now a corporal, signed up again—just in time for the Civil War. This time he rose quickly through the ranks, brevetted to first lieutenant "for gallant and meritorious service" at the Battle of Trevilian Station, in Virginia in 1864, the largest all-cavalry engagement of the war.

When peace finally returned, Bendire was again sent west with the cavalry, to California, then to Fort Lapwai, in Idaho, in 1868, where he stayed for the next three years. He was growing into the solid, balding, round-faced man shown in later photographs, a startlingly long mustache forming a stiff inverted V. Life on a frontier outpost hadn't changed much, and boredom was still a daily challenge. It appears it was partly to combat this that he began to study birds, a natural outgrowth of his interest in hunting. In particular, Bendire collected bird eggs while he was posted in Idaho, and threw himself into this new hobby with abandon—and with scientific precision, becoming intimately familiar with western birdlife. In fact, he collected almost everything natural, from mammals and reptiles to fish and fossils. Transferred to Arizona, he stepped up the pace, sampling the Mexican-flavored fauna of the Southwest.

Many of these specimens Bendire shipped to Washington, to Audubon's old protégé Spencer Fullerton Baird. Though as a young man Baird missed out on that trip up the Missouri, he'd come to sit

Having almost single-handedly created the National Museum of Natural History at the Smithsonian, Spencer Fullerton Baird used his connections to forge a network of military officers across the western frontier that collected birds and other specimens from distant outposts. *Courtesy of the Smithsonian Institution Archives*

at the center of a far-flung web of collectors and ornithologists, many of them, like Bendire, U.S. Army officers. (It didn't hurt that Baird's father-in-law was General Sylvester Churchill, the inspector-general for the army.) Baird, who came to the Smithsonian only four years after it was founded, had almost single-handedly created the National Museum of Natural History, taking charge of the moldering specimens already on hand, and augmenting them with his own extraordinary collection, which filled two railway boxcars.

Now, every week, new specimens flowed into Washington from the far corners of the continent, gathered by smart field scientists like Charles Bendire, who were constantly nudged, congratulated, encouraged, and chivvied by Baird. Prospective collectors were issued precise, written instructions on what to gather, how to acquire and prepare their specimens, and how to ship them back to Washington. Baird never spared the pen in advancing his cause; he sent an average of thirty-five hundred letters a year to his many collectors. Some of the names on the specimen labels would be famous for other reasons, like George B. McClellan, who (a decade before he would become commander of Union forces in the Civil War) collected twenty-five new species of mammals and ten new reptiles while searching for the source of the Red River in Texas.

Little wonder, then, that Bendire wanted the zone-tailed hawk for Baird and the Smithsonian. He thought about shooting it, but he wanted a peek in that nest even more, since no one had yet described the eggs of this species, and he was interested in observing their behavior. Tying off the horse, he shinnied up the tree as the hawk and its mate flew about, shrilly calling. In the cup of the nest, he found "but a single pale bluish white unspotted egg," which he pocketed. But because most hawks lay two or three eggs, he knew the clutch wasn't complete, and decided to come back in a week or two and collect the rest of the set, along with one of the parents.

In early May, Bendire's duties finally allowed him to return to the nest, where one of the adults sat tight on the eggs until he rapped the trunk of the tree with the butt of his shotgun. He was going to shoot, but because the hawk seemed tame, only flying a short distance away, he decided to wait until he'd checked on the eggs, then collect the adult. Leaving his shotgun in its scabbard, he started up the tree.

"Climbing to the nest I found another egg, and at the same instant saw from my elevated perch something else which could not have been observed from the ground, namely, several Apaché Indians crouched down on the side of a little cañon which opened into the creek bed about 80 yards farther up," Bendire wrote some years later. "In those days Apaché Indians were not the most desirable neighbors, especially when one was up a tree and unarmed; I therefore descended as leisurely as possible, knowing that if I showed any especial haste they would suspect me of having seen them."

The problem was, what to do with the eggs? Bendire hated to abandon them, so in the scant seconds he had to think, he popped one into his mouth ("and a rather uncomfortably large mouthful it was, too"). Sliding down the cottonwood, forty feet to the ground, he got on his horse and rode hell-for-leather the five miles back to camp, expecting an attack at any moment, cradling the egg against the jolts and jars of the ride, his jaw muscles swelling, trying to breathe, trying not to gag. And then, safely at camp, trying to remove the precious egg without breaking it, his breath coming in labored gasps.

"I returned to that place within an hour and a half looking for the Indians, but what followed has no bearing on my subject," he reported laconically, saying that he mentioned his near brush with the Apache only "to account for not having secured one of the parents of these eggs." His jaws ached for days thereafter, and when he "blew" the egg, removing the contents to prepare it for his collecting, he found it slightly incubated—in part by his own body heat.

A German immigrant who joined the army and changed his name, Charles Bendire began collecting bird skins and eggs to stave off boredom on lonely frontier postings. His hobby sometimes came close to killing him—he once escaped pursuing Apaches with a rare hawk egg tucked in his mouth. *Courtesy of the Library of Congress*

Although his zeal for ornithology was unmatched—and would later bring him to wide recognition—in a sense, Bendire was a bit of an anomaly among Baird's network of collectors because he was a cavalry officer. Most of Baird's best collaborators were members of the Army Medical Corps—highly educated men with scientific training and a bent for natural history, traveling on the army's nickel to places that were too remote (and frequently too dangerous) for civilians to reach, joining military expeditions or tagging along on federal railroad and boundary surveys.

Some were solid professionals, while others were cut from more colorful cloth. Adolphus Heermann was the son of an army doctor, elected to the Academy of Natural Sciences when he was just eighteen; he made two trips to California, the second in 1853 with the army crew surveying railroad routes along the thirty-second parallel. He discovered several new species of birds, including the gull that now bears his name, an honor bestowed by his friend John Cassin. Heermann sent back east crates full of skins and eggs (and appears to have coined the term *oology*, for the collection and study of eggs) but he always traveled with trunks of luxury items, including a decorated incense burner that raised more than a few eyebrows on the frontier. Suffering from the debilitating effects of syphilis, Heermann died, in 1865, of a gunshot wound while hunting—perhaps as a result of a stumble brought about by his illness.

Yet Heermann seems positively drab when compared with John Xantus, for whom a number of western birds were named, including Xantus's murrelet and Xantus's hummingbird. He was a Hungarian émigré whose life is shrouded in mystery, most of it a smoke screen generated by Xantus himself, who appears to have been born Xántus János—or perhaps Louis Jonas Xántus de Vesey, L. X. de Vesey or one of several other variations he used. He claimed to have been an officer in the Hungarian army, with ties to nobility, a political prisoner who escaped to England, and to have held a succession of jobs in the United States after emigrating there in 1850 (or '51), including canal digger, bordello piano player, and university professor—though, as is usually the case with him, there is evidence for virtually none of this.

What is known is that by 1855 he joined the U.S. Army as a hospital steward, where he came under William Hammond's wing. Hammond was as different from Xantus as could be imagined— the scion of an old, respected Maryland family, he would later rise from his frontier postings in Indian country to become Surgeon-General of the United States at age thirty-four, survive political backstabbing that resulted in his court-martial on trumped-up charges, and see his name later cleared by Congress even as he did pioneering work in the field of neurology. But in the 1850s, he was assigned to the cavalry as a surgeon, fighting the Sioux at Fort Riley, Kansas—and collecting birds for Baird.

Xantus was unhappy as a steward, but under Hammond's guidance, he blossomed as a collector; between the two of them, they sent back dozens of species. With Hammond's patronage, Xantus was able to join a variety of western expeditions and postings, including a railroad survey through the southern Plains and a coastal survey of California. (He later claimed to have also taken part in a naval exploration of the south Pacific, discovering dozens of new islands, and even had his portrait painted in the uniform of a navy captain—a trim, dashing fellow, with dark goatee and mustache, the gold epaulets flashing on his shoulders. In fact, he was at the time an enlisted man at Fort Tejon in the southern Sierras of California, where his claim to fame was discovering a flycatcher he named for Hammond.)

Xantus left a great deal to be desired from a military standpoint—his commander on the coast survey called him "the most unreliable man ever"—but Baird valued his collections of birds, fish, and a great deal more. Despite his many shortcomings, Xantus was skilled at parlaying his connections into employment, eventually becoming U.S. Consul in Colima, Mexico, before returning to Hungary to work with the national museum there—and continuing to spin stories about his fictitious American adventures.

However, the most important ornithologist to come out of the Army Medical Corps was Elliott Coues,* whom Baird (and Baird's close associate John Cassin) had befriended when Coues was a young man growing up in Washington, DC. He had a classics-heavy education, but was even then more interested in birds than anything else: "The inflection of the Prairie Warbler's notes was a

---

*Although most birders pronounce it *coos*, he and his family pronounced their surname *cows*.

much more agreeable theme than that of a Greek verb, and I am still uncertain whether it was not quite as profitable," he later wrote.

The winter of 1858, he began collecting bird skins (and harvesting wild flax by hand to use to stuff them), starting with a field sparrow he shot in February, and spent all of his free time at the National Museum under Baird's tutelage. It paid off; two years later, Baird secured for him a berth on a cruise to Labrador, where he collected puffins, murres, and other subarctic birds for the museum. While he was completing school, Coues produced a flurry of papers on birds, including the description of a new species of shorebird he'd discovered in the museum's collection and which he named Baird's sandpiper, for his mentor. It was a foretaste of his remarkable productivity in the years to come.

At nineteen he was in medical school, shortly thereafter participating in a (presumably illegal) body-snatching to obtain a cadaver for study, and by 1862, at age twenty, he was a medical cadet in the Union Army, pulling hospital duty in Washington. In 1864, however, Baird tugged the strings that would set Assistant Surgeon Coues firmly on his career—an appointment to Fort Whipple, near Prescott, Arizona. Another collector was heading to the field, but maybe Baird recognized even then that Coues was of a different caliber; the man who came back from the frontier would eventually eclipse even Baird as the leading ornithologist of his day.

Next to Audubon, Coues is probably the most complex and interesting character in American ornithology and, as with Audubon, not always the easiest one to like. He was enormously talented and hugely energetic, producing a body of work all but unsurpassed— not only in ornithology, where he became one of the giants of its golden age, but mammalogy, history, and other fields as well. He wrote voluminously, not just for scientists but for the general public, and was one of the first popularizers of science for the average reader.

He spent much of his later life editing a succession of journals by early western explorers, fifteen volumes in all, from Lewis and Clark to Rocky Mountain trappers, hunting down old manuscripts, even as his health faltered, and bringing their often forgotten narratives to wide attention. Coues had a healthy (at times smug) opinion of his own abilities, although as his biographers have written, "To those who would charge that Coues' lack of modesty was unbecoming, we will . . . say that he had little to be modest about."

But Coues could also be a petty and hectoring man, merciless in attacking those with whom he disagreed. His disdain for "the opera-glass fiends," as he called the first birders (especially women involved with the young Audubon movement), was bottomless, yet he was also an early and vocal champion of women's rights, a position that eventually cost him his faculty position at the National Medical College. He was generous with his time and influence on behalf of those just entering the field; Coues's patronage would prove instrumental in launching the career of the young bird artist Louis Agassiz Fuertes in the 1890s, and he collaborated with some of the first important women ornithologists and bird writers, like Florence Merriam Bailey and Mabel Osgood Wright.

His personal life was a mess. He was married three times, the first through a dalliance that resulted in pregnancy. The young lady lost the baby in a miscarriage, but Coues, under pressure from her brother, went ahead with the marriage for appearance's sake; he departed for his first army post the following day, then had the union annulled six months later by a special act of the Arizona territorial legislature. His second marriage, which lasted almost twenty years, devolved into a bitter, hateful conflict perhaps triggered, and certainly made worse, by his prodigious womanizing. He shared with his third wife, a wealthy widow named Mary Emily Bates, not only a commitment to women's rights but an interest in spiritualism and the occult, to which he lent his considerable prestige as a leading scientist—much to the dismay of his colleagues. Although he later broke publicly with one branch of spiritualists, the Theosophists, whose presidency he had once held, he remained interested in occult subjects his entire life.

Most of that was yet to come, however, when Coues set off for the Southwest in 1864, his Army commission and his orders tucked in his bag along with his collecting gear. Coues described himself in those days as a "slender, pale-faced, lantern-jawed, girlish-looking youth without a hair on lip or chin," a description reinforced by a photo taken that same year, showing the newly commissioned assistant surgeon in his uniform, a shock of hair curling up over one ear and brushed back from his forehead, eyes wide-spaced and his mouth slightly open as though about to speak. Clean-shaven in the portrait, he soon grew a beard in the fashion of most cavalry soldiers, and in later years it flowed down over his chest.

For the next two years, Coues roamed across New Mexico and Arizona, then west to the coast of southern California. He amassed a large collection for Baird, including a new warbler Baird named for Coues's sister Grace. In what by now was an almost obligatory episode for naturalists, he accumulated a rum keg full of reptiles and amphibians that was, predictably, drunk dry by thirsty soldiers. But he was an army officer in hostile country, and much of his time was spent chasing, or being chased by, Indians. His discovery of

A complex, often bitter and difficult man, Elliott Coues was also a brilliant scientist, one of Baird's military collectors who rose to become the one of the leading ornithologists of the late nineteenth century. *Courtesy of the Smithsonian Institution Archives*

the least Bell's vireo came during a raid on the Apache, and on another occasion, Coues quickly stripped off the skin of a rare subspecies of rattlesnake and wrapped it around the barrel of his rifle for safekeeping, all while he and his companions were being chased on horseback by pursuing warriors.

It was dangerous work; as his biographers note, among Coues's most poignant memories was hearing the song of a phainopepla during the burial of a comrade who had been killed, dismembered, and burned by the Apache. Back-and-forth raids between whites and Indians were as ceaseless as they were bloody, but despite this, Coues eventually developed a respect and sympathy for his former enemies, regretting his part in what had at times been little more than massacres by the soldiers.

Perhaps not surprisingly, then, given the violence, Coues wasn't especially fond of the Southwest. Not just the bloodshed but the aridity and starkness of the desert landscape bothered him; he didn't like Hispanics much at all, and even the incessant howling of coyotes annoyed him. But the scientific novelty of it all was a constant joy. To be "thousands of miles from home and friends, hot, tired, dirty, breathless with pursuit, but holding in my hand and gloating over some new and rare bird, I feel a sort of charitable pity for the rest of the world."

For the next sixteen years, Coues bounced back and forth between frontier assignments and periods in the East. He traveled to the Dakotas in 1872, then the next year joined a party surveying the American/Canadian border, traveling up the Missouri to the Rockies. In 1876, as naturalist for the U.S. Geological Survey, he was back in the mountains again, this time in Colorado. When not in the field, he was cranking out publications like his landmark *Key to North American Birds* in 1872, *Birds of the Northwest* in 1874, and *Birds of the Colorado Valley* in 1878 (as well as such medical treatises as "Aneurism of Aorta, Innominnate and Carotid Arteries"). Though still in his mid-thirties, he was rapidly gaining a reputation as one of the most important naturalists in the country—which makes his 1880 assignment back to Fort Whipple, Arizona, a puzzling one. Coues blamed his by now embittered wife, and there is evidence to suggest the move may have been prompted by another of his illicit affairs. In any event, even Baird couldn't help him this time, and after a year of protests from the wilderness, Coues resigned his commission and left the army in disgust.

Out of the military, Coues landed on his feet. He began to write about natural history for the popular press and lectured widely, while drafting forty thousand zoological and anatomical definitions for the *Century Dictionary*, a task that took eight years. He brought out new editions of his two most important books, and he helped to create the first professional ornithological organization in the country. His work, and that of other writers (many of them women) he mentored and encouraged, helped stoke the emerging popularity of birding and nature study in the general public—though, contradictory to the end, he was by no means always well-inclined to bird-watchers.

ONE OF THE WOMEN with whom Coues corresponded, and whose ornithological work he aided, was the only female collector active on the Western frontier—Martha Maxwell, a remarkable, self-made woman who carved out a national reputation despite her gender and the considerable odds that fate stacked against her.

Born, in 1831, in the steep-sided mountains of northern Pennsylvania, Martha Ann Dartt got a love of nature—and her self-reliant, sharply feminist streak—from her unusually independent grandmother, while her steadfast belief in the value of education came from her scholarly stepfather. She moved with her family to Wisconsin, then attended Oberlin College, in Ohio, the first coeducational institute of higher learning in the country. Yet even there she bristled at the disparity between the privileges enjoyed by male students and the constraints placed on women.

A lack of funds, however, brought her college career to an end after little more than a year. Therefore, she jumped at the offer from a successful Wisconsin businessman, James Maxwell, to chaperone two of his children to Lawrence University in Appleton, Wisconsin—and to continue her own education at the same time.

Not long after, she learned that Maxwell, a widower twenty years her senior, had even more serious interests in mind; he proposed to her, a fairly brusque, businesslike offer made by letter. She, after long consideration, accepted in an equally no-nonsense manner.

It's hard to say what she later thought of the bargain; she was responsible for six children, the youngest of whom had been living in deplorable conditions despite their father's relative affluence. A few years later, Maxwell's businesses collapsed in a financial panic, and he lost everything. Leaving the children—including a new daughter of their own—in 1860 Martha and James joined the hordes headed to the newly discovered gold fields of Colorado.

It wasn't what they'd hoped. James didn't strike it rich mining, though Martha made a decent living for them by building and managing a boardinghouse in Denver. After three years, the distance widening in their marriage and her daughter growing up without her, Martha left James to return to Wisconsin—where, in a stroke of luck, she was offered a job doing taxidermy for a local professor.

Martha Maxwell had no experience with stuffing animals, but she'd become curious about the process in Colorado and now found she was naturally adept at it. When in 1868 she allowed James to persuade her and their daughter to join him again in Colorado, she threw herself into collecting and mounting specimens. She must have been a dervish of activity; that fall at the Agricultural Society fair in Denver, she exhibited more than one hundred specimens, from hummingbirds to eagles, arrayed on cottonwood branches in lifelike poses. The public reception was ecstatic, in large part because Maxwell had struck on a variety of techniques that made her mounts far more lifelike and artistic than was typical of the day. The following year, she wrote to the Smithsonian for advice on how to identify the unknown birds she was collecting, and began a correspondence with Spencer Baird. In 1873 she opened the Rocky Mountain Museum in Boulder (moving it later to Denver)—confiding to Baird that she hoped it would become "a kind of academy of science, perhaps an adjunct to the State university." In 1876 she was asked to represent Colorado at the Centennial Exposition in Philadelphia, with an enormous display of her work.

The exhibit was a smash—the idea of a petite woman (Maxwell was less than five feet tall) toting a gun through the wild mountains, shooting birds and beasts and then mounting them in such fluid ways, mesmerized many of the estimated ten million fairgoers who attended. Cougars leapt from cliffs of fake rock onto the backs of running deer, heavy-antlered elk stood among trees full of birds, and turtles lay next to a flowing stream. There were buffalo, pronghorn, bears, and bighorns. And in case anyone missed the point, Maxwell posted a sign in front of the display that read simply, "Woman's Work."

The display won Maxwell a bronze medal, and turned her into an instant national celebrity. When the expo ended, she took her exhibit to Washington, where Elliott Coues first encountered her. He was mightily impressed by her work; many of the birds and mammals had been collected in the same part of Colorado he'd just explored, and Maxwell was not only able to show him specimens of the rare black-footed ferret he'd sought unsuccessfully, but she was able, for the first time, to explain the previously unknown details of this rare weasel's habits. Coues eagerly agreed to prepare an annotated catalog of the mammals in her collection, and Smithsonian researcher Robert Ridgway was already at work on one for the birds. In it, Ridgway named for Maxwell a subspecies of eastern screech-owl that she had collected—the first time a woman had been so honored for a bird she had discovered.

All but lost amid the mounted Rocky Mountain wildlife she brought to the Centennial Exposition in Philadelphia in 1876, Martha Maxwell sits in a display she slyly titled "Woman's Work." (The image is a detail from a stereo photograph; for full image see www.hsp.org.) *Courtesy of the Historical Society of Pennsylvania*

That tribute aside, it may be stretching the term to call Martha Maxwell an ornithologist, at least in the word's meaning by the late nineteenth century—a trained scientist pursuing the serious, academic study of birds. Unlike her contemporary Graceanna Lewis, John Cassin's female protégé in Philadelphia, Martha Maxwell lacked an accomplished mentor at her elbow and a respected institution in which to flourish, or she might well have gone on to scientific success. But she was an unusually accomplished naturalist in her own right, supplying Ridgway, Baird, and others with specimens, and warmly acknowledged for her assistance in their publications. And she did it all on her own, managing to overcome the handicap of living and working thousands of miles from the East Coast centers of science.

It's also worth noting that even though both Maxwell and "real" ornithologists collected birds, what they did with them was radically different. When Elliott Coues or one of his colleagues made a bird skin, it was a stiff pole of a specimen—beak sticking straight ahead, cotton in the eyes, wings closed, legs neatly folded and a label tied on with thread—easy to store with dozens of others in a shallow drawer. There was no attempt to make the thing look alive, since the purpose was simply to serve as a permanent museum record.

Martha Maxwell's mounted birds and mammals, on the other hand, were primarily a form of entertainment, but with the implicit idea of inspiring and educating those who came to see them. As her biographer, Maxine Benson, has pointed out, this put Maxwell in the vanguard of museum development, although she was then and still remains overlooked as a pioneer in the use of large habitat groups. (She also had to support herself and her family, so some of her work was wholly commercial and, at least to modern eyes, of questionable taste—like her tableaus of monkeys sitting around a table, playing cards.)

Although the eastern exhibits brought her fame, as did the publication of an 1879 biography, *On the Plains,* by her half-sister Mary Dartt, they did not bring Martha Maxwell much in the way of income, and her final years were difficult. She made yet another attempt to finish her education, briefly attending a women's program at the Massachusetts Institute of Technology, but money grew increasingly tight. When she was not yet fifty, her health began to fail, and ovarian cancer killed her, in 1881. Her daughter wrote to Coues for advice on having the Smithsonian procure her mother's collection, but instead the specimens were trundled off to storage, entrusted to a man who proved to be a cheat. Many were sold off piecemeal, and those remaining were allowed to deteriorate beyond salvage, many of them sitting outside in the snow through a long, wet winter until they fell to bits—a sad legacy for a ground-breaking naturalist.

ORNITHOLOGY HAD once been the province of inspired amateurs; now it had solidified into a profession, and professional institutions were growing up around it, although their genesis was sometimes humble. A group of bird-crazy young men in Cambridge, Massachusetts, started gathering on Monday evenings in the early 1870s in the home of a twenty-year-old named William Brewster, to discuss birds and read from Brewster's treasured octavo edition of Audubon. Within two years, the gathering had grown into a formal society, which the members named after Thomas Nuttall, the former Harvard scientist who had accompanied the Wyeth expedition to Oregon half a century earlier.

The Nuttall Ornithological Club was the first of its kind in the country, and its roster was a future who's who of ornithology and natural history, including Brewster and Theodore Roosevelt, who joined while a sophomore at Harvard.* "Resident" members lived near Cambridge and met weekly, but the club also invited from around the country "corresponding" members like Coues, taking advantage of the first real opportunity to create a collegial association, and to debate (in person, and in the pages of the club's journal) the issues of the day.

One surprisingly divisive issue, which pitted many noted ornithologists against one another, became known as the "Sparrow Wars." North Americans in the late nineteenth century were infatuated with the idea of bringing to the New World foreign birds, especially those from Europe, like the nightingale and skylark, that were famed in art and literature. The fad was global; so-called acclimatization societies sprang up not only in North America but Australia, New Zealand, South America, Europe, and elsewhere, moving around game birds, songbirds, big game and small game mammals, fish, garden flowers, crops—a worldwide game of biotic shuffleboard.

The vast majority of introductions fizzled completely, or almost so. Hundreds of species, from exotic game birds to tropical finches, were stocked, but only a handful managed to hang on. Eurasian tree sparrows, brought to Saint Louis in 1870 among dozens of European birds imported from Germany, were the only ones to survive—and just barely, remaining restricted to the same

---

*Not everyone was impressed with the future president. Charles Batchelder, a founding Nuttall member, wrote later that T.R. "seemed a bit too cocksure and lacking in the self-criticism that, in our eyes, went with a truly scientific spirit."

stretch of Mississippi Valley to this day. Skylarks, released on Vancouver Island in British Columbia in 1903 with support from the provincial government, have maintained a low (and declining) population ever since, while across the channel on the mainland, Asian crested mynahs, which initially numbered in the thousands and spread as far south as Seattle, appear to be dwindling away to nothing. Would that the same fate had befallen the mynah's relative, the European starling—the most notorious success (if that is the word) of the acclimatization movement. Introduced to New York in the 1890s, it was the benefactor of a society whose goal was to bring to North America every species of bird mentioned in the works of Shakespeare. (Lucky us, the Bard referred to a starling in a single line in *Henry IV.*)

The house (or English) sparrow was a darling of the acclimatization crowd, promoted as a natural control on agricultural pests like cankerworm. The first were released in Brooklyn in the 1850s, where they thrived, and by the 1870s, people were happily shipping crates of them all over the country. In Boston, the city was providing them with nest boxes on Boston Common, while the city forester was employed to kill predators that might harm the imports, including eighty-nine northern shrikes—an astonishing number of this rare northern migrant—shot in the winter of 1876–77.

Many ornithologists were aghast, seeing the aggressive sparrows displace once-common yard birds like eastern bluebirds and tree swallows. But others, notably Nuttall Club member Thomas M. Brewer, loudly advocated for the sparrows, and when a majority of club members took a position against the introductions, Brewer shot back, lambasting them in print as "overmodest young gentlemen." Coues entered the fray on the side of the club (and against the sparrow), and the argument roiled newspapers across the East. With time, the sparrow opponents were proven sadly correct, but by then the genie was out of the bottle. The house sparrow spread like a prairie fire, blanketing the East in just a few decades and (with the help of additional introductions in San Francisco, Salt Lake City, and elsewhere in the West) reaching from coast to coast by 1900.

Another issue of debate was a more fundamental one—how to classify North American birds, and what to call them. It had been a thorn since Catesby's day, and while Baird had done much to smooth the wrinkles, there was still plenty of disagreement among the experts. The matter came to a head in the early 1880s with the publication of dueling bird lists—a new edition of Coues's *Check List of North American Birds,* and *Nomenclature of North American Birds* by Robert Ridgway at the Smithsonian, who did much to popularize Coues's idea of adding a third Latinized name to the old two-name Linnaean system, for describing subspecies like Martha Maxwell's screech-owl.

Ridgway had grown up in the Midwest during the Civil War, besotted with birds from his earliest recollection, and with a talent for painting them that was evident even in his teens. When he was fourteen, and puzzled by the identity of a bird, he sent a drawing of the mystery species to the federal director of patents in Washington, DC—a man whom, as Ridgway later observed, "did not 'know a hawk from a handsaw,'" but who gave the letter to Baird over at the Smithsonian. Baird in turn identified it as a purple finch and struck up an encouraging correspondence with the boy. In typical Bairdian fashion, the older man soon finagled Ridgway—not yet seventeen years old but clearly a prodigy—a position as naturalist on a survey of the fortieth parallel from Colorado to California, and by the time Ridgway was twenty-two, he was working for Baird at the Smithsonian.

Ridgway and Coues got crossways of each other fairly soon thereafter; Ridgway had published an article on color variation in birds, and Coues, characteristically pricklish, felt his own work on the subject had been slighted. The breach never really healed, and the two men remained professional rivals for decades, even as their reputations grew to dominate the field. With the publication of their competing checklists, ornithologists could now choose from four versions of ornithological reality—Baird's original list, one by Ridgway, and two by Coues, one from 1873 and his latest effort. Each differed in significant ways in taxonomic order and how species, subspecies, and their corresponding names were handled, and rifts began to develop throughout the ornithological world along these multiple fault lines.*

To break the logjam, Coues proposed convening a congress of ornithologists, who would by common consent thrash out the differences and come up with a single, official inventory of North America's birds. In fact, he said, while they were at it, why not create a truly national professional organization? The Nuttall Club was the jumping-off point for the new entity, its leadership and invited members largely drawn from the Massachusetts group's rolls.

---

*Nor are such disagreements a thing of the past. While taxonomy was once based almost entirely on physical structure, the advent of DNA analysis has brought revolutionary change to the field, as scientists reassess—and continue to argue over—the relationships between groups of birds. For birders, this upheaval is most evident in the constantly changing order in which species appear in their field guides. For example, loons were long considered the most primitive of North American birds, and came first on both the checklist and in field guides. But recently they were bumped back, now coming behind waterfowl (ducks, geese, and swans) and gallinaceous birds like pheasants, turkey, and quail.

For three days in September 1883, twenty-one of the country's leading ornithologists gathered in the American Museum of Natural History in New York and created what they dubbed the American Ornithologists' Union, modeling it on the British Ornithologists' Union, which had been founded in 1858.

One of the main tasks of the fledgling AOU was settling the discrepancies between Coues's and Ridgway's lists, and in 1886, the first official checklist of North American birds was published, covering the area north of the Mexican border along with Baja, Greenland, and Bermuda. (The checklist has since gone through seven editions and forty-seven supplements and now covers more than two thousand species from Colombia to the North Pole, including the Caribbean and Hawaii.) Gone was the welter of local, colloquial names; now the only official name for a bird, be it in English or Latin, was the AOU name. Likewise, the AOU ruled on the evidence for whether a bird was a full species or merely a subspecies—a responsibility it holds today, with an immediate impact on birders who keep close watch on their life lists. Finally, the AOU also began publishing a journal, *The Auk,* which replaced the Nuttall *Bulletin,* though naming it after the great auk—a flightless, extinct seabird of the North Atlantic—caused a fair bit of harrumphing among some members.*

Ornithology was still overwhelmingly a boys' club, but some cracks were beginning to show. Unlike the Nuttall Club, which refused to allow women (and which continued to do so for the better part of a century), the AOU elected its first female member only

---

*Naming ornithological journals after birds living and extinct was and is popular; the British Ornithologists' Union started the trend with *Ibis,* and today there are *The Condor, Cotinga, Babbler, Emu,* and *Sandgrouse,* to name but a few around the world, as well as an even larger number that draw their titles from Latin bird names, including *Strix, Hirundo, Picoides, Ardea,* and *Buteo.*

two years after its founding—though it's hard to imagine how any ornithological organization could have refused Florence Merriam. Her brother, C. Hart Merriam, was chief of the federal Biological Survey and one of the AOU's founders, but his sister's election wasn't a case of nepotism—both siblings had a passion for nature, especially birds, that was encouraged from an early age. Born in upstate New York and educated at all-women's Smith College, Florence spent as much time outside as she could, leading bird walks while in college and, later, focusing on nature study as an antidote to "that most abhorred and abhorrable occupation of plain sewing, with housekeeping and bookkeeping."

While still in college Merriam began to write—not scientific papers, but articles for popular magazines like *Bird-Lore,* about the excitement of watching birds rather than collecting them. Birds were not her only interest; she spent time in Chicago, working on behalf of women's issues, and there contracted tuberculosis. One

Not long out of college, twenty-six-year-old Florence Merriam published *Birds Through an Opera-Glass* in 1889—a breezy, informal book that showed readers how to identify live birds in the field, instead of specimens shot for collections. It was, in a sense, the first field guide to American birds. *Courtesy of the Smith College Archives*

common treatment for the disease was the dry western air, and she headed to California, Arizona, and Utah, penning a frank book about Mormons, before she turned her attention to western birds.

In 1896 she published *A-Birding on a Bronco,* which was warmly received by both the public and the ornithological community, then followed it up with *Birds of Village and Field* two years later, after moving back east. In 1896 she married Vernon Bailey, a biologist who worked for her brother at the Biological Survey; the Baileys spent decades traveling in remote parts of the West and Southwest, equal partners in field research. She wrote the authoritative *Handbook of Western Birds* in 1902, and *Birds of New Mexico* in 1928, for which the AOU gave her its Brewster Medal, its highest prize for ornithological research and the first ever bestowed on a woman.

But Florence Merriam Bailey's most lasting contribution to bird study may have been her first book, published when she was just twenty-six and not long out of college—a collection of her *Bird-Lore* articles, titled *Birds Through an Opera-Glass,* which appeared in 1889. Chatty, informal, and funny, its purpose was to catch the imaginations of readers and make them curious enough about birds to go outside and find them—not with a shotgun, but with a pair of opera glasses, the only useful (though barely) optics available in the 1880s.

"Focus your glass on the meadow, and listen carefully for the direction of the sound. As the lark is very much the color of the dead grass that covers the ground when he first comes north, and of the dry stubble left after the summer mowing, he is somewhat hard to see. When you have found him, it is a delightful surprise to see that the brownish yellow disguise of his back is relieved . . . by a throat of brilliant yellow, set off by a large black crescent."

And so it went for seventy species—how the birds lived, where to find them, how to identify them, with woodcut illustrations to help the process along. While Coues and Ridgway had been battling it out for primacy in the arcane world of ornithology and taxonomy, young Florence Merriam had invented the first popular field guide—and the study of birds would never be the same.

IN THE 1880s the idea of birds as objects of simple observation was still a fairly revolutionary one—growing in acceptance, certainly, as the popularity of Merriam's book shows, but very much a minority view. To the general public, birds were usually seen through a strictly utilitarian lens—either as valuable for sport, food, or pest control, or viewed as vermin to be stamped out when their behavior conflicted with human interests. "Economic ornithology," which tried to justify the existence of birds by tallying their positive or negative impact (mostly on agriculture) was all the rage; Foster Beal, who worked for many years at the Biological Survey, examined the stomach contents of more than thirty-seven *thousand* birds, which led him to calculate, among other things, that a single species, the American tree sparrow, destroyed 196,000 bushels of weed seeds every year in Iowa.

That may seem a trifle silly to us, but birds needed all the help they could get. Until federal legislation protecting native wild birds passed following World War I, oversight was limited to the state and local levels, and there was precious little of it. With few exceptions, if it flew, it was considered fair game. What constituted a game bird in those days was radically more inclusive than today—not only waterfowl and gallinaceous birds like quail and pheasants, but shorebirds, waders, and many songbirds. Robins, red-winged blackbirds, and "ricebirds" (bobolinks) were as likely to appear on the menus of upscale urban hotels as pork chops and roast beef. A stroll through a busy market square in New York, Chicago, or Baltimore would reveal "calico snipe" (ruddy turnstones), "robin snipe" (red knots), "grass-birds" (buff-breasted sandpipers) and "doughbirds" (Eskimo curlews, today probably extinct).

Market shooting for the table and to supply the millinery trade, which used bird skins and feathers as hat decorations, was exploding in the late nineteenth century. While many—including some ornithologists—saw the supply of wild birds as inexhaustible, others were starting to sound a warning. George Bird Grinnell, Lucy Audubon's old pupil and a founding member of the AOU, was using his pulpit in the pages of *Forest and Stream* magazine to raise the alarm. The astonishingly swift collapse of the passenger pigeon population added impetus to the calls for conservation, as did the near extermination of the great bison herds, an issue that J. A. Allen, one of the founders of the Nuttall Club and the AOU, hammered away at in the popular press. It was the first time most Americans read about a new and disturbing concept: extinction.

But ornithology itself did not escape the lash of public condemnation. The growing number of bird-watchers and nature lovers looked at the scientific types, with their shotguns and drawerfuls of skins and eggs, and were increasingly horrified. Even worse, in many eyes, were the professionals who made a living collecting birds and their eggs. John Burroughs, probably the most influential nature writer of the late nineteenth century, had qualms about how much scientific collecting was justified, but he saved his real anger for the ones who did it for money.

Every town of any considerable size is infested with one or more of these bird highwaymen, . . . I have heard of a collector who boasted of having taken one hundred sets of the eggs of the marsh wren in a single day; of another who took, in the same time, thirty nests of the yellow-breasted chat; and of still another who claimed to have taken one thousand sets of eggs of different birds in one season . . . I can pardon a man who wishes to make a collection of eggs and birds for his own private use . . . but he needs but one bird and one egg of a kind; but the professional nest-robber and skin-collector should be put down, either by legislation or with dogs and shotguns.

Burroughs's hated professionals were filling an enormous demand. The late nineteenth century saw a mania for natural history collections, not only among professional ornithologists and museums but at all layers of society. Victorian households were commonly decorated with "glass bird cages," which ranged from little tableaus of a couple dozen stuffed songbirds, mounted on branches and displayed under a glass dome that sat on the family mantel, to enormous mahogany cases jammed with hundreds of specimens, including hawks, herons, and waterfowl. Infancy was no protection; many displays included nests full of stuffed baby birds. Taxidermy shops cranked out these collections to meet the growing demand, usually using whatever local species they could find, but there was a lively import business as well; for a handsome price, you could buy a case filled with dozens of species of glittering South American hummingbirds.

Eggs were the focus of the most extreme form of collecting fever, however. Oology, the study and collection of eggs carefully blown clean of their contents, was a genuine rage in North America and Europe during the late nineteenth and early twentieth centuries, with tremendous competition to assemble the most complete collections of eggs, usually taken not one at a time but in entire clutches from the nest. The excess was extraordinary; one "oologist" boasted of owning a hundred and eighty peregrine falcon clutches comprising more than seven hundred eggs, out of a collection totaling twenty thousand of many species. Magazines like *Ornithologist and Oologist* facilitated the sale of eggs around the world, and a single blown egg of a California condor might fetch $350, at a time when that sum would buy a small house. (Interestingly, although egg-collecting is a long-gone fad in North America, it remains all too alive in Great Britain, despite its illegality. Even today, the nests of rare raptors, like ospreys and eagles, must be guarded twenty-four hours a day in the UK, lest egg thieves strike.)

Ornithologists kept their noses in the air when the subject of private collectors and suppliers came up—perhaps to avoid the odor of hypocrisy, since few had much compunction about dealing with professional suppliers. The AOU pushed what became known as the model law, which urged municipalities to ban the killing of birds, or the collection of their eggs and nests, except for those who could demonstrate a "scientific" reason for doing so. In 1886, for example, a young Harvard student named Arthur C. Bent, who had begun his own collections some years earlier, applied to the Boston Society of Natural History for a permit to take birds and their eggs, having first pledged not to break state laws prohibiting "wanton destruction of birds or birds' eggs, or killing birds for merely ornamental purposes." The following year, when he applied directly to the state for his permit, he noted that he had a "small collection, consisting of slightly more than 100 eggs and between 50 and 60 species of birds."

Although Bent would go on to make an extraordinary contribution to our understanding of birds, the country was awash with hobbyists like him who had cabinets full of eggs and skins. And even the most august of academic ornithologists got hopelessly caught up in the chase. Although they could, with complete validity, argue that the number of birds collected for museums was as nothing compared with the vast amount of natural mortality (to say nothing of human carnage at the hands of market-gunners), that line of reasoning only worked for common species—and ornithologists in the late nineteenth and early twentieth centuries were rabidly interested in acquiring the rarest specimens they could.

Among some of the worst examples are the Carolina parakeet and ivory-billed woodpecker, two species which by the 1890s were clearly in desperate straits. The rarer they became, the greater the frenzy to get them for museum collections. Roughly 660 parakeets from Florida were shot and stuffed for collections in the last two decades of the nineteenth century. William Brewster, in whose attic the Nuttall Club had begun, made trips to Florida hunting for parakeets and ivorybills, as did Ridgway, C. Hart Merriam, Frank M. Chapman, and many other top ornithologists.

Birds they couldn't get themselves, they paid for; over the years, Brewster bought sixty-one ivorybill skins, many of them from people like South Carolina collector Arthur Wayne, who even advertised ivorybills for sale in the AOU's journal, *The Auk*. In just three years, from 1892 through 1894, Wayne and his workers killed forty-four of the huge woodpeckers in Florida, and he's blamed for wiping out the species entirely along the Suwannee River, where it had once been fairly common.

There was no excuse for this bloodbath, and accounts like this make it hard to take a balanced view of collecting overall. In most cases, however, the scientists were right—collecting had no effect on bird populations at all, and was a vital, unavoidable step in studying them. (And it remains so today, though to a much more limited degree.) This was especially true in the nineteenth century, when ornithologists were encountering hundreds of new species in a confusion of morphs, geographic races, and plumages, and without any published material like field guides to help them sort out everything. Optics were primitive at best, and the only way to sift through the confusion was to collect and scrutinize specimens.

Consider the red-tailed hawk, one of the most variable raptors in North America. Almost everyone, birder or not, can recognize this big, chunky buteo, with its brick-orange tail, brown back, and dark bellyband, right? Except that there are fourteen subspecies of redtails, ranging from the extremely pale "Fuertes" redtail of southwest Texas and Mexico to the richly colored birds of the north. They come in light and dark morphs unrelated to age or gender, and in the West there is a striking rufous morph, to boot, not to mention plumage differences between adults and immatures. Figuring out how all these redtails fit into the larger scheme of things took the better part of two centuries, and the puzzling still isn't over. Audubon described Harlan's hawk, the often chocolate-colored redtail of Alaska, which winters on the Great Plains, as a new species, although it was later downgraded to a subspecies. But some specialists, basing their argument in part on an examination of study skins, believe Audubon was right in the first place and maintain that Harlan's hawk is a full species in its own right.*

Sparrows are even worse. There are eighteen recognized subspecies of fox sparrows, and an ongoing argument about whether they make up one single species, or four closely related ones. Depending on which expert you believe, there are between two dozen and thirty-nine distinguishable subspecies of the song sparrow, but early ornithologists named *fifty-two* different varieties. All have the trademark streaky breast with a dark central spot that birders rely upon for identification, but those from the Southwest are pale, lightly streaked and rusty, while song sparrows from the Pacific Northwest are gray and sooty, and those just down the coast in California have dramatically black streaks. The first time I saw an Aleutian song sparrow I mistook it for a fox sparrow, so large, heavy-billed, and dark was it. Only by gathering specimens from across the song sparrow's range, and patiently comparing sizes, colors, and shapes (along with details of the birds' life histories, songs, and behaviors) were scientists able to make sense of this profusion of variation on a single theme.

The bloodless sport of field identification, as birders practice it today, wouldn't have been possible without the underpinnings of museum collections—not only the enormous task of bringing order to a continent's worth of species and subspecies, but also the creation of the field guides on which we all depend. From the earliest

---

*Actually, it's even more complicated than that. Judging from the painting of the bird that Audubon collected in Louisiana in 1829 and named "Black Warrior *harlani*" for his friend Dr. Richard Harlan, the bird was apparently not, in fact, what we now call a Harlan's hawk at all, but rather a juvenile dark-morph western redtail. The actual type specimen from which the written description was made, however, now in the British Museum, does appear to be a "Harlan's" redtail.

guides to the most recent, the experts still rely to a significant degree on museum collections. The result was that as collection-based ornithology progressed in the mothball-scented corridors of museums, it permitted wider and more accurate identification of birds in the field—often by people with little scientific background who looked askance at the collectors. As the number of bird-*watchers* increased, there was an increasing demand for better means of protecting birds, and the tension over this issue became palpable by the end of the nineteenth century. It was simply no longer necessary for anyone interested in birds to shoot them in order to study them.

Even as the world was changing and the rationale for universal collection waning, Elliott Coues remained firm in his belief that the path to ornithological wisdom issued from the muzzle of a shotgun. Collecting wasn't just the best way to study birds, it was the only way. How many birds should a beginning ornithologist collect? Coues asked rhetorically. *"All you can get*—with some reasonable limitation," was his answer—though modern birders would gasp at what he meant by "reasonable."

> Say fifty or a hundred of any but the most abundant and widespread species ... Your own "series" of skins is incomplete until it contains at least one example of each sex, of every normal state of plumage, and every normal transition stage of plumage, and further illustrates at least the principal abnormal variations in size, form, and color to which the species may be subject; I will even add that every different faunal area the bird is known to inhabit should be represented by a specimen, particularly if there be anything exceptional in the geographic distribution of the species. ...
> Begin by shooting every bird you can, coupling this sad de-

struction, however, with the closest observation upon habits . . . Fifty birds shot, their skins preserved, and observations recorded, is a *very* good day's work.

Nor was it merely to better know the local birds that one was encouraged to shoot. "Birdskins are a medium of exchange among ornithologists the world over," Coues observed; "they represent value—money value and scientific value. If you have more of one kind than you can use, exchange one for species your lack; both parties to the transaction are equally benefited." If you didn't use a shotgun, you weren't an ornithologist, and Coues had little use for the "Audubonians," as he called them. "There are too many inspired idiots among them, who fancy they have a God-given mission not to hide their light under a bushel," he fumed in 1899, just a few months before his death.

The shotgun people are mostly made of sterner stuff; they are realistic and can be cultivated, educated, and really helped in various ways. But the opera glass fiends! They always live too near the great heart of nature to know anything of her head or hands, or do a stroke of sensible work, even to protect the birds. . . . One woman wrote to say she was so unhappy because the cats in her neighborhood killed birds. We were going to write back and suggest that she collect the murderous felines and read the Audubon circular to them; but we restrained ourselves and advised her to feed the cats.

Such snide comments were far from rare. Charles B. Cory— the incoming president of AOU, a wealthy Boston Brahmin who used his money to amass a collection of nineteen thousand bird skins from the Caribbean and the Gulf of Mexico—was asked in 1902 to address an Audubon meeting. He declined, sniffing, "I do not protect birds. I kill them."

No doubt Cory's witty little retort drew chuckles and backslaps at the next AOU meeting. But the "Audubonians" weren't amused. Yes, it was a movement largely born of, and propelled by, women of means and leisure. But whatever the old boys in the AOU thought, the Audubonians were poised to become one of the most potent forces for bird protection the continent would ever see, and to change permanently the way most Americans thought about birds.

5

Angry Ladies

IT WAS THE THIRD WEEK of December, a chilly, overcast Sunday morning just a slow cup of coffee after daybreak. Most of the world was asleep, but Amy and I, a heavy tripod balanced on my shoulder, were splashing through cold puddles, counting birds.

We were a few miles from Tilghman Island on the Eastern Shore of Maryland, a flat, jigsaw-puzzle landscape of interlocking peninsulas, coves, and tidal creeks, of cordgrass marshes, fields, and soggy pine-oak forests. A few miles up the road was the tourist town of Saint Michael's, around which lay an imaginary circle fifteen miles wide. This day, as in every December since 1953, good weather or bad, dozens of birders combed that circle, trying to tally every bird of every species within it.

I stepped in a puddle and winced, realizing I'd put off getting new hiking boots a little too long when frigid water flooded through a long split in the seam above one sole. It was worse with the next step—I could see that the entire meadow was flooded a few inches deep from here on to the edge of the bay—but after a minute my foot was numb enough that I didn't notice. Much.

Amy and I were taking part in a Christmas Bird Count, a venerable tradition whose roots, more than a century old, lie in the great movement for bird protection, which both rose out of and helped give birth to birding as a modern pastime. We were on the Jean Ellen duPont Shehan Audubon Sanctuary, a 950-acre peninsula of forest, field, and wetlands. Amy had been the sanctuary's first and only manager, but after eight years, this was her final day on the job—the next morning we were packing up the remainder of her things for the move to Pennsylvania, where I lived. So this last Christmas Bird Count on the sanctuary was a bittersweet one for my wife, who loves the tidal creeks and marshlands of the Chesapeake, who had lived her whole life by the water but was giving that up for the mountains.

To our right was a shaggy field of switchgrass and big bluestem, matted down by an early snowstorm, while to our left lay a big woodlot of loblolly pines and southern red oaks, tangles of greenbrier clotting the edge like green concertina wire. Among the brambles, lots of birds were flitting; the air was full of the metallic *plink* calls of white-throated sparrows and the sharp *tsk* notes of juncos, like the disapproving sound you make with your tongue. It was a cold, damp morning; no wonder the juncos sounded peeved at our disturbance.

We stopped, glassed the greenbrier, and tried to sort how many of each species was milling around in there. "I've got twenty-seven whitethroats and fifteen juncos," I said, after a minute. "Seventeen juncos," Amy corrected me, not dropping her binoculars. "And a cardinal somewhere back in the woods."

"And a brown-headed nuthatch," I said; two can play at one-upsmanship, and I could hear the little bird's nasal call from high up in a pine.

"Actually, there are two nuthatches, and a red-bellied wood-pecker." I should have known better; Amy's ears are sharper than mine. "Anything else?" she asked, scratching the totals in a small notebook, which she jammed in her pocket, hurrying along.

We splashed down the rain-filled ruts of the truck path to the edge of Leadenham Creek, a wide estuary dotted here and there with duck blinds built on pilings, way out in the center channel. Duck season was closed, though, and none of the birds bobbing in the light chop were decoys. I lowered the tripod from my shoulder and aimed the scope across the bay; Amy would sweep the fore-ground and middle of the creek, and I'd use the heavier magnifica-tion to pick out the birds huddled against the far bank, maybe a quarter-mile away. Buffleheads sheltered against a rocky seawall, along with scaup (at that range, I could only guess at which of the two species), mallards, and a few black ducks. I blinked against the wind, trying to clear the tears from my eyes, struggling to resolve the long, white bodies of larger ducks into either male common goldeneyes or male common mergansers, while keeping the totals for each species straight in my head. Three canvasbacks, five more buffleheads, one tundra swan; the list grew as I panned the scope from right to left.

We swung wide, into another field of shorter grass where a mass of Canada geese were feeding, the sentries around the edges snapping to attention and giving a few warning honks as we came into view. Amy said she'd take the flock of sparrows working the edge of the tall grass and brush as I started counting up the increas-ingly nervous geese, and she finished before me. As I lowered my glasses and said, "One hundred and eighty-one," the whole flock of Canadas broke into flight, their black wings making a sibilant racket as they clawed for altitude.

"Well, that was good timing," I said brightly.

"Except that they're going to fly over to Cherry Tree Cove with all the geese we haven't counted yet," Amy said sourly, watching them veer south. "Or else *those* geese will decide to join these birds, and they'll all take off." She clomped off through the sodden grass. Clearly, her own imminent departure was making my sweetheart a little testy.

A Christmas Bird Count is, as the name suggests, all about numbers—and therein lies its surprisingly dark origin. The CBC, as it is universally known, grew out of the bloody holiday tradition of a "side hunt" or "match hunt," in which teams of marksmen would fan out on Christmas Day, shooting essentially anything that moved. The team that accumulated the largest pile of game was declared the winner, and birds were the commonest victims— not just game birds, but virtually anything unlucky enough to fly into shotgun range.

Even a dedicated hunter like Frank M. Chapman could be moved to revulsion by the sheer waste of a match hunt. A banker who had left a promising career in business to pursue his interest in birds, Chapman was by the turn of the last century a rising star at the American Museum of Natural History in New York, and the founder and editor of the popular magazine *Bird-Lore*. Why not challenge the idea of a match hunt, he reasoned, with something that combined competition and conservation? He bruited the idea among friends and colleagues, got an enthusiastic response, and on Christmas Day 1900, twenty-seven people hit the woods, field glasses in hand, in twenty-five locales from New Brunswick to

Louisiana to California. (One participant, a Wisconsin boy named Alexander Wetmore, would go on to direct the Smithsonian Institution.) By the end of the day, the teams had tallied more than eighteen thousand birds of ninety species, and the Christmas Bird Census (later Count) was born.

The popularity of the event grew rapidly, but it's hard to imagine what Chapman would make of his brainchild today, more than 106 years after its founding. He'd be proud, no doubt; while the side hunt is thankfully a thing of the past, the CBC has become the largest, longest-running wildlife census in the world, encompassing the western hemisphere from one end to the other. In 2005–06 there were 2,056 Christmas Bird Counts, each taking place within its own fifteen-mile-wide circle, scattered from Prudhoe Bay on Alaska's North Slope, across Canada, and down through the lower forty-eight and Mexico, Central America, the Caribbean, and as far south as Tierra del Fuego in Argentina. Almost fifty-seven thousand participants recorded birds of more than 650 species in North America and another 1,500 or so species in Latin America. The total was a seemingly breathtaking 61.5 million individual birds, but that pales with the record-setting year of 1988, when millions of nomadic blackbirds appeared within some count circles, boosting the numbers to an eye-popping 193 million.

Chapman had been agitating for years on behalf of birds, looking for ways to awaken people to the increasingly desperate situation of the continent's birdlife. Side hunts were far from the worst of it; a leading cause of destruction was the millinery industry and its slaughter of birds to supply the whims of fashion. While still a banker in the 1880s, Chapman had been inspired by attacks on the plume trade by the newly organized AOU, and by prominent ornithologists like George Bird Grinnell, who had been lobbying tirelessly for greater wildlife protection, on the editorial pages of his influential magazine *Forest and Stream*.

Largely forgotten today, Grinnell was one of the leading figures in American conservation at the end of the nineteenth century. *Forest and Stream* was widely read and enormously influential (Teddy Roosevelt was a contributor), and through it, Grinnell advocated for the creation of national parks, wilderness preservation, and an end to market hunting. He was instrumental in founding the AOU, the Society of American Foresters, the Boone and Crockett Club (which was among the strongest advocates for game laws), and the New York Zoological Society, along with more than half a dozen other groups.

Although he was involved in the AOU's first bird-protection efforts in 1886, Grinnell felt broader measures were needed, and in an editorial in February of that year, he proposed the creation of "an Association for the protection of wild birds and their eggs, which shall be called the Audubon Society." He outlined a pledge that all members would take, promising to work against the senseless destruction of birds, their eggs and nests, and to refrain from using bird skins or feathers as decoration or on clothing.

While the threats against birds were legion, the greatest enemy was market hunting, especially to supply the millinery industry. Fashion in the 1880s had taken wing—and head, and tail, and plume, all stripped from wild birds and arrayed on increasingly flamboyant hats. The greatest demand were for aigrettes, the long, airy, impossibly delicate breeding plumes grown each spring by herons and egrets. Milliners told naïve buyers that the feathers were plucked harmlessly from live birds, or collected beneath nests, but this was feel-good hogwash; gunners shot the birds in their breeding colonies and stripped them of their skins, leaving their eggs and chicks to die and bringing many species to the brink of extinction. Wrote one eyewitness:

> There, strewn on the floating water weed, and also on adjacent logs, were at least 50 carcasses of large white and smaller plumed egrets—nearly one-third of the rookery, perhaps more—the birds having been shot off their nests containing young. What a holocaust! Plundered for their plumes. . . . There were 50 birds ruthlessly destroyed, besides their young (about 200) left to die of starvation! This last fact was betokened by at least 70 carcasses of the nestlings, which had become so weak that their legs had refused to support them and they had fallen from the nests into the water below, and had been miserably drowned.

A single great egret—the "long white" of the plume hunter—has thirty to fifty aigrettes cascading down its back,* each feather worth roughly twice its weight in gold in the late 1890s. The carnage beggars belief. In London at the height of the craze, a ton and a half of aigrettes passed through one firm's salesroom in a single year; given that each feather weighed less than a fourth of an ounce, that meant that almost two hundred thousand birds had been shot to supply them, never mind the multiplying loss in eggs and chicks. Overall, the plume trade was chewing through an estimated 200 million birds a year. No wonder Grinnell and his colleagues foresaw a catastrophe.

---

*Often thought to be tail feathers, the long aigrettes are actually highly specialized scapular feathers, anchored at the base of the wings and lying, when at rest, down the back and protruding beyond the tail. In courtship displays, the egret raises the feathers, creating a stunning nimbus of filmy white around its body.

Wading species like egrets, and seabirds like terns and gulls, were the primary victims, but almost any bird was at risk, from sparrows to hawks. In 1886, Chapman famously took two afternoon strolls down Fourteenth Street, then Manhattan's main shopping district. "There, notebook in hand, I recorded, when I could identify them, the names of the birds which, usually entire, were seen on the hats of passing women," he recalled some years later. "In light of existing conditions the results seem incredible." Indeed; of the seven hundred hats he saw, 542 sported dead birds or feathers, and Chapman noted some forty species of birds. They ranged from songbirds like Baltimore orioles, blackburnian warblers and scarlet tanagers to a saw-whet owl, sixteen bobwhites, and twenty-one flickers.

The response to Grinnell's proposal was swift and encouraging—thousands of people signed his pledge, and hundreds of local Audubon societies sprouted across the country. Luminaries like Oliver Wendell Holmes and the celebrated abolitionists John Greenleaf Whittier and Rev. Henry Ward Beecher lent their significant weight to the movement, which found common cause with progressive goals in general.

But while Grinnell was writing to the largely male audience of *Forest and Stream,* made up of hunters, naturalists, and scientists, his message found its greatest resonance with women. Florence Merriam, then still a student at Smith College, helped organize a chapter at the school and was able to pull strings to get no less an authority than John Burroughs to lead the young ladies on a series of bird walks. The local chapters, in turn, recruited schoolchildren by the score, knowing (as did Grinnell, who wrote many children's books) how effectively kids could reach adults. By the time Grin-

As a boy, George Bird Grinnell was tutored by Lucy Audubon, and he created the first Audubon Society in 1886 to stem the destruction of wild birds. It soon foundered on its own success, but Grinnell had laid the groundwork for later and far more successful efforts. *Courtesy of the Library of Congress*

nell incorporated the Audubon Society the following year, it had some thirty-nine thousand members of all ages, and its own publication, *Audubon Magazine,* with its namesake's portrait on the cover.

And then the whole thing collapsed under its own weight. By the end of 1888, the demands of running the society and publishing a second magazine had grown too great. In retrospect, Grinnell's plan seems hopelessly idealistic—a national society with no dues structure, no governing body other than a hodgepodge of local chapters, and supported by a shower of free publications supplied by Grinnell and *Forest and Stream.* Income was supposed to be generated by magazine subscriptions, but these were voluntary and most Audubon members declined to pay the six cents an issue. Grinnell was no business lightweight, but it appears he either did not think through the consequences of his proposal, or perhaps hadn't counted on the burden of its success, which was shouldered by the overworked *Forest and Stream* staff.

He was also discouraged by the lack of progress against the fashion industry. Despite its flourishing membership, the Audubon Society made little headway in changing the way Americans used bird skins and feathers. The AOU's model law was quickly adopted by some states and then just as quickly dropped or gutted of any enforcement power when milliners, taxidermists, and egg collectors fought against it. The slaughter continued unabated; the fashion-conscious continued to snatch up every new feather-bedecked bonnet that appeared in shop windows.

Grinnell, whose faith lay in the power of reason and who had expected to sweep the field once women were informed of the horrors behind their hats, gave up the fight. In December 1888, the second and final issue of *Audubon Magazine* appeared; a month after, Grinnell announced that he was closing shop. "Fashion decrees feathers, and feathers it is," he conceded bitterly. "For the great majority, self-restraint can only be secured by the dictates of fashion, which are stronger than penal legislation." The Audubon Society was dead.

Men had tried to mobilize the country to protect birds, and they had failed. Now it was the women's turn.

USING FEATHERS as adornment is probably as old as humanity, and plumed hats had come in and out of fashion for centuries. But the craze for using feathers and bird skins on hats took off in North America shortly after the Civil War; *Harper's Bazaar* featured articles about this European trend as early as 1868, and in the decades thereafter, milliners pushed the boundaries of taste and excess further and further, until eventually whole "families" of stuffed birds perched around ersatz nests, glass-eyed bird heads sprouted out of boas of feathers, and ducks and prairie-chickens lay upside down, feet skyward, as though displayed in a butcher's window.

Grinnell's acidic remarks notwithstanding, the fight for bird protection wasn't entirely dead in the water. In 1894 a Pennsylvania school superintendent named Charles Babcock established Bird Day, modeling it on Arbor Day (with which it was often paired), and the observance quickly spread across the country, aided by official proclamations in dozens of state legislatures. Congress, pushed hard by Grinnell, had finally closed Yellowstone to hunting, and two years earlier, President Harrison had established the first federal wildlife reserve, in Alaska, presaging the national wildlife refuge system that Teddy Roosevelt would create in 1903.

But the pivotal event in bird conservation—and in the growth of birding as a hobby for millions—came in 1896, on a cold winter day in Boston, when Harriet Lawrence Hemenway sat down in the parlor of her fashionable Back Bay home to read.

Thirty-nine years old, Mrs. Hemenway sat at the apex of New England society. Fifteen years earlier, at the age of twenty-four, she had married Augustus Hemenway, uniting two of Boston's most prominent families. Her family, the Lawrences, traced their impeccable Brahmin status back to Revolutionary War Major Samuel Lawrence, and their tremendous wealth to Harriet's grandfather, who with his brother had founded one of the most successful business partnerships in New England, laying the groundwork for the region's enormous textile industry. Augustus Hemenway Jr.'s blood might not have been quite so blue (as such fine distinctions were made in Boston society) but his father, Augustus Sr., had amassed an enormous fortune in South American silver mines, Caribbean sugar plantations, and other ventures, largesse that Augustus Jr. would in later years shower on Harvard and other institutions.

Harriet Lawrence Hemenway was an arresting woman; a portrait by John Singer Sargent shows a direct gaze, sharp chin, and wide-set eyes. Thick brown hair is piled on top of her head, and she is in the act of tucking a white water lily in the bosom of her black gown. Given that the water lily was the symbol of pregnancy—a condition few polite women would discuss publicly in those days, much less declare in a portrait—it was a provocative pose, but Harriet Lawrence Hemenway was unafraid of controversy. Her family had been ardent abolitionists, and she had made a point of opening her home to Booker T. Washington at a time when others refused to take in the black orator.

Every great organization has its founding legend, and thus it is with the modern Audubon Society. As the story is usually told, Mrs. Hemenway was a clueless society matron adorned with bird skins and feathers until that January morning in 1896 when she sat down to read a bloodcurdling account of the killing of herons and egrets in Florida for the millinery trade. With this, she experienced a road-to-Damascus conversion and became a champion of conservation.

While compelling, this version of history overlooks the fact that Harriet and Augustus Hemenway were both longtime birdwatchers and lovers of the outdoors, and it seems unlikely that she was unaware of the controversy surrounding the millinery trade; *Harper's Bazaar* and other women's magazines had been writing about it for years, even as they carried advertisements for the newest fashion offerings.

It's clear, however, that reading that fateful article finally galvanized the formidable Mrs. Hemenway to the sort of action hardwired into her by her family's activist past, so she invited her cousin Minna B. Hall over for a cup of tea and a bout of strategizing. Together, they sifted through the *Blue Book*, the register of Boston society, and identified women of substance and influence who might be open to their message of bird protection. What followed was a series of meetings over tea. "We marked the ladies of fashion who would be likely to wear aigrettes on their hats or in their hair. We sent out circulars asking the women to join a society for the protection of birds, especially the egret. Some women joined and some who preferred to wear feathers would not join," Miss Hall said.

Among the women they brought into the fold were Elizabeth Cabot Agassiz, the first president of Radcliffe College and widow of the famed Harvard biologist Louis Agassiz, and Sarah Orne Jewett, a popular novelist who had written a short story about a girl protecting a heron. "Although Harriet Hemenway knew where the strings of power lay, she preferred to work them behind the scenes," writes Frank Graham Jr. in his superb history of the movement, *The Audubon Ark*. "She was aware that if a society to protect birds were to be successful, it would need to reach beyond her own circle." And beyond her own gender; women lacked even the right to vote, and reality dictated that for the movement to have a prayer of success, there would have to be prominent men at its helm. At an organizational meeting that February, Hemenway convened not only her social peers, but an august representation of important male naturalists and civic leaders; at the next meeting, they chose William Brewster, founder of the Nuttall Club, as president of what they called the Massachusetts Audubon Society.

The new society borrowed freely from Grinnell's model, not only in name but also in approach, such as the pledge not to harm birds, which children were asked to sign in order to become members. The group sold calendars and bird charts to raise money (though much of the initial support came quietly from the Hemenway fortune) and plowed it back into educational materials for schools, broadsides against wearing bird skins, and leaflets on how to attract birds, and the evils of allowing one's cats to roam outside. A reprint of the essay "Woman's Heartlessness," by the well-known poet Celia Leighton Thaxter, was an especially effective tool.

The remade Audubon movement spread rapidly; in less than two years, there were 111 chapters across Massachusetts—and while men were on the masthead of the state organization, all but a handful of the local chapters were headed by women, which made up 80 percent of the society's membership. Some of the state efforts were likewise run by women like Mabel Osgood Wright, a popular nature writer and colleague of Elliott Coues's who headed the organization in Connecticut.

Such rapid success cannot be credited only to Harriet Hemenway's tactical brilliance. Audubon was a product of its time, which was shaped to a great degree by the robust women's club movement of the late nineteenth century, through which upper- and middle-class women exerted what they saw as their moral imperative to fight evils, from poverty to alcohol. The temperance drive was a tremendous motivating force, giving women for the first time a national political outlet and experience they could apply to other battles, including the fight for universal suffrage. When Hemenway and Hill began to spread their message about birds, it was to a tightly knit network of women activists already dealing with a myriad of topics—ground troops handy to the cause. The white, angelic egrets were "feathered innocents" (in the words of a General Federation of Garden Clubs resolution) and the fact that women themselves were driving the demand for plumes lent the effort special weight, because wearing feathers, it was believed, robbed women of the high moral ground on the many other issues of concern to them.

Bird-watching itself was a growing force. Florence Merriam wrote in 1898 of "this increasingly popular branch of nature study," and gave examples of how many birds might be in one's own neighborhood:

> In a shrubby back yard in Chicago, close to one of the main thoroughfares, Mrs. Sara Hubbard has seen fifty-seven species in a year, her record for ten years being a hundred species. In an orchard in Brattleboro', Vermont, Mrs. E.B. Davenport has noted seventy-nine species in a year . . . In the larger cities, cemeteries and parks offer rare opportunities for bird study. Dr. W.C. Braslin gives a list of seventy-six species for Prospect Park, Brooklyn, while Mr. H.E. Parkhurst has himself seen ninety-four species in Central Park, and as many as a hundred and forty-two have been recorded altogether.

Whatever the impetus, the new Audubon message spread like a grass fire. By 1900 there were associations in twenty states (Frank Chapman had given the inaugural address "Women as a Bird Enemy" to the Washington, DC, chapter, which hosted a feather-free millinery exhibit), and by 1901, thirty-six. In 1905 they came together to form the National Association of Audubon Societies.

Their inspired choice as the association's first president was William Dutcher, an insurance agent and self-taught ornithologist who had worked with Grinnell to form the first, ill-fated Audubon society, and who was appointed chair of the AOU bird protection committee about the same time Harriet Hemenway founded Massachusetts Audubon. Dutcher was a dervish of activity on the protection front, helping to create new state Audubon chapters, lobbying for Bird Day celebrations, reinvigorating the AOU committee, and pushing that group hard in directions it was not always eager to go.

When the noted artist Abbot Thayer proposed paying for wardens to police the bird-nesting islands along the Atlantic coast, the idea was dismissed by most AOU members. "Where he should have received encouragement, *i.e.*, among ornithologists, he met with discouragement, for he was told it was impossible to raise funds for the work," Dutcher chided the group in its journal, *The Auk*. So Thayer put up much of the twelve thousand dollars himself, and Dutcher and the Audubon societies oversaw the work, which stretched from Maine to Florida. Some of the biggest remaining wading bird colonies lay in the watery wilderness of south Florida, a state that had just passed legal protection for the birds. The rookeries would be under the care of a former bird hunter named Guy Bradley, a new father to whom the $35-a-month warden's salary seemed like a godsend. Instead, it was a death sentence; three years later, Bradley was gunned down by a plume hunter he was trying to arrest, becoming bird protection's first martyr, and (thanks to the publicity over his murder and that of two more wardens, Columbus McLeod and L.P. Reeves, in 1908) propelling the movement forward.

Remarkable strides had been made. The first national success was the passage of the Lacey Act, in 1900, which made it a federal crime to sell in one state birds or game shot illegally in another—a move that, coupled with wider passage of the AOU model law, finally began to choke off market hunting. The Audubon societies were by no means the only force pressuring state and federal lawmakers on behalf of birds, but they were crucial, especially on the state level, battling hundreds of bills that would have rolled back or watered down newly enacted safeguards. They also held the AOU's feet to the fire when it seemed ready to compromise with the milliners on only partial protection for birds. At last, in 1913—thanks to hundreds of thousands of letters and telegrams from the public—Congress passed bills effectively shutting down the remaining feather industry and granting protection to all migratory birds; when a judge struck down the latter as unconstitutional, the measure was recast as a treaty with Great Britain (on behalf of Canada), then codified in 1918 as the Migratory Bird Treaty Act, which remains the bedrock federal protection for all native wild birds.

The more Dutcher and others pushed for bird protection, however, the less eager the AOU as a whole seemed about the whole topic. Concerned that legislation would deprive scientists of the right to collect birds and eggs as they saw fit, many in the organization grew decidedly cool to the subject. This sometimes boiled over into the kind of open, sneering hostility that AOU president Charles Cory had revealed in his "I don't protect birds" comment, and Coues's carping about overly sentimental "Audubonians."

Dutcher, though, certainly saw the potential force of the Audubon movement, and Grinnell gave it his blessing, serving as a trustee for the new association. Teddy Roosevelt, then governor of New York, lent his support: "I do not understand how any man or woman who really loves nature can fail to try to exert all influence in support of such objects as those of the Audubon Society," he wrote to Chapman, who published the letter in his newly founded *Bird-Lore,* the "Official Organ of the Audubon Societies." The magazine's motto was "A bird in the bush is worth two in the hand."

Roosevelt wasn't the only notable in the pages of *Bird-Lore,* which eventually became today's *Audubon* magazine; the first several issues, beginning in February 1899, featured John Burroughs writing about warbler migration, articles for children by Florence Merriam Bailey, a poem about song sparrows by Ernest Thompson Seton, and an article on caring for cage birds by Olive Thorne Miller that urged readers—if they must keep a bird—to treat it "as if he were a sentient being, instead of a piece of furniture." (Not everyone was impressed by the new publication. Coues, terminally ill and even crankier than usual, wrote in his competing journal, *The Osprey,* that with *Bird-Lore,* Chapman was "toying with ornithology in amateurish fashion, and will have to guard against dilettantism, if he would not degenerate into mere prettiness or virtuosity.")

The charge of sentimentality carried some validity; a lot of what was being written about birds in the popular press, especially for women's publications, was hopelessly mawkish. But many of the women writing for *Bird-Lore,* like Florence Bailey, Mabel Wright, and Cordelia Stanwood—women who were the public face of the Audubon movement—were generally clear-eyed pragmatists about wild birds, although Wright often heavily anthropomorphized her subjects, and she (like Seton) occasionally crossed the line into fiction with what Burroughs and Roosevelt attacked as "nature-faking."

Cordelia Stanwood's story is an especially fascinating, if somber, one. Born to an old Maine family, she worked as a school-teacher and principal until in 1904, at age thirty-nine, she suffered a nervous breakdown and retreated to her family's farm near Mount Desert Island, where she remained for the rest of her long life. Odd and reclusive, prone to off-putting outbursts, she never-theless became one of the most respected amateur ornithologists of the early twentieth century, and one of the first to make good use of photography, toting a heavy Eastman glass-plate camera and tri-pod through the boggy woods to document the nests of thrushes, warblers, and other northern birds. Chapman gave her much en-couragement and direction, and in turn she wrote articles for lay readers in *Bird-Lore*, while her meticulous field observations— relayed through long correspondence with Chapman, Burroughs, Edward Forbush, and other prominent naturalists—were particu-larly critical to understanding the life histories of many birds. But she struggled for years to make a living for herself, braiding rugs and weaving baskets to help make ends meet. "Too proud to accept help from anyone, even her siblings, she was reduced in her old age to selling greeting cards from door to door," notes Marcia Bonta in her history of women naturalists.

Other women who were not as directly linked with Audubon, but who propelled nature study to the national forefront, include Anna Botsford Comstock, a writer and leading proponent of na-ture education, Gene Stratton-Porter, who wrote the Limberlost books, and Fannie Hardy Eckstorm, a friend of Florence Bailey's from Smith College, who wrote a number of bird-study books before shifting her attention to anthropological work in her native Maine.

But easily the most important—and visible—figure in the early Audubon movement was Mabel Osgood Wright, who served as Chapman's associate editor at *Bird-Lore* and wrote voluminously on birds and nature, while turning her home in Connecticut, which she named Birdcraft after her best-known book, into a haven for wildlife. Wright, who was among the first women elected to AOU membership, was a potent force on behalf of Audubon, founding the Connecticut state chapter and, after the national association was formed in 1905, serving on the association's board for the next twenty-three years.

Photos of Mrs. Wright show a no-nonsense woman with a firm jaw and a fashionable (though assuredly bird-free) bonnet. Her husband was an Englishman, James Wright, who dealt in rare books. For so public a woman, relatively little is known about her personal life; even her autobiography is less revealing than one would hope, though it appears her father, an Episcopal priest, encouraged her interest in nature. "How or why Wright learned so much about birds or why she felt compelled to fight for their protection is not known," shrugs Deborah Strom in her survey of important female bird writers. "It is not even clear whether Wright had children, although it seems unlikely that she did."

Wright was a confidant of most of the leading ornithologists of her day, but where their focus was scientific, she understood the importance of reaching as wide an audience as possible, especially children. Wright's 1907 book, *Citizen Bird*, cowritten with Elliott Coues, features three children: Nat, his sister (nicknamed Dodo, but clearly the brighter of the two), and their country-bumpkin friend Rap. Kindly old Doctor Hunter teaches them about the

The most visible figure in the early Audubon movement was Mabel Osgood Wright. A protégé of Elliott Coues, the author of bestselling books on birds, and the founder of the Connecticut Audubon chapter, she was among the first women elected to AOU membership. *Courtesy of the Library of Congress*

songbirds surrounding their farm, and the patriotic importance of protecting the Sky Sweepers, Wise Watchers, and Weed Warriors, as he styles some of the groups of birds. It was economic ornithology again, this time for kids. "Every time you children deny yourselves the pleasure of taking an egg from a nest, or think to spread a little food for hungry birds," he tells them, "you are adding to the food supply of your country . . . So we must learn to love and protect this feathered neighbor of ours, who works for his own living as well as ours, pays his rent and taxes, and gives, besides, free concerts to the public daily. He certainly deserves the name Citizen Bird."

In much of the bird writing in the first two decades of the twentieth century, there is a marked but understandable overreaching to make almost every species of bird appear valuable to humans. Wright and Coues credit the rose-breasted grosbeak with "earning his living helping farmers clear their fields of potato-bugs," even though the grosbeak is a canopy species rarely seen in crop fields, while the eastern kingbird is "a good friend to horses and cattle, because he kills the terrible gadflies. Eats a little fruit, but chiefly wild varieties, and only now and then a bee." (At the time, beekeepers tended to shoot kingbirds on sight, believing them a threat to their hives.) T. Gilbert Pearson, who succeeded Dutcher as Audubon's president after the latter was disabled by a stroke, felt compelled to burnish even the ivory-billed woodpecker's credentials: "An analysis of the food . . . indicates that this species, were it not for its small numbers, might be of considerable economic value. The insects which form the animal portion of its food are mostly of an injurious nature."

Not only were birds generally portrayed in the most favorable economic light, they were also held up as moral symbols. This was best exemplified by Gene Stratton-Porter, whose Limberlost novels were wildly popular around World War I. Stratton-Porter centered much of her writing in her beloved Limberlost swamp of Indiana, populating the stories with the birds, insects, and creatures she studied there. "Porter, a quintessential Victorian, viewed the preordained habits of the animals she studied as analogs for human family life," write Felton Gibbons and Deborah Strom. "In nature study she found the keys to defining wholesome Christian values. She offended no one and pleased everyone—educators, religious leaders, and her young readers." It was a recipe the public craved; while critics today dismiss her treacly, up-by-the-bootstraps plots, her books sold more than ten million copies in her lifetime.

Citizen Bird also gave its readers a dose of morality that makes a modern birder cringe—not only making the case for "good citizens" like swallows and seed-eating sparrows, but condemning as "really bad cannibals" bird-eating raptors like goshawks and sharp-shinned hawks. Such good bird/bad bird judgments were ubiquitous in the first half of the twentieth century, from backyard birders to the most prominent scientists, and the most common victims of this bias were raptors.

"From the economic standpoint only a few birds . . . may be said to be thoroughly undesirable," wrote ornithologist George Miksch Sutton in 1928. "The Goshawk is a savage destroyer of small game and poultry. His smaller cousins, the Sharp-shinned Hawk and Cooper's Hawk, are killers. The Great Horned Owl is destructive at times. Other hawks and owls, the Crow, Kingfisher, Starling, and other species have some destructive or undesirable habits, but they are not altogether bad."

One of the more remarkable vendettas pursued against "bad" birds was that of Althea Sherman, an idiosyncratic midwesterner who in the 1890s gave up teaching in favor of ornithology when she returned home to Iowa to tend to her aging parents. Over the years, she spent countless hours hunched in blinds, observing the lives of birds on her farm, compiling extraordinarily detailed life history accounts for many species, including chimney swifts that she lured to a specially constructed tower peppered with peepholes through which she could observe the inhabitants. For her work, she was the fourth woman elected to the AOU.

But along the way, Sherman drew some very firm conclusions about which species deserved her hospitality. After discovering that the screech-owls and American kestrels she'd been studying were eating songbirds (no more than a fifth of their diet, but still) she declared them *aves non grata*. But her greatest venom was directed at the house wrens she had once attracted. In March 1925 she published a paper in *The Wilson Bulletin* titled "Down with the House Wren Boxes," and she let fly with both barrels. The house wren was, she charged, "a felon . . . on trial for high crimes and misdemeanors," and she and others had long witnessed its "criminal character," in the way wrens will toss out the eggs of other cavity-nesting species, like bluebirds or tree swallows. She railed against those who encouraged house wrens, saying they act "precisely like the parents of vicious children, refusing to believe the evil things their darlings do."

"Capital punishment has not been demanded, though if no steps are taken to stop his unrestricted breeding it is safe to predict that the time will come when all true bird lovers will wring his neck as cheerfully as they now wring the neck of the pestiferous English Sparrow," she predicted.

Sherman was correct in charging that house wrens will destroy the eggs, and occupy the nest boxes, of other species, but her wholesale attack was beyond the pale. In the next issue of the journal, the editor's note acknowledged the receipt of many letters, both of protest and support, and said the ball was now in the court of the wren defenders: "The main question right now is the determination of the House Wren's status as a good or bad citizen. Let us endeavor to keep an open mind; and above all, let us be willing to know the facts, even though we may choose to exercise a bit of sentiment in our personal attitude toward this bird." Sherman pressed the attack, a few months later publishing a second article detailing, as she said, "additional evidence of the viciousness of this species" and attacking "the contemptuous leering of incredulity" that had met her original remarks.

Sherman's comments had so churned the birding waters that Witmer Stone, the editor of the competing journal *The Auk*, felt compelled to editorialize on the bird's behalf. "The Wren's methods are no worse than the parasitic habits of the Cowbird, the predacious habits of certain Hawks and Owls or the egg destroying propensities of the Blue Jay, and why have not these birds a perfect right to practice their living in the way that nature has ordained that they should? The Wren is no more a 'felon' for destroying the nest of a bluebird than is a Flicker for destroying a nest of ants."

If the whole wren brouhaha seems a little farcical today, such attitudes had a tremendous impact on bird conservation. In the view of even leading conservationists, not all birds were created equal. Songbirds—eaters of insects and weed seeds, lovely to see and lovelier to hear—were at the apex, along with game species; nest predators like jays were well below the salt.

It was especially hard to muster support for raptors, although by the 1920s and 1930s, a few farsighted conservationists were battling the prevailing wisdom about "bad birds" and lobbying for the protection of birds of prey as well. One of the most important was a strong-willed New Yorker named Rosalie Barrow Edge, whose relationship with Audubon was a rocky one. It says a lot about Mrs. Edge by knowing that Audubon president T. Gilbert Pearson called her "a common scold"—and that she considered it a compliment.

Audubon had grown beyond anything Harriet Hemenway might have imagined. By the end of the 1920s, there were 125 state and local associations, but most of the power was concentrated in the national board and its staff, led by Pearson.* Almost five million schoolchildren across the country had been exposed to nature through the Junior Audubon program (including a boy in Jamestown, New York, named Roger Tory Peterson), and Audubon was beginning to assemble a network of sanctuaries, starting with the enormous Rainey Wildlife Sanctuary, in Louisiana.

The organization had also become, in the eyes of many conservationists, overly bureaucratic and cautious, too polite to fight a down-and-dirty battle when the need arose, and altogether too cozy with munitions manufacturers and other advocates of extremely liberal laws for waterfowl hunting, including the use of bait, live decoys, and bag limits of up to twenty-five ducks a day. (After all, many of its original leaders had themselves been avid sportsmen, who loathed the plume trade but felt that waterfowl hunting was harmless.) When it became known that the society was profiting from muskrat trapping on its Rainey Sanctuary (the royalties from pelt sales were coyly marked as "rental" income on

---

*It's ironic, therefore, that Massachusetts Audubon is today a proudly independent organization, not part of the National Audubon umbrella.

the balance sheets), the critics howled even louder, even though the sanctuary managers believed muskrat control was necessary to protect the marsh grasses on which migrant geese fed.

The greatest critic of all was Edge, a New York socialite and battle-scarred veteran of the suffrage movement, who in the 1920s took up birding in Central Park following the collapse of her marriage. Among the friends she made was Dr. Willard Van Name, a zoologist at the American Museum of Natural History. On vacation in Paris in 1929, going through her mail from home, the fifty-two-year-old Edge found a pamphlet from Dr. Van Name titled "A Crisis in Conservation," charging that Audubon was derelict in its responsibility to birds, especially waterfowl. It electrified Mrs. Edge, and she acted with characteristic force. Back in New York she, Van Name, and one or two others formed what they called the Emergency Conservation Committee, and launched a frontal assault on the National Association of Audubon Societies.

It was a nasty fight; in order to distribute Van Name's pamphlet to all Audubon members, Edge and the committee successfully sued for the organization's mailing list, and the court case generated wide and unpleasant publicity for Audubon. Edge and her supporters mounted a three-year proxy fight to take control of the Audubon board, and while they lost, all the negative publicity took a serious toll, with membership falling by 60 percent. In the end, Pearson was forced to resign as president and many of the changes Edge and the ECC pushed were adopted, including an end to trapping on the Rainey sanctuary. Crowed journalist Irving Brandt, an ECC member, "At last a miracle, physiologically impossible, was achieved in the field of morality—the National Audubon Society recovered its virginity." In the words of Audubon historian Frank

Graham Jr., "Rosalie Edge sailed almost without warning into the very center of the conservation establishment and shook it by the scruff of its neck as no one has before or since."

Edge has been called one of the most important—and over-looked—forces in American conservation. She and the ECC were critical in the creation of Kings Canyon National Park and the en-largement of Yosemite, in California, the protection of western big game, and finally achieving national park status for Olympic Na-tional Monument, in Washington, which had been whittled down to barely half its original size by giveaways to the timber industry. But her most notable achievement came, again, through a failure of National Audubon—one that had much to do with the good bird/bad bird dichotomy of the 1930s.

In 1928 George Miksch Sutton—later famous as an ornitholo-gist and bird artist, but then a biologist for the state of Pennsylva-nia—published a brief article in *The Wilson Bulletin* about a curious choke point in hawk migration along the Kittatinny Ridge, the front range of the Appalachians in the eastern half of that state. Hawks migrated past there in great numbers, he reported, and gun-ners shot them from an old sand mine on a high promontory. In 1931 Sutton published another paper, this time about the large number of goshawks turned in for bounty from the site.

That next autumn, a young camera shop owner from Philadel-phia named Richard Pough decided to see for himself—and when he climbed to the ridgetop, he was shocked by the carnage. Return-ing several times that fall, Pough, his brother, and a few friends gathered rank after rank of dead hawks, falcons, and eagles from the woods below the shooting stand, laid them in morbid rows and photographed them. He published a letter in *Bird-Lore* about the slaughter, worked through the Hawk and Owl Society he helped form, even tried to interest the Lord's Day Alliance in the issue of Sunday shooting—anything to stop the killing.

Pough (who would later go on to found the Nature Conservancy) finally had a chance to make his case to a number of national conservation leaders, including the ECC and Audubon, which were then at each other's throats. The meeting ended, Mrs. Edge recalled, with the understanding that Audubon would buy the ridgetop, which was for sale for back taxes. But nothing happened for another year. Unbeknownst to conservationists, a local gun club was debating whether to buy the mountain themselves as a hawk-shooting preserve. Finally, Rosalie Edge could wait no longer. In June 1934 she met Pough in Pennsylvania and agreed the ECC would lease two square miles of the ridge for five hundred

When National Audubon did nothing to stop the slaughter of migrant hawks in the Appalachians, Rosalie Edge stepped in, founding Hawk Mountain Sanctuary, the first refuge in the world for raptors. Mrs. Edge was also instrumental in the creation of other natural areas, including Olympic National Park. *Courtesy of Hawk Mountain Sanctuary*

dollars, with an option to buy the rest for three thousand more. J. A. Baker, Audubon's headstrong new director, moved belatedly to try to take over the lease and assume control of the sanctuary, but Mrs. Edge would have none of it. Hiring a tough young ornithologist from Massachusetts named Maurice Broun as curator/warden, she created Hawk Mountain Sanctuary as an independent, private conservation organization.

Today Hawk Mountain is one of the most important institutions in the world for raptor research and protection, but in the early years, simply keeping the migrant birds safe was a dicey proposition. With Broun on the promontory counting the passing birds, it usually fell to his petite wife, Irma, to intercept the arriving gunners, mostly coal miners and Pennsylvania Dutch farmers from the surrounding communities. All were armed, many had been drinking, and most were unhappy, to say the least, about the change in fortunes on the mountain. But private property was something these tough men understood, and angry words aside, conflicts were few.

Rosalie Edge and the ECC bought the ridgetop to protect the hawks from harm, but once the sanctuary was open, an unexpected thing occurred. Visitors started streaming in, often traveling from Philadelphia or New York to see the migration, bumping up the rutted mountain road and climbing the last mile or so to the lookout. They came by the dozens, then the hundreds, and soon the thousands. Weekends were so busy that cars lined the narrow road. Broun was reporting fifteen thousand or more raptors each fall, and not everyone believed him; his reports of dozens of golden eagles each year—a western bird almost unknown in the East—brought scoffs and jeers, so much so that Broun took to charging five dollars for each eagle he showed to skeptics. To support the sanctuary, the Brouns collected a two-dollar annual fee. One day some years later, Mrs. Edge opened a letter from Gilbert Pearson; a check for two dollars fluttered out. Would she enroll him as a member of Hawk Mountain, he asked? The hatchet was buried.

BIRD-WATCHING WASN'T popular only at Hawk Mountain. In the previous fifty years, birding and nature study had blossomed across North America; John Burroughs's books sold more than a million copies, while the books of Ernest Thompson Seton—despite "nature-faking" charges—sold more than two and a half million. When Mabel Osgood Wright's *Birdcraft* entered its ninth edition, in 1936, she could look back with justifiable satisfaction at the changes she'd seen.

> More than twenty years ago this simple record was first sent forth . . . Since then the scene has changed, and a great awakening to the value and beauty of bird life has swept the land. The Audubon movement has not only stimulated knowledge by its fine biographical bird leaflets adequately illustrated, issued by The National Association, but this knowledge has created the general desire to protect the bird.
>
> Not only is the wild bird conceded to be an inheritance of the people, but the people have constituted themselves the trustees of its liberty.

In the years between world wars, more and more people were taking to the field, despite the desperate economy and ominous political news. The increasing availability of European optics made it easier to see birds, and the publication of the first truly useful field guides made it at last possible for beginners to identify what they were seeing. Frank Chapman's idea for an annual Christmas Bird Count was growing by leaps and bounds; from the original twenty-five counts in 1900, the event had expanded to almost two hundred and fifty sites by 1940, with thousands taking part, and their results being printed in *Audubon Field Notes*. Bird-watching was becoming less an oddity and much more of a mainstream activity. Bird clubs were popping up in many urban areas; the trend that began with the Nuttall Club, and with the Delaware Valley Ornithological Club in Philadelphia in 1890, accelerated in the years around World War I. Sometimes these morphed into Audubon chapters, with an emphasis on education and preservation, while others (like the venerable DVOC) remained focused on research and field birding.*

One of the enduring myths about modern bird study is that professional ornithology and recreational birding split asunder in the late nineteenth and early twentieth centuries, never the twain to meet. As with most folklore, there is a kernel of truth to this; there was a lot of open hostility in those days, over divisive issues like specimen collecting, and the snobbery that often afflicts entrenched academics when laymen encroach upon their field of expertise. But the fact is that the chasm between birders and academic ornithologists has never been as deep or as permanent as many believe; ornithology remains one of the branches of science most enriched by

---

*And, unfortunately, on maintaining a boy's club; The Nuttall Club forbade women for much of its first century and the DVOC, for all its strengths, did not finally allow female members until the shamefully late date of 1982.

the work of dedicated amateurs, and it's hard to find a full-time or- nithologist who isn't also a recreational birder. With the rise of so- called citizen-science in the past thirty years, the line has become even blurrier, with breeding-bird surveys, atlases, migration counts, and a host of other projects, designed by scientists but ex- ecuted by millions of birders who combine sport and research every time they head for the woods.

But there were certainly some testy moments when things were still sorting themselves out. The biggest headache of all, from the professionals' perspective, was the "opera-glass observers" show- ing up at club meetings and reporting rarities based not on a spec- imen in the hand, which anyone could examine or challenge, but on sight records.

It's the sort of thing that happens at every monthly bird club and Audubon chapter meeting across the country. The president dispenses with the bits of business—field trip reports, a call for volunteers to help with the weekend birdseed sale—while the eve- ning speaker is fussing with the projector. And then comes the question: "So, who has any sightings to report?"

One after another, members rise to tell what they've been see- ing, from the banal to the breathtaking. The audience is usually at- tentive, because you never know what's going to emerge, and a birder who's a good showman knows how to play the audience, waiting for the commonplace stuff—reports of cardinals and song sparrows at backyard feeders—to die down, then casually drop- ping a bombshell that will get everyone murmuring.

But if the report seems to be coming from out of left field—a bird wildly out of range or season, especially one reported by a be- ginner or someone whose credibility is in doubt—then glances are exchanged among the elders of the tribe; eyebrows are lifted, lips are pursed, heads are shaken ever so slightly. The graybeards start asking questions—politely, of the "Any chance it was a thus-and-such?" variety—but the more surprising the report, the more vigorous the grilling. Some clubs are notorious for the intensity of their inquisitions, and take pride in their rigor. That's because sightings are the heart and soul of modern birding, central to the whole business, and the only way the clan can determine if the observation is valid is to poke and prod until the observer is sore.

That's such an accepted part of birding today that it's hard to imagine the tectonic mental shift it required back in the days of shotguns and specimens. With so many novices getting into birds, filling the minutes of their local bird clubs with reports of their sightings, many of the scientists grumped and harrumphed to one another about how far the ornithological world had fallen. As early as 1883, the Nuttall Club's *Bulletin* was slamming the idea: "It is to be hoped . . . the observations made by those who have 'become acquainted' with birds in this way will never be put into print as a contribution to ornithology."

Yet try as hard as they might, shotgun ornithologists couldn't keep sight records out of the game. More than fifty years after the Nuttall Club complaint, Witmer Stone—generally a supporter of the wave of new amateurs coming into ornithology—objected that bird-watchers armed with new field guides were muddying the water with all sorts of dubious records. He cited an "olive-sided flycatcher" reported in March, sitting by a springhouse and wagging a tail—a bird that, as all of Stone's readers knew, was certainly just a run-of-the-mill eastern phoebe. Even worse, Stone said, "is the element of competition which naturally creeps in."

During a Christmas Bird Count, "Even the most careful individual observer will, more or less unconsciously, give a record the benefit of a doubt if it adds one more species to his team score." In the end, Stone said, "The present day arguments on the possibility of identifying closely related species in the field is of no scientific consequence."

If they were being honest, though, even the most specimen-oriented ornithologists admitted that field glasses provided a window on birdlife, especially behavior, that a shotgun and stuffed skin never could. With an army of eager bird-lovers now found the length and breadth of the continent, it fell to a single (and singularly driven) man to harness their enthusiasm and newfound skills to spectacular ends—the Smithsonian Institution's twenty-one-volume series *Life Histories of North American Birds,* which stands as one of the most striking achievements of ornithology.

Where the focus of bird study had once been on collecting, as a means of simply sorting out what species were what (and where they were found), by the end of the nineteenth century there was a growing emphasis on how birds lived—their diet, courtship and nesting behaviors, migrations, and more. The idea of a single resource compiling life history information dated back to Spencer Baird in the 1850s, but not until 1892 did Charles Bendire—no longer being chased through the Arizona desert by Apache but now curator of the Smithsonian's egg collection—publish the first of an expected six volumes on the subject.

Bendire was an oologist, and his book, not unexpectedly, focused heavily on nests and eggs, with lavish color plates of game bird, owl, and hawk eggs. But Bendire went beyond a narrow oology viewpoint to report on the lives of the birds themselves. A second volume appeared in 1895, but two years later Bendire, just sixty, died of kidney disease, leaving the great work unfinished. An egg collector named William Ralph took over, but he died in 1907 without publishing anything further. That was when the unusually persistent Arthur Cleveland Bent stepped into the breach.

Born in 1866, in eastern Massachusetts, Cleveland Bent was a frail and sickly child whose father began taking him on long outdoor excursions to build his health. It worked; a collegiate boxing career followed, and throughout his long life, Bent chopped wood and lifted weights almost daily to stay in shape. The boy became hooked on birds and, with his friends, began collecting skins and eggs, but after he graduated from Harvard he went into business, eventually becoming a successful manufacturing and public utility tycoon.

But he never lost his interest in birds, a passion that once almost cost him his life. In 1896, he scrambled up a huge, dead oak tree near his home, aiming to collect the eggs of a pair of barred owls nesting in a deep cavity. He used no safety harness and strapped no climbing irons to his feet, but merely shinnied up the tall trunk to the hole—as he had done on countless occasions.

But this time, when Bent reached into the opening for the eggs, he slipped and fell, his arm jamming itself into the narrow cleft at the bottom of the owls' hole. He was stuck, in excruciating pain, and a long way from help. Before somehow wrenching free and plummeting to the ground—a drop that should have killed or crippled him—he hung there for twenty-five agonizing minutes. This is not an estimate; Bent could see the village clock in the distance, and meticulous to the bone, he carefully noted the duration of his ordeal, which left him with a permanent tremor in his right hand.

Not long after, he began submitting articles to the ornithological journals, although he didn't get serious about ornithology until he started to ease out of business in his mid-forties, with comfortable means that permitted him to crisscross North America from Newfoundland to the Aleutians. His collection eventually reached thirty thousand eggs (now in the Smithsonian), and although he was an amateur, he later rose to become the president of the AOU. He was also one of the first people Harriet Hemenway approached when she founded Massachusetts Audubon, not long after Bent suffered his climbing accident.

After Bendire's death, several of Bent's associates urged him to take up the task of completing the life history series. It was 1910; he was in his mid-forties, still managing many of his business ventures, and over the previous few years, he'd begun to travel widely. No doubt he recognized that finishing Bendire's series would crimp his style, but with his old Nuttall Club friend Charles Batchelder pushing him, he agreed to complete the six-volume set as Bendire had originally planned. Once he dove in, though, Bent realized he would have to start essentially from scratch, and he told his friends, "It will be my life work." He was right about that. He was then forty-four years old, and over the next forty-four years he produced nineteen volumes, with an additional two in the later stages of preparation at the time of his death, in 1954. And Bent, made comfortable by his success in business, never accepted a dime in salary from the Smithsonian for all his work.

It was a monumental undertaking, not only in terms of the sheer mass of information, but how he obtained it. Bent combed the scientific literature, of course, quoting experts from Wilson and Audubon to the leading ornithologists of the day, and he also included much of his own scholarship, including his pioneering observations of Bicknell's thrush. But he also became the clucking, chiding mother hen to a network of more than eight hundred correspondents—many of them highly skilled amateur ornithologists like himself—scattered from the Arctic to the tropics, from the halls of science to the most remote outposts imaginable. The observations of a clerk at a Hudson's Bay Co. fur trading post in northern Canada carried as much weight as those of the most eminent professor.

Bent's correspondents sent him letters detailing the minutiae of avian life, from the number of eggs in a great-horned-owl nest near Dried Meat Lake, Alberta, (three) to descriptions of the call of the elegant trogon in Arizona ("almost like the chattering of our gray squirrel") to the habits of the yellow-rumped warbler on its wintering grounds in Costa Rica. The introduction to every volume carried the same put-up-or-shut-up message:

> The reader is reminded again that this is a cooperative work; if he fails to find in these volumes anything that he knows about the birds, he can blame himself for not having sent the information to
>
> —The Author.

It took Bent nine years, until 1919, to produce the first volume, covering diving birds, but after that, a new volume—ranging from three hundred to more than six hundred pages each—was published every few years. The last came out in 1965. Comprising 9,500 pages of text, the *Life Histories* were at once enormously informative and immensely readable, and they remain incredibly relevant today; no other single resource contains as much sheer information on the continent's birds, and Bent's series is still one of the most-cited works of ornithological literature.*

While the pooh-bahs of ornithology were grousing about amateurs and their damnable sight records, ornithology had changed forever around them. The shift from specimens to observation— from the dead bird to the living one—was a gradual but inexorable process, and one that was being driven both by intense birders and a new crop of behavior- and evolution-focused scientists.

Perhaps no one in the professional community did more to smooth the way for this new manifestation of bird study than Ludlow Griscom. A New York–born ornithologist who started his career working under Frank Chapman at the American Museum of Natural History, and then moved to the Museum of Comparative Zoology at Harvard, Griscom had been fascinated by the challenges of field identification all his life. As a boy, he'd been deeply embarrassed when he reported a rare Bicknell's thrush at a meeting of the stuffy old Linnaean Society. "The resultant storm of criticism rendered me practically speechless," he recalled. "Then and there I planned to do my best to become a reliable observer and to investigate the scientific possibilities of sight identification."

And he did. An oft-told story claims that one of the old-school shotgun ornithologists challenged Griscom to identify a warbler high in the treetops. A female Cape May, the young man said—a gutsy call, because this is a notoriously tricky bird to identify. *Bang.*

---

*No one attempted to duplicate the feat until the early 1990s, when the *Birds of North America* project—described as "Bent for the 21st Century"—was launched. It took three major institutions (the AOU, the Cornell Lab of Ornithology, and the Academy of Natural Sciences), employing dozens of editors and hundreds of authors, a decade to match what one dedicated amateur and his legions of collaborators had achieved half a century earlier.

The warbler falls; it is a Cape May. And that one? *Bang*—another correct identification. And *bang,* another, until at last the doubting Thomas is convinced.

True? The story was told by one of Griscom's own students, so it might well be, but the factuality of it almost doesn't matter; the story has been told so often because it boils down the emergence of modern birding, with its reliance on the binocular instead of the gun, into a simple parable—the dawn of a new age in a single morning in Central Park, instead of the protracted, messy, far more complex process it actually was, taking more than fifty years.

But in many ways, Griscom was the fulcrum of the shift. His master's thesis in 1915 was a treatise on duck identification, and in the decades to follow, he proselytized a new, cutting-edge approach to birding, one that entailed looking for just the most important field marks—not the laundry list of minute physical description found in most bird books of the day, but the handful of distinguishing characteristics that separated one species from another, like wing bars, eye stripes, or a phoebe's wagging tail. Griscom, more than anyone else, proved that it was possible to coax an identification from a distant bird using nothing more than trained eyes and ears, and a knowledge of field marks. He and his friends were also among those who more or less invented the notion of birding as a competitive sport—pitting one birder's list against another's, or setting a birder against him- or herself, trying to better previous marks.

While he acknowledged the problem with sloppy identification and inaccurate sight records, Griscom not surprisingly viewed the explosion in the popularity of birding as an enormous plus for ornithology.

With the great growth in recent years of interest in bird-study, there has undoubtedly been an increase in poor sight-records and misidentifications . . . It is true that the modern flood of sight records makes the writing of a local avifauna a far more complex and difficult task than the old-fashioned ones, based on the comparatively small number of birds shot. But it is also true that the modern avifauna is far more complete, detailed, and accurate than the old. For every poor record there are at least fifty good ones, which have greatly extended our detailed knowledge of birds in every State of the Union. If scientists can justly complain of their troubles, when science becomes too popular, let them at least remember, that like everybody else they cannot get something for nothing. And what they have got is the assistance of the enthusiastic, reliable amateur.

When Griscom wrote of "enthusiastic, reliable amateurs," he might have had in mind a band of eight or nine eager teenagers from the Bronx, who treated him as something of a birding god, shadowing his footsteps, learning his field methods, even aping his inflections of speech and how he parted his hair. They called themselves the Bronx County Bird Club, and they came together in the mid-1920s, attending meetings of the Linnaean Society at the American Museum of Natural History, where Griscom was a curator.

The Bronx club was a tight-knit group, but they made room for one more fellow—a shy, skinny bird nut from southwestern New York, whom they met in 1925 when the seventeen-year-old visitor attended an AOU meeting at the museum. The boy moved to the city two years later, to start art school, and became the first non-Bronx member of the BCBC. He stayed three years, working when he had to, birding when he could, absorbing everything Griscom and the other hotshot New York birders had to teach. When he left for Boston in 1931, it was with all the ingredients he needed to revolutionize birding—for the young man was Roger Tory Peterson, and he had an idea for a new kind of bird book.

6

Becoming a Noun

MY WIFE AND I own a lot of bird books—a ridiculous number of them. They fill shelves in our offices, our bedroom, our living room; they sit stacked in corners, on the bureaus, on chairs, on the floor; when we're not looking, I think they multiply, like rabbits. We have books we swear neither of us bought, but there they are, nevertheless. The ones we use less frequently occupy countless boxes in the attic and garage, through which we are forever scrabbling to find whatever tome we need. We have discussed, with perfectly straight faces, the need to buy a larger house simply to store our books.

In this, we are not alone; most birders are also bird-book collectors. And like most birders, we have a particular weakness for birding field guides, which take up one entire wall of my office and a good chunk of the living-room bookcase. But of course, it isn't just bird guides—we own field guides to seashells and reptiles, ferns and insects, marine mammals and mushrooms, trees and plankton, lichen and fish, frogs and wildflowers, seaweed and sedges. We have field guides to tracks, to bones, to the little heaps of plucked feathers one finds after a hawk has finished eating. We have field guides—yes, plural; at least three of them—to animal scat in all its infinite, excretory variety. Somewhere around here I have a field guide to roadkill. Honest.

Field guides make the natural world knowable; they are the first entry point for most people into the diversity of life on the planet. One can shuffle through life noticing little more than dandelions and roses, but open a field guide and you confront the fact that there are literally thousands of species of wildflowers, from tiny alpine forget-me-nots in the Rockies, with flowers barely a quarter-inch wide, to spectacular lady's-slipper orchids rising from soggy fens, with pink and white blossoms that would make anyone stop and stare. If you're open to wonder, this will be a staggering discovery. What had been a blur begins to resolve itself into myriad distinct shards, each unique, each lovely. Putting a name to a thing may not be, as the old proverb holds, the first step to wisdom—but it is often the first step to appreciation.

And the diversity of guides these days bids fair to rival the diversity of the organisms they celebrate. There are more bird guides than anything else, and if we do not—yet—have a guide for each of the thousands of species of birds on the planet, it can sometimes seem that way. There are the standard field guides, the whole-avifauna books that cover an entire continent's or region's worth of birds in one volume—dozens for North America and parts thereof, as well as Europe, Africa, Asia, Australia, the Pacific Ocean, the Antarctic, the West Indies, the Middle East, and, generally speaking, anywhere else with birds (meaning everywhere else). Increasingly, you can find guides at the country level—the birds of New Zealand, or Indonesia, or Thailand; birds of Belize, or Venezuela, or Kenya; of China, India, Morocco.

They keep publishing new ones, and we birders keep buying them. Although I've never been to Colombia, I have two copies of *Birds of Colombia*, which was until recently also the only field guide for neighboring Peru, where I have traveled several times. (There is now a guide to Peru, and I've ordered a copy.) I have two copies of the 850-page Colombian guide because my original became so badly stained and mildewed from repeated trips to the Amazon that I bought a replacement. But of course I couldn't bear to part with the first one—sentimental value, you see—so they both sit on the shelf, next to *The Birds of Ecuador*. The latter is a boxed, two-volume set comprising ninety-six color plates and sixteen hundred pages of text (roughly one for each of the country's species of birds), and weighs in at six pounds. I've never been to Ecuador, either—but I have the book, just in case.

There are video guides, audio guides, computer software guides, and of course regional guides. If you're like us, you can buy guides to the birds of the Blue Ridge Mountains, the Rocky Mountains, the Cascade Mountains; the desert Southwest, the Monterey peninsula and bay, the western Aleutians, and Central Park; Lake Erie, the lower Rio Grande Valley, the Lehigh Valley, the Hudson Valley, and the Lahontan Valley, just to name a very, very few. These are mostly where-to-go guides, mind you, but they're still part of the juggernaut. The sound you hear is our shelves sagging.

There are family-specific guides to owls, to hawks, to pigeons and doves; to nightjars, to swifts, and to Arctic-nesting plovers; to New World warblers and Old World warblers, and to "cuckoos, cowbirds and other cheats," in the words of one guidebook to this cadre of nest parasites. The more thorny the identification puzzles posed by a group, the more abundant the guides, which explains the embarrassment of good books on gulls, raptors, and shorebirds. There are reference guides that treat every single bird in North America, and every single bird in the world. One entire shelf in my office groans under the expanding weight of the *Handbook of Birds of the World,* now up to volume twelve of an expected sixteen. The *Handbook* had me at hello—big, lavishly illustrated volumes compiling every significant fact about every one of the more than nine thousand species of living birds on Earth. Okay, they're not field guides unless you do your birding with pack animals; altogether, the twelve volumes weigh more than one hundred pounds. But they branch from the same family tree.

How did all this start? Field guides are a fairly recent innovation; for most of human history, identification knowledge was passed along directly, person to person. ("See these berries, Throg? Don't eat 'em, or next thing you know, the clan will be smearing your body with red ochre and burying you under the cave floor.") Even after the invention of mass-produced books, the idea of combining art and words on the printed page for the express purpose of identifying natural objects took a very long time to germinate.

Asked to pinpoint the birth date of the field guide, any well-informed birder will point to the autumn of 1934, when that socially awkward, twenty-six-year-old schoolteacher published *A Field Guide to the Birds.* Even today, more than a decade after his death, in 1996, Roger Tory Peterson remains the world's most famous birder, his celebrity resting largely on the general recognition that he invented the birding field guide. Which would be laurels enough for any man, even one as talented and driven as Peterson—except for one niggling little fact. Roger Tory Peterson did nothing of the sort.

THE BASIC CONCEPT of a field guide to birds was already more than a century old by the time the boy from Jamestown, New York, came along. What Peterson did was *reinvent* it, make it cheap, handy, and accessible to the general public. Peterson himself was always very clear about his role in the process, carefully listing the many sources of inspiration and precedence that led up to his landmark publication.

The first "field guide," in any practical sense, was the *Manual of the Ornithology of the United States and Canada,* the two-volume set that Thomas Nuttall published in 1832 and 1834, just before joining the Wyeth expedition to the Pacific Northwest. Nuttall's book borrowed rather too freely from Wilson, sometimes with (though most often without) giving due credit, and his own experiences were mostly restricted to the birds of the Northeast—he was, after all, primarily a botanist. But it was the first time someone had compressed the sum of North American ornithological knowledge into a compact form, and its woodcut illustrations, while simple, added tremendously to its value.

Of course, it was "compact" only in comparison with the lavish volumes of Wilson and, a few years later, Audubon. Nuttall's books ran to about eight hundred pages of dense text, but compare that with Audubon's four folios, each the size of a small table, which together cost the modern equivalent of forty thousand dollars. If a scientist were heading for the field and needed a reference to keep in the saddlebag, it was Nuttall's *Manual* they invariably packed, and it remained in print, and in use, through the beginning of the twentieth century.

The final decades of the 1800s, however, saw a flurry of new works on bird identification—all of them aimed at scholars, all of them presuming that the first step in identifying a bird was shooting it. By far the most influential of these was Elliott Coues's *Key to North American Birds,* which first appeared in 1872 and went through five editions by 1903.

Comprehensive, painstaking, authoritative—Coues's *Key* was all of these. But it was also unwieldy; at its heart was the kind of dichotomous key long beloved of specialists with a specimen in hand, but a trial to anyone without a lot of expertise and plenty of time to devote to thumbing through its pages. Each key led the reader to another key, moving down the taxonomic ladder at last to the subspecies level, with ever-finer gradations of size, shape, and plumage. For example, to distinguish the subspecies of the Carolina wren, *Thryothorus ludovicianus,* a reader was confronted with the following choices:

CAROLINA WRENS. Of largest size in this group; length up to 6.00 [inches]. Tail decidedly shorter than wings. Back uniform in color, without streaks or bars; wings and tail more or less barred crosswise; belly unmarked; a long superciliary stripe; rump with concealed white spots. Eggs colored.

Analysis of Species and Subspecies
Reddish-brown above, rusty whitish below; tail regularly
barred throughout. Wing 2.40 . . . *ludovicianus*

Similar; more heavily colored; rusty-brown below. Wing
  2.75. Florida . . . *ludovicianus miamensis*
Grayish-brown, more extensively barred on flanks;
  barring of tail irregular; small; wing 2.25. S.E.
  Texas . . . *ludovicianus lomitensis*
Darker brown, most extensively barred on flanks, barring
  of tail irregular; small; wing 2.25. N.E. Mexico . . .
  ludovicianus berlandieri

The illustration, a woodcut of a Carolina wren from a late edition of Nuttall (which, in turn, was copied from Audubon) would be hard for a novice to recognize as that species—but the art was meant to be secondary to the measurements and the exhaustive, almost feather-by-feather descriptions of each geographic race that followed the key. "GREAT CAROLINA WREN. Upper parts uniform reddish-brown, brightest on rump, where are concealed white spots; a long whitish superciliary line, usually bordered with dusky streaks . . . Below, rusty or muddy whitish, clearest anteriorly, deepening behind, the under-tail coverts reddish-brown barred with blackish. Wing-coverts usually with dusky and whitish tips . . ." And so it went, for half a page.

Used properly, a key is an almost failsafe way to identify a specimen—but the hurdles are obvious, and all but block anyone with a novice's interest and experience. To make bird study accessible, bird *books* would have to become more accessible—a shift that occurred as the world marked the change from one century to another.

Frank Chapman, who would later play such a pivotal role in the bird protection movement, said that discovering a copy of Coues's

Key for sale in a bookstore in 1885 marked a turning point in his life. "For the first time, I learned there were living students of birds, worthy successors of Wilson and Audubon," he said, and the discovery led him to abandon his career in banking in favor of ornithology. But even though he long praised Coues's work as one of the benchmarks of bird study, he recognized that it left a good deal to be desired for the more casual bird student, especially the growing numbers who preferred to watch birds rather than collect them.

In 1895 Chapman published *Handbook of Birds of Eastern North America,* a seminal book in which the balance began to swing from shotgun to field-glass ornithology—at least incrementally. The book was still built on keys—keys to the families, keys to the species (the key for wood warblers was eight pages of eye-crossing small type). But Chapman arranged his keys with an eye to color and obvious traits a more casual user would notice in the field, and his was the first guide to use many of the common song transliterations we still use today, such as the Carolina wren's *tea-kettle tea-kettle tea-kettle.*

Fifteen years later, Chapman revised his book, including an extensive new introduction on "The Study of Birds in Nature." In his autobiography, he wrote, "The day of the bird collector had passed and the day of the bird student had come. It was to this group, practically nonexistent when the first *Handbook* was written, that the new work was addressed."

Chapman's growing army of bird students had more and more resources available to them. Florence Merriam, who had written for Chapman in *Bird-Lore* magazine, published *Birds of Village and Field* in 1898 and *Birds Through an Opera-Glass* the following year, both with an informal style and a focus on field-identification; they were among the most popular books of their day, and as noted earlier, one can make a case for *Opera-Glass*, in particular, being the proto–field guide. But it covered only the seventy most common eastern and midwestern species, and gave most of its attention to life history information salted with a heavy dose of romanticism, as in this description of the American robin: "His sentiment is the wholesome every-day sort, with none of the sadness or longing of his cousins, the thrushes, but full of contented appreciation of the beautiful world he lives in."

Merriam understood the growing popularity of bird-watching, and certainly saw the need for a book that dealt with the puzzles of field identification. But instead of taking the logical next step and creating a book that zeroed in on how to identify birds, Merriam—by now married to biologist Vernon Bailey—stepped back into the scientific fold. She and her husband coauthored *Handbook of Birds of the Western United States* in 1902, using photographs of museum skins instead of the far more useful woodcuts, and freighting it down with dichotomous keys, creating a book of lasting value to scientists and dedicated amateurs, but leaving the general public in the cold.

Keys were all the rage. In 1904 a thirty-four-year-old Massachusetts schoolteacher named Ralph Hoffmann published *A Guide to the Birds of New England and Eastern New York*, a now sadly forgotten trove of information about the region's birdlife, illustrated with ink portraits. As with Merriam's book, many birding historians point to Hoffmann's handbook as one of the crucial ur-guides. But to narrow down an identification, Hoffmann had his readers turn first to—you guessed it—a series of seasonal keys. Under the key for winter, there were nineteen species lumped as "brown or brownish," from the flicker—"flies to or from trees; rump white"—to the American tree sparrow "in small flocks on ground;

wing-bars white; breast unstreaked, with small dusky spot in cen-
tre." And on through every other major color, and six seasonal
keys (summer, fall, winter, and three spring migration months).
Putting a name to a bird using Hoffmann was possible—with practice, and much patience—but newcomers to bird-watching no
doubt found it an insurmountable climb.

It fell to Frank Chapman to make the next significant contribution to the development of the field guide, with his 1903 *Color Key
to North American Birds*—a work whose sole aim, he said, was "the
identification of the bird in the bush." The *Color Key* marked several dramatic firsts, especially its *visual* approach to identification.
Each species was illustrated with a drawing, eight hundred in all,
tinted with colored ink. Judged as art, the drawings were stiffly
done and crudely colored, but the idea, the author explained, was
not to create "perfect reproductions of every shade and tint of the
plumage of the species, but . . . to present a bird's characteristic
colors as they appear when seen at a distance."

Chapman also jettisoned the usual taxonomic arrangement by
family and genus, and grouped his songbirds by their most obvious
colors and habits—"Perching Birds Marked with Yellow or Orange" (eighteen pages of them), or "Perching Birds Chiefly Brown
or Streaked" (twenty-two pages). Instead of Merriam's cheerful,
chatty text, or the kind of detailed descriptions he'd used in his
Handbook, he condensed the written material into a single, clipped
paragraph for each species and subspecies that covered the basics of
plumage, voice, and range.

There were obvious drawbacks to the *Color Key;* the art was
weak, and while there were no illustrations of female or juvenile
plumages, the book was cluttered with subspecies, some of which

A banker who abandoned a promising career to study birds, Frank Chapman left a remarkable legacy both in science and conservation, making several important strides in the evolution of the modern field guide. *Courtesy of the American Museum of Natural History Library*

were essentially indistinguishable in the field. But for the first time, an expert had created a single book specifically for bird-watchers, designed to aid field identification, dependent primarily on illustrations, and covering the avifauna of the entire continent north of Mexico. This was no small feat, and it would be more than sixty years before anyone else attempted it.

Chapman's *Color Key* was a reasonable success, so much so that he brought out a second, expanded edition in 1912. But in the meantime, Chapman's illustrator, a young man from Worcester,

Massachusetts, named Chester Reed, had been busy—and the books he published in 1906 would quickly eclipse everything else that had been written for beginning birders.

Nature was the Reed family business; Chester's father, Charles K. Reed, a onetime housepainter, billed himself as a "Dealer in Instruments and Supplies for Ornithologists, Oologists, Entomologists, Botanists, Mineralologists and Taxidermists. Also, Birds' Skins, Birds' Eggs, Minerals, Shells and Curiosities." (The senior Reed had acquired the business in the 1880s from Edward H. Forbush, who went on to become a noted New England ornithologist.)

Unfortunately, the elder Reed fell afoul of New York Audubon in 1904, accused of taking birds and eggs in violation of the new protection laws, and he moved away from selling eggs and skins. Books, however, were another aspect of the Reed family business, and a successful one at that. Starting in 1901, they began to publish a high-end monthly magazine, edited by Chester, called *American Ornithology*, devoted to a series of life-history sketches in each issue, and which was later released in book form "for home or school." But Reed's biggest success was two oddly shaped little books that appeared in 1906, published by Doubleday. They were long and narrow, about the size of a modern checkbook, each simply titled *Bird Guide;* one covered waterbirds, game birds, and raptors, and the other covered songbirds of North America from the Great Plains east. Each page had a color painting and several hundred words of text describing the bird's plumage, voice, and range.

Reed's guides were a sensation, becoming, almost overnight, the most popular guidebooks for anyone just starting to watch birds. Why did they catch on, when Chapman's far more comprehensive *Color Key* did not? The price probably had something to do with it; at just seventy-five cents per volume, they were within the reach of most people, including parents looking for a gift for children, whereas Chapman's book cost more than three times as much. Unlike Reed's previous work for Chapman, here the artist could create attractive paintings of the birds in a swatch of their habitats, and he often included females and immatures. But it was the practicality of the book that won the most converts—instead of a three-hundred-page brick like Chapman's *Key,* these guides were truly pocket-sized. They were easy to use, fun to read, not too intimidating in their scope, and people gobbled them up. They sold three hundred thousand copies in five years, and more than half a million by the early 1930s.

The Reed books were obviously not without their flaws; they depicted only some of the birds, and covered only part of the continent. But for most bird enthusiasts, they presented an easy first step into birding. Read the memoirs of almost any naturalist, birder, or ornithologist who came of age before the Depression, and a Reed guide usually plays a central—often decisive—role; time and again, you find the phrase "the book that changed my life." A gift from a doting grandparent, a loan from a perceptive teacher, a chance encounter on a library shelf—however it happened, Reed's little books provided the spark to countless birders. Alan Devoe, a popular nature writer in the first half of the century, reminisced (tongue firmly in cheek) about how, armed with his Reed guides, he made one stunning discovery after another around New York City.

> Prowling the fields and thickets with boyhood's rapt attentiveness, I was constantly coming upon some bird that was obviously no common species but must be a great ornithological rarity. Perhaps (who could be sure?) it might be a

species hitherto unknown. . . . Then, at home in the evening, there would be the magical delight of thumbing through Chester A. Reed's "Bird Guide," in search of the identity of the bird I had just seen. And presently—sure enough!—there it would be. A scissor-tailed flycatcher, to the life. Unmistakable. There would be a fresh excitement in going out for the next bird-walk, for there was always a chance that a similar piece of good luck might come my way again. Indeed it virtually always did. There were *birds* in those days, I tell you.

Chester Reed did not live long enough to appreciate the importance of his guides; he contracted pneumonia and died in 1912, just thirty-six years old. His father repackaged the eastern books into one volume, adding more information, and published a guide to western birds the year after his son's death. It's interesting to wonder—had he lived longer, continuing to refine his ideas and his art—whether Chester Reed would have pulled all of the strands together to create the first real, functional field guide. Instead, using a century's worth of false starts and incremental improvements, it fell to Roger Tory Peterson, who as a boy cherished his Reed guides, to make the final big leap to the modern bird guide.

ALL HIS LIFE, Peterson made a point of crediting those whose encouragement and ideas were crucial to his development as a birder and a field guide author. At the head of the line stood Blanche Hornbeck.

Although she only taught in the Jamestown, New York, schools for a single year, beginning in the fall of 1919, the pretty, red-

Roger Tory Peterson (right) shares a cup of coffee with Maurice Broun on Hawk Mountain's North Lookout, probably in the late 1940s. *Courtesy of Hawk Mountain Sanctuary*

headed Miss Hornbeck changed young Roger's life. He'd always been interested in nature, but when Miss Hornbeck started a Junior Audubon Club in her class, distributing the illustrated leaflets from the National Association of Audubon Societies, Roger Peterson fell hard for birds. Soon he and a school chum, Carl Hammerstrom, were roaming all over Jamestown, armed with their Reed guides. On their very first excursion, the boys found a brown bird, fluffed up, asleep on a tree; they thought it was dead, but when they touched it, it exploded into flight, yellow quills flashing—a northern flicker, the image seared into Peterson's brain for life. From then on, he was hooked. He arranged his paper route to hit the best birding spots, sometimes starting as early as 2 A.M., and skied through the winter woods every other afternoon to refill as many as twenty feeding stations. With his paper money, he bought a pair of opera glasses and a camera. In high school, his idea of showing a girl a good time was frog-marching her seventeen miles on a bird walk.

As he progressed through school, Peterson made it clear to everyone, including his disapproving teachers and worried parents, that he would make a career of birds. But when Peterson graduated (two years early, at age sixteen), he decided to throw his lot with art, not ornithology. He'd always been adept at painting and drawing, and so he took a job decorating lacquered cabinets, while continuing to paint birds in his free time. That same year, 1925, he traveled to New York City for an AOU meeting at which two of his own paintings were on display. He met the boys of the Bronx County Bird Club and their mentor, Ludlow Griscom, along with several of his artistic heroes, including Francis Lee Jaques and Louis Agassiz Fuertes, who gave the shy boy a sable watercolor brush.

One person Peterson had hoped to meet in New York, but didn't, was the Canadian naturalist Ernest Thompson Seton, whose book *Two Little Savages* had been one of the lad's favorites—and which would prove to be enormously influential to him.

Born in England of Scottish descent, Seton immigrated to Canada with his family in 1866, when he was six years old. A talented artist and an avid naturalist, at nineteen he won a scholarship to the Royal Academy of Art in London, but his health declined so drastically that within two years, his family brought him home—to die, they thought.

Instead, Seton recovered and joined his older brothers on their homestead in Manitoba, where he ignored farm duties in favor of chasing birds, studying wildlife, and learning from local Indians. He began to write about natural history and to correspond with prominent naturalists, from Elliott Coues and Teddy Roosevelt to Frank Chapman, whose *Handbook of Birds* Seton helped illustrate. His experiences across North America formed the core of his writing, including a period with wolf hunters in New Mexico that gave rise to his famous tale "Lobo, the King of Currumpaw"—although Seton's tendency to anthropomorphize his heroic subjects also left him open to charges of "nature-faking" by John Burroughs and others, including Roosevelt himself.

By 1900 Seton had moved to Connecticut and was deeply involved in creating a youth movement he called Woodcraft, based on Native skills and philosophies, which would prove critical to the emergence of the Boy Scouts in England a few years later. Seton was going to publish a how-to guide to woodcraft, but his friend, the writer and poet Rudyard Kipling, suggested he weave the information into a novel instead.

The result, published in 1903, was *Two Little Savages,* the tale of a teenaged boy named Yan and his friends, who live the life of Indians for a summer near a Canadian frontier town; Seton salted it with many of his own experiences as a boy, escaping to the woods around Toronto to get away from his abusive father. Through the story and hundreds of illustrations, Seton showed how to make a tepee and moccasins, stuff an owl, identify common trees, make a fire-drill, and other outdoorsy crafts. It was the sort of thing that nature-mad readers like Peterson just devoured.

But Yan struggles with how to identify birds.

By and by he got a book that was some help, but not much. It told about some of the birds as if you had them *in your hand*. . . . One day he saw a wild Duck on a pond so far away he could only see some spots of colour, but he made a sketch of it, and later he found out from that rough sketch that it was a Whistler, and then [he] had an idea. All the Ducks were different; all have little blots and streaks that are their labels, or like the uniforms of soldiers.

Yan goes to a taxidermy shop, where he uses the stuffed birds as models, sketching dozens of them. "These he afterward carefully finished and put together in a Duck Chart that solved many of his riddles about the Common Ducks." Seton supplied his readers with two black-and-white plates showing what he called "far-sketches" of twenty-four species of ducks, the view approximating what one would see at a range of about fifty yards. The birds are tiny and the sketches schematic, but instantly recognizable—the vertical white bar on the chest of a green-winged teal, the black rump of a gadwall, the white body and cheek spot of a common goldeneye, or "whistler." The captions were brief and to the point: "Gadwall or Gray Duck (*Anas strepera*). Beak flesh-coloured on edges, feet reddish, a white spot on wing showing in flight."

With his duck illustrations, Seton was expanding on something he'd created a few years earlier to illustrate an article in *The Auk* about raptor identification—a plate showing hawks and owls overhead, drawn simplistically and schematically. Never mind that one rarely sees owls soaring overhead; these were really the first true field guide plates anyone had ever created.

Seton never capitalized on his invention, however. As a boy, Peterson and his chums hunted for a book with just the kind of "far-sketches" Seton created for ducks, but covering all the birds. Such a book didn't exist, but the idea lodged in Peterson's mind, even after he moved to New York to attend art school. There, he joined the Bronx County Bird Club and absorbed everything he could from Griscom, who was almost single-handedly creating the new sport of competitive birding, with its focus on field identification and lists.

> Griscom was our god, and his *Birds of the New York City Region* was our bible. Every one of us could quote chapter and verse. We used his terminology and even his inflection when we pronounced something as "unprecedented" or "a common summer resident." It was quite logical that we should choose Griscom for our role model, for he represented the new field of ornithology. He bridged the gap between the shotgun ornithologist of the old school and the modern birder with binoculars and telescope.

"Had it not been for Ludlow Griscom and his disciples, I could never have produced the Peterson field guides," Peterson wrote not long before his death. "These super birders taught me the fine points of field recognition while I, trained academically as an artist, attempted to pull things together and give them visual form." If not for them, he said, birding for him would never have been more than a hobby.

Instead, the idea for a true field guide, which had its beginnings back in Jamestown with *Two Little Savages,* began to gel. Bill Vogt, a friend from the Bronx club, talked Peterson into tackling the project, and when Peterson protested that he lacked name recognition, it was Vogt who suggested he test the waters with several magazine articles on gull and waterfowl identification. Peterson began to work seriously on the guide after leaving New York in 1931 to teach art at a prestigious prep school in Boston, and by 1933, after endless late nights over the typewriter and drawing table, he had a first draft ready to show to publishers. Again, it was Vogt (himself a successful drama critic and novelist) who began to shop the manuscript around.

The initial results were far from encouraging. It was the Depression, publishers were hurting, and the first half-dozen that Vogt approached turned the guide down. Finally, Houghton Mifflin, whose editor Francis Allen was a member of the Nuttall Club and the chair of Massachusetts Audubon, accepted it—but only on certain conditions. The press run would be limited to two thousand copies, and Peterson would have to forego royalties on the first thousand. Such cautions were unnecessary; the first run sold out in a week at $2.75 a pop, and the presses have kept rolling ever since.

Peterson's subtitle, "A Bird Book on a New Plan," summed up how different his first *Field Guide to the Birds* was. The goal was to create a handbook "wherein live birds can be run down by impressions, patterns and distinctive marks, rather than by the anatomical differences and measurements that a collector would find useful." The book itself was only about seven and a half inches by five, and two hundred pages long, perfect for slipping into a back pocket or knapsack. It covered birds of the East and Midwest only. The text was terse, like Chapman's, but peppered with memorable descriptions, and the field marks were culled from many years in the field with Griscom and his crew. Salient points were printed in italics for quick reference: "Parula Warbler: Descr. $4\frac{1}{4}$–$4\frac{3}{4}$. *Male*:——The only *bluish* Warbler with a *yellow* throat and breast."

There were thirty-six plates, four in color and the rest in black and white, jammed with small illustrations that grouped together similar species; ink drawings of less colorful species appeared with the text. "No attempt has been made to make 'pretty pictures,'" one reviewer noted approvingly, "but instead the figures on a plate are all drawn in a slightly conventionalized manner, so that the distinguishing field marks . . . may be more easily recognized." In a stroke of genius, Peterson added small arrows to the plates, pointing to the same critical field marks mentioned in the text—what came to be known as the Peterson Identification System.

Not everyone embraced it with undiluted enthusiasm. A reviewer for the journal of the Wilson Ornithological Society's *Wilson Bulletin* chastised Peterson for not including recognizable subspecies of several midwestern birds and for leaving out range information—the latter a fault Peterson quickly corrected in subsequent editions. In fact, the book began evolving almost from the moment of publication. Revisions appeared in 1939 and 1941, adding illustrations and text and including more range and song information, and a western guide came out in 1941. Once World War II was over, Peterson undertook a major revision of the eastern guide, which was published in 1947 and remained the standard for the next thirty-two years. In 1960 he published a guide to the birds of Texas, featuring many of the Mexican species that cross the

The genius of Peterson's 1934 guide was that it boiled down sophisticated identification information into concise, pithy text and illustrations that were almost schematic in their simplicity—the kind of "far sketches" he'd unsuccessfully sought as a young birder in western New York. *Courtesy of Houghton Mifflin Co. and the Roger Tory Peterson Institute*

border, along with the amalgam of western and eastern species that make that state so ornithologically rich.

At the same time, the Peterson field guide series, modeled on the original, blossomed beyond birds. While Peterson kept oversight on the series and wrote or illustrated a few himself (such as guides to European and Mexican birds, and to eastern wildflowers), the franchise grew beyond its namesake author to eventually encompass more than fifty subjects, from freshwater fish to the night sky, prairie ecosystems to edible plants, and beetles to venomous animals. New titles continue to appear regularly, and the Peterson series has become one of the gold standards of American publishing.

It also cemented Roger Tory Peterson's reputation as the iconic bird-watcher, the very personification of the tribe. That odd, tripartite name was as recognizable (and as exotic) as "yellow-bellied sapsucker," even to folks who couldn't tell a chickadee from a mallard. The writer E. B. White, himself a more than casual birder, had a little fun with this in *The New Yorker* in 1959:

> *Birds have their love-and-mating song,*
> *Their warning cry, their hating song;*
> *Some have a night song, some a day song,*
> *A lilt, a tilt, a come-what-may song;*
> *Birds have their careless bough and teeter song*
> *And, of course, their Roger Tory Peter song.*

By Peterson's death, in 1996, a month short of his eighty-eighth birthday, he had been draped with two dozen honorary degrees, won almost every major conservation award in the world, and received the nation's highest civilian honor, the Presidential Medal of Freedom, presented by President (and avid birder) Jimmy Carter. But perhaps the most lasting tribute was all those little books. His eastern guide had gone through four major editions and forty-eight printings, and his eastern and western books together had sold more than seven million copies. Nor was he finished; when he died, Peterson had all but completed the final plate for a fifth eastern edition, which was published posthumously, in 2002. Even without its author, the phenomenon keeps right on rolling.

It's hard to overestimate the impact that Peterson's guides have had on the world—not just on birding, but the way we as a culture think and feel about nature itself. Millions of people whose eyes were opened to the natural world in the pages of a Peterson guide provided the impetus for the modern environmental movement—a role he would have been too modest to accept himself, but which others have long recognized. "In this century," ecologist Paul Ehrlich said in the 1980s, "no one has done more to promote an interest in living creatures than Roger Tory Peterson." Pete Dunne, eulogizing his friend and mentor in the pages of *Birding* magazine, wrote, "It could be argued that without Roger Tory Peterson, there would be no environmental movement. Without the guides that made the world understandable and real, there would be no mass of people to anchor such a movement."

That influence even shaped the language of birding, turning "Roger Tory Peterson" from a proper noun into something more universal and ultimately timeless. Nearly a century after his birth, no matter where birders gather, you can still hear it—on spray-drenched winter jetties, buggy summer tidal flats, or the spring woods on a cool morning when the warblers form a shimmering, musical sheet of life through the treetops. Someone will lower their glasses, turn to their companion, and say, "I don't recognize that bird—I need to check my Peterson."

FOR ALL THAT, I have to confess here that my first field guide was not a Peterson; I didn't even own one of the legendary books for the first decade or more of my serious birding career. As a little kid already crazy about nature, I had a variety of books on birds, of course, but none of them were true field guides, and like Alan Devoe with his trusty but incomplete Reed's guide, I filled in the considerable gaps they left with my enthusiasm and imagination. I spotted all manner of rarities at our Pennsylvania feeders, including an "Oregon junco," with its buffy flanks, that was just like the painting in one of my books—which did not show a female slate-colored junco (as they were still called in those days), the bird I'd actually spotted. The closest thing I had to a guide was *How to Know the Birds*, a Peterson book from 1949 that taught the basics of birding.

Then, in 1969, when I was ten, I used my allowance money to buy a serious, adult bird guide—but instead of the iconic Peterson, I picked its only real competitor, *Birds of North America,* one of the Golden Field Guide series. Why not Peterson? I can't honestly recall; it might have been as simple as the Golden Guide being on the bookstore shelf that day, and not the other. I was certainly familiar with the great man's guide, since I'd checked out the library's copy over and over again.

But later, when I had learned enough about birding to make a comparison, I still thought I'd made the right decision. The publication of several new field guides in the 1950s and 1960s had spurred something of an identification arms race, as Peterson and his competitors pushed each other into adding more and more features to their books. The Golden Guide had several things the Peterson lacked—it covered all the birds of North America (the first guide to do so since Chapman's *Color Key*), so it was the book I packed when I made my first trip to the Rockies a couple of years later. All the birds were depicted in color, with the accompanying text and a range map (missing from Peterson) on the facing page—no flipping through the book.

It was far from perfect; the maps were too small, the text was too brief, and the book wasted valuable space on "sonagrams," visual representations of bird sounds that only someone with a Ph.D. in acoustics could interpret. Nevertheless, I wore out that book. The binding cracked, and I glued it back together with aquarium cement; it cracked again, and I literally sewed it up with heavy thread. After it (and I) fell into a river, I dried it out in my mother's oven. I underlined the important points on its wrinkled text, and I aped the Peterson System and made little arrows pointing to field marks on the paintings. I checked off birds in the index as my life list grew with each field trip and migration season. With its soft cover (another feature I liked), the book developed a permanent curl from riding in my hip pocket.

The very fact that birders like me had a choice in field guides was still a pretty new thing in the 1960s—though in retrospect, the pickings were fairly slim compared with the embarrassment of riches in the genre today. Peterson's *Field Guide to the Birds* so dominated birding that for more than a decade, no one challenged it. The first to do so was a series of guides sponsored by National Audubon and written by Richard Pough, the conservationist who first raised the alarm about raptor shooting at Hawk Mountain in the 1930s and who would later found the Nature Conservancy. *Eastern Land Birds* appeared in 1946, and while it borrowed some ideas from Peterson, like breaking the continent into manageable chunks, it went a step further, concentrating only on land birds. This allowed Pough and his illustrator, the gifted bird painter Don Eckelberry, to devote more space to each species, but the results were a bit awkward; Pough's book encompassed passerines, woodpeckers, swifts, and hummingbirds, but while he included owls and cuckoos, he excluded hawks and doves. (A second volume, covering water, prey, and game birds, came out in 1951, and a third, on western birds, in 1957.)

The Pough books did reasonably well, but the Golden Guide was the first book to give Peterson's a real run for its money. The senior author was Chandler S. Robbins, a federal wildlife biologist and bird-bander whose career is the stuff of legend, including creation of the North American Breeding Bird Survey, now in its fifth decade. (It has also been an extraordinarily long career; Robbins finally retired at the end of 2005, at age eighty-seven, and still maintains the kind of active field schedule that would exhaust people half his age.) Robbins is also a rabid birder, as one statistic makes clear: he has participated in more Christmas Bird Counts—more than 350 at last tally, including many each year—than anyone else in history.

The artwork was by Arthur Singer, a Long Island illustrator who grouped five or six species per page, showing most of the ages, genders, and seasonal plumages a birder might encounter. Singer also borrowed an idea as old as Wilson and Audubon, to show the birds in a bit of their habitats—a Lucy's warbler nesting in a tree cavity, or a northern mockingbird singing from a TV antenna. Like most artists, Singer had to rely on museum skins and photographs for reference while he was working, but he took many of the finished paintings to a bird-banding station so he could double-check the fidelity of the colors against the real thing before shipping them off for printing.

For naught, it appears; one of the drawbacks of the original Golden Guide was the poor color reproduction. But it also begs the question—why, in an age of high-speed color photography, were field guides still using paint and brush, a technique that hearkened back to the days of illuminated manuscripts? The fact is, illustrations and photographs each present their own suite of strengths and weaknesses. An illustrator can boil down a lifetime of experience to create a single, idealized portrait of what a birder *should* see, but it's filtered through the artist's style, bias, and draftsmanship skills; a photograph does away with most of these flaws, and presents an image of what the bird *does* look like—but only at one instant in time, under certain lighting conditions and in a single pose, and within the constraints of the lens, exposure, and type of film.

Arguments about the relative merits of art versus photos have been around for a long time. People tried to produce photographic guides at least as far back as Florence and Vernon Bailey's 1902 western handbook, with its photos of specimen skins. Allan Cruickshank, Peterson's old friend from the Bronx County Bird Club days, published a "pocket guide" to birds in the early 1950s that married ink illustrations by Don Eckelberry with color photos by Cruickshank's wife, Helen. It didn't work very well, and the result, sadly and ironically, was a book by one of the best field birders in the country that was of limited value as an identification guide.

But the notion of a photographic field guide didn't go away. In 1977 the *National Audubon Society Field Guide to North American Birds,* written by John Bull and John Farrand Jr., made a splash— the first all-photographic guide to the continent's birdlife. It and a western version by Miklos Udvardy, with more than six hundred color photos each, were an odd mix of success and failure. The books were bestsellers, even as most serious birders and bird book reviewers excoriated them. They attacked the grouping of birds by color instead of taxonomy; the separation of illustrations from text; and most vehemently, the use of photos instead of paintings.

If nothing else, the guides proved that it's hard—some would say impossible—to get a single good, well-lit photograph that shows all the important field marks on every bird. It became something of a parlor game, when things got slow on the hawk watch or along the beach, to trot out one's favorite gaffe among the Audubon guide's pages—the herring gull backlit so that its upperparts looked almost as dark as a black-backed gull's, for instance, or the Old World oriole from the wrong hemisphere whose photo crept in by mistake.

But that didn't stop millions of people, mostly beginning birders, from buying the books. With sales like that, it's no wonder that a few years later the same publisher, Knopf, tried again—but they also learned from their mistakes. The *Master Birding Guide* was a three-volume set, again sponsored by Audubon, again illustrated largely with photographs (multiples for most species, allowing for easier comparisons), again edited by John Farrand. But this time it was aimed at the very group—serious birders—who griped so much about the first; more than sixty of the best birders were even enlisted to write the species accounts.

The result was an excellent, if pricey, reference work—but three volumes, each more than four hundred pages long, was hardly a field guide. As the *Master Guides* showed, birding had progressed dramatically by the early 1980s, especially in the sophistication of field identification. None of the pocket-sized guides had kept up, and when Peterson released the much-anticipated fourth edition of his eastern guide in 1980, the response was predictably heavy sales, but a lot of sniping from prominent birders that the sport's guru hadn't kept pace with advances in the pastime he'd done so much to popularize. Yes, Peterson's remained the best guide for beginning and intermediate birders, but those who were more experienced were hungry for a guide that synthesized the state of the art in field identification.

It fell to the National Geographic Society—hardly the first organization one thinks of when it comes to birding—to try to meet that need. In 1983 the society published what is universally known as "the Geographic guide,"* and it was an immediate hit. It was wonderfully inclusive, illustrating not just all the breeding species in North America but also most of the rarities, accidentals, and

---

*It is formally titled *Field Guide to the Birds of North America*, just like half a dozen other books before and since; one problem with field guides is an utter lack of imagination in what they are titled.

exotics one might reasonably expect to find, even if you were bird-ing the far western Aleutians or the borderland mountains of the Southwest. It showed the differences between juvenile shorebirds and adults in nonbreeding plumage (something previous guides had ignored), and it devoted pages to confusing groups, like gulls. *This* was what serious birders—and those hoping to improve their skills—had been looking for.

Or was it? Even granting that birders are a tough crowd to please, there were at least as many brickbats as compliments for the Geographic guide. It was created by a committee, and it certainly looked like it; the illustrations were painted by more than a dozen artists, and ranged in quality from terrific to absolutely wretched, although replacement plates in subsequent editions tempered some of the complaints. Nor were birds painted to scale, so that the woodcock, for instance, appeared to be several times the size of a Wilson's snipe. But for all the grumbles, the Geographic guide was a huge step forward.

The 1980s and 1990s also saw the flowering of specialty guides and handbooks that focused on specific groups, like P. J. Grant's *Gulls,* Peter Harrison's *Seabirds,* and a volume on shorebirds by Peter Hayman, John Marchant, and Tony Prater. All of these authors were Brits, which isn't surprising, given Europe's (and es-pecially the UK's) history of pushing the envelope of field identi-fication techniques. The Europeans were also trying innovative approaches to general field guides. In 1992 a Swede named Lars Jonsson published *Birds of Europe,* an extraordinary blend of Jons-son's considerable talents for both art and birding in a guide that was as beautiful as it was groundbreaking. These were birds that moved, that *breathed,* true to the fluidity and grace of the real thing; although many of his plates were detailed, Jonsson often used quick, almost impressionistic gesture sketches that captured the quality of the bird, instead of the static, feather-by-feather renderings common in American guides. It was the contrast between using what the Brits call "jizz"—the general, almost instantaneous impression of a bird—versus a laborious, field-mark-by-field-mark approach.

The revolution in European guides was not unnoticed on this side of the Atlantic, although it would take a while for the seed to sprout. Meanwhile there were more and more specialty guides for the enthusiast to buy—books devoted to North American raptors, or to hummingbirds, or sparrows, or warblers. They were filled with information a birder could use, but who could carry them all? The Peterson series guide to warblers alone was 650 pages long. A birder needed a card catalog to keep track of all the guides in his or her knapsack, and a Sherpa to carry them. Couldn't somebody, please, come up with the kind of revolutionary guides the Europeans had?

TUCSON, ARIZONA, in midsummer; it was almost eleven o'clock at night, and the mercury outside was still in the upper nineties, with the blanket of humidity that comes with the monsoon rains. The American Birding Association had taken over one of the big hotels in town for its annual conference, and despite the hour, and the heat, and the fact that most of them had been up since four A.M. (and would be up at that hour again the next morning), a few of the field trip leaders were sitting outside the hotel bar, shooting the breeze.

Jeff Bouton got a final beer and sank into one of the soft chairs in the lounge. He took a pull, sighed, and asked, "I ever tell you about the first time I met Peterson?"

Like a lot of hard-core birders, Jeff has lived an interesting life, one whose thread always followed where the birds led; I knew about his time as a hawk bander and field biologist, for instance, and his years guiding in Alaska, but I'd just learned that evening he'd once managed a karaoke bar, and did a stint in a Chuck E. Cheese costume. (Today he's a writer and a highly respected specialist with one of the big birding optics manufacturers.) But in the mid-1980s, Jeff was seventeen, one of the young turks of birding, hired for the fall to count hawks at Cape May, New Jersey. Jeff was maybe a little too full of himself in those days, and when the grand old man himself came to town for a visit, Jeff found his opinions outrunning his manners at a get-together he and Peterson were both attending.

"The fourth edition of his eastern guide had come out a few years earlier, and that's what everyone was talking about. I guess I was opening my mouth—anyway, Peterson turned and asked me what I thought about the new guide. And I figured, what the hell? So I told him the truth—that I thought the hawks were all too generic, as though the buteos, for instance, had all been drawn from the same general outline."

To Jeff's shock, Peterson placidly agreed. "He said that yeah, hawk ID had come a long way, but that he was too old to go back and completely revise everything. He said it would be up to the next generation to create the new revolution in field guide. In fact, he said, 'It will be up to that young man over there in the corner,' and he pointed to someone behind me."

Jeff said he turned, following Peterson's finger, and found he was looking at another of Cape May's young birding phenoms, a twenty-something with a shock of dark hair and an almost painfully quiet personality, a man who, like Lars Jonsson, was a supremely talented birder and artist—a shy fellow named David Sibley.

IN THE MID-1980S, Peterson was one of the very few people who knew that David Allen Sibley had a mission and that it had been driving him for most of his life.

Sibley was born in 1961, in Plattsburgh, New York, along Lake Champlain, but by the time he was five, his family had moved to northern California. His father, Fred Sibley (who went on to become the curator of birds at Yale's Peabody Museum), was at the time directing the Point Reyes Bird Observatory, on the California coast near San Francisco. His job included a lot of bird banding, and he'd take his boys along on chilly mornings, when they'd help their dad set up the mist nets, then make the periodic rounds with him to collect the birds; David showed an unusual aptitude, given his age, for extracting the birds from the delicate netting. Years later, Sibley still recalls the almost electric shock he felt as a seven- or eight-year-old the first time he held a live bird in his hands.

Right from the start, David was serious about birds, bird identification, and bird art—he started drawing when he was five and never stopped. It didn't hurt that he was growing up in the kind of household where he might find a California condor in the garage. (The bird, a starving chick, had been rescued by Sibley's father.) He spent hours staring at Arthur Singer's paintings in *Birds of the World*, at the work of Fuertes and Eckelberry. It may have been in the blood, since his older brother Steve shared a passion for both birding and art, and he couldn't have been in a better place. The Point Reyes crowd included some of the best birders on the West

Coast, and David soaked it all up. By age twelve, living back east, he was obsessively photographing the birds his father captured—top view, bottom view, wings spread. He kept drawing, getting better, learning to handle various media. Roger Tory Peterson, a family acquaintance, gave the lad a friendly critique. His first attempts were, not unexpectedly, fairly crude, but he was a boy with a plan—because even then, David Allen Sibley knew he wanted to create a field guide. Not just any old guide, either—the best anyone had ever seen.

Although his dream came early, it remained a largely secret ambition for many years. In his late teens, Sibley was thinking about a book on the warblers of North America, covering virtually

For more than a decade, David Sibley—working as a birding tour guide leader—crisscrossed North America repeatedly, working against a self-imposed goal of finding six hundred species a year and accumulating the experience to produce the most successful field guide since Peterson's. *Photo by Scott Weidensaul*

every aspect of their ecology, life history, and identification. He tried to convince his parents to let him drop out of high school and chase birds; they said no. He thought to follow his father into academic ornithology, and he headed off to college at Cornell University, home of the famous Lab of Ornithology. But classrooms weren't for him, and he dropped out after a year, the vision of a field guide still beckoning.

He became something of a bird bum—the perfect education for an incipient field guide author. In 1981 the Cape May Bird Observatory hired him as a hawk counter, placing him in the middle of perhaps the single best place for birding in North America—and among some of the hottest birders on that side of the continent. He banded birds in Massachusetts (where he met his future wife, another intern, Joan Walsh) and worked in the studios of Cornell's Library of Natural Sounds.

He also became a leader for a company called WINGS, which conducts birding tours around the continent. Sibley was always on the move, ranging from the Florida Keys to south Texas to the cold, foggy islands in the Bering Sea of Alaska, working against a self-imposed goal of finding six hundred species a year—always birding, always sketching, always painting, trying to capture the beauty and character of each species.

In barely more than a decade, Sibley accumulated a lifetime's worth of experience with virtually every species of North American bird—and found, to his growing frustration, that what he was seeing through his binoculars or scope, and trying to show to his clients, wasn't what even the best field guides showed. He, and the other expert birders with whom he spent time in the field, had moved the craft of bird identification to a new level—winnowing out not just species from species, but the intricacies of subspecific identification, the puzzles of odd and transient plumages. It was almost as big a leap as the old shotgun-to-binocular jump that Griscom and his colleagues had made.

The existing guidebooks hadn't kept up. Sibley decided his book would be the most comprehensive birding field guide ever. "I wanted a book that would show every plumage and every subspecies, at rest and in flight," he later wrote. "A book that would give details on the plumages and habits of each species, describe songs and calls, and show the complete distribution of each species."

It was still something he rarely mentioned aloud, even to his wife. Joan recalled a camping trip through the west Texas mountains in 1987, soaking in a hot spring after weeks on the road. "It was clear the book wanted to be born, and we sat in the hot water talking about the scariness and hubris of saying out loud, 'Sure, I'm going to do a field guide to the birds of North America,'" she told an interviewer years later. "It takes a fair amount of chutzpah. But once he said it aloud a few times—in the dark, full moon, in the hot water in west Texas—it just started to seem real."

He had already shared the secret with one notable person, though. Three years earlier, Sibley had taken part in the first World Series of Birding, the brainchild of his friend Pete Dunne from New Jersey Audubon. Teams of crack birders from across the country would fan out over New Jersey and see who could tally the largest number of species within the same twenty-four-hour period. The idea was to raise birding's profile, have some fun, and generate money for conservation. (The WSB has been a huge and ongoing success, but more about that later.)

For his team, Dunne had tapped Sibley, along with two other high-octane New Jersey birders, Bill Boyle and Pete Bacinski. But the star power was provided by Peterson, who asked to be on the team. (It was, Pete often quipped, "a little like having the Pope ask if he can go to church with you on Sunday.") By the end of the day, Dunne's "Guerrilla Team" had racked up a winning 201 species— and Sibley had nervously confessed to Peterson his plans for a field guide. The man who did more than anyone to create modern birding gave the shy young birder his enthusiastic endorsement, though he must have heard such dreams from many an incipient author.

Or perhaps Peterson already knew this guy was different. Over the years, Sibley had been experimenting with many different designs and approaches for his epic project. His art was more and more widely published, although it was usually his ink drawings rather than color work. His first field guide was *Hawks in Flight,* a 1988 collaboration with Dunne and Clay Sutton that took the European approach to identification—putting the emphasis on the general, holistic impression of the bird, rather than specific field marks. Instead of paintings, Sibley created hundreds of ink drawings, many little more than silhouettes—and he generated a buzz among serious students of birding. No less a person than Peterson said that Sibley's "sense of flight and shape are unparalleled."

His main field guide project was never far from his mind, though. Sibley was torn between Lars Jonsson's very artistic approach, which had appealed to him ever since he first encountered the Swede's work in 1980, and other guides (especially the Mitchell Beazley *Birdwatcher's Pocket Guide,* another British title) that sacrificed artistic splash for lots of visual information. But it wasn't until 1993, when he went birding in Europe himself, that he had his eureka moment. The kid who'd grown up in a birdy household, with a father and older brother on whom to depend instead of a book, found himself for the first time actually *using* a field guide—flipping from page to page, trying to locate unfamiliar birds. Back home, while working on a painting of eared and horned grebes, the proverbial lightbulb suddenly snapped on in his head, and Sibley knew he'd found the perfect mix of art and science.

The key, he realized, was not only how far to pare a painting to its essentials—the balance between expression and precision—but also how to arrange the birds on the page, so the reader would get the most information in the simplest, most direct way. Field guides are all about sorting through confusing similarities; part of Sibley's genius was his decision to align the most similar birds and plumages across the page. Opening the guide, a reader would generally find facing pages with four species of birds. Flying birds seen from the top and from the bottom would form twin lines across the upper third of the page; then perched birds ranging from the drabbest (usually juveniles) at the top, to the most colorful plumage (usually breeding males) at the bottom.

The book was, in an almost literal sense, the culmination of a lifetime's work—a decade and a half of fieldwork, six years struggling with the right artistic and design approach, and once he'd settled on a design, five more years at the drawing table, producing the finished plates. Now that he had a template for how to present each species, the trick was translating all the minutiae of bird identification that he'd accumulated in the field and putting it onto paper. He soon realized that his goal of showing every subspecies and every plumage was unrealistic—the song sparrow alone has at least two dozen subspecies, for instance, and they are not sharply differentiated but tend to blur, one into the other, across the species' continental range.

But where other guides would show one or two examples, Sibley filled a page with almost a dozen song sparrows—big, sooty birds from the Aleutian Islands, pale rusty ones from the Southwest, the California race with its distinctive black markings. Red-tailed hawks, which come in a bewildering array of adult and immature plumages, light and dark morphs, and regional subspecies, were depicted in no fewer than forty paintings, along with a series of in-flight silhouettes.

It makes obvious sense to show hawks in flight, but Sibley's greatest single advance for field identification may have been to do the same for all of the 810 species he illustrated—a departure from every previous guide, which tended to relegate flight drawings to the largest and most conspicuous species. For instance, spotted thrushes, like the wood thrush and veery, have a large, pale bar running the length of the underside of the wing—a very distinctive field mark, but one that no previous guide had shown, since thrushes were only shown perched.

From 1994 through 1999, Sibley hammered away at the plates, producing more than 500 that comprised more than 6,600 individual illustrations in all. Those years' worth of sketches and observations were boiled down into a stack of paintings more than two feet high. "It was as though I'd spent a lifetime collecting recipes—now I was finally in the kitchen, trying them out," he told me.

The result, *The Sibley Guide to Birds,* was released in October 2000, to immediate acclaim. The *New York Times,* drawing comparisons to Audubon and Peterson, said, "Once in a great while, a natural history book changes the way people look at the world." The world of birding certainly agreed; it became the fastest-selling field guide in history, with the first hundred thousand selling out in just two weeks. Six years later, sales were approaching three-quarters of a million copies.

As popular as the Sibley field guide was, it had a clear drawback—its size. Even though the artist had pared down the text to the bare minimum (deleting most habitat information, for example) it still came in at a whopping 540 pages and more than two and a half pounds, making it hard to comfortably carry in the field. In 2003 Sibley released two smaller, pocket-sized regional guides, one for eastern birds and one for western species, compromising by including fewer illustrations, but more text describing behavior, habitats, and vocalizations.

One reason Sibley's guides were such huge hits was their obvious quality; for serious birders, there was (and is) simply nothing else in their league. But their success also had to do with something much more fundamental—the number of birders had exploded, and the potential market was enormous.

Birding is no longer the realm of a few slightly dotty seniors and obsessive teenaged boys—it's utterly conventional, absolutely mainstream. The days of this being some fringe hobby are long gone; and that change started shortly after World War II. By the late 1950s and 1960s, birding was catching fire, breaking free of the quiet, musty, academic approach that had marked it in earlier decades. A cadre of new faces—mostly young, mostly male, who combined a mania for birding with an almost mystical ability to ferret out rare species and new hot spots—were setting the pace. And while most of birding's growth had previously been centered on the East Coast, it's no surprise that, like so much else in postwar America, the modern birding boom really hit its stride in that epicenter of trends: California.

7

Death to Miss Hathaway
(How birding became almost cool)

I WAS A CHILD of the 1960s, and even though I spent an abnormal amount of time outside chasing birds and snakes and anything else I could find, I pretty much grew up with television.

Westerns, *Dragnet,* old movies, and especially sitcoms—they molded my view of the world. I wondered, for example, why my parents slept in one bed, when Rob and Laura Petrie on the *Dick Van Dyke Show* slept in neat little single beds. (So did Lucy and Desi. It was another example, I assumed, of how decidedly strange my parents were, and I made a point of never mentioning this quirk to my friends.)

For a while, though, my favorite show was *The Beverly Hillbillies,* which I caught in reruns every Saturday morning. I thought the Clampetts were a stitch, especially Granny, with her spring tonics, and the possum hunting, the "cee-ment pond" and the rest of the antics—though if I were being honest with myself, it was probably because I had a bit of a crush on Elly May.

I loved pretty much everything about *The Beverly Hillbillies,* that is, except for one thing.

I *hated* Miss Jane.

MISS JANE HATHAWAY—the tall, mannish spinster played by Nancy Kulp, who'd pop up with a pith helmet and a pair of binoculars, so starchy, so prim, so nerdy, though no one used that word in those days. None of which mattered, except that she was a birdwatcher—and I knew bird-watchers weren't really like that.

Not that I actually knew any bird-watchers, mind you, except for myself. But I already suspected I was a pretty odd kid—the whole poking-under-logs thing was a tip-off, since most of my friends were much more into football than finding salamanders or garter snakes. Likewise, I was alone in our neighborhood in deciding to tan (with questionable success) the hide of a road-killed woodchuck. Or in raising thirty monarch butterflies in my bedroom, which smelled of caterpillar droppings for weeks. Or— well, the list is a long one.

If I'd thought about it, I suppose I would have realized that my bird-watching was also a little off center from what a normal rural Pennsylvania twelve-year-old was supposed to be interested in. I hunted and fished and joined the Boy Scouts, like most of my friends, but I just accepted the fact that I liked all things natural, and birds were a big part of that, whether they were chickadees at the feeder or the Cooper's hawk nest I found in the woods behind the house on a stifling June day. My mother intercepted me heading out wearing a heavy winter coat, my dad's work gloves, and my grandfather's hard hat, with a stepladder over my shoulder; I was going to shinny up the tree for a peek at the chicks, and I knew I had to protect myself from the adult hawks. I should have considered protecting myself from my mother.

Bird-watching was just this pretty cool thing I enjoyed, among a lot of pretty cool things (did I mention the ring-necked snake that lived under my bed?). Then one day I flipped on *The Beverly Hillbillies*. There was Miss Jane and Professor P. Caspar Biddle (actor Wally Cox, playing to nerdy type) and their dweeby little friends, prancing around in their tweeds and sensible shoes, with binoculars around their skinny necks and spectacles perched on their ridiculous faces.

I stopped, frozen by the flickering images on that little black-and-white set, as the awful truth hit me.

Wait a minute, I thought. They're bird-watchers.

I'm a bird-watcher.

But they're *really, really weird*.

Which means . . .

Aw, *crap*.

I GOT OVER IT, of course. The mortification didn't last too long, because I figured I'd rather mess around with birds than be popular, which was a long shot in any event. But it was my first taste of the stereotypes under which birding has long labored—the spinster bird-watcher, the maiden aunt, the geeky professor spouting Latin. I was the only bird-watcher I knew, but even then, I suspected Miss Jane and Professor Biddle were cut from thinner cloth than the rest of us—that they wouldn't, for example, wind up clinging to the trunk of a tree thirty feet above the ground, being dive-bombed by great horned owls trying to defend their nest, the way I'd been. (My folks hadn't intercepted me that time, unfortunately—it's a miracle the owls didn't knock me to the ground.)

That heroic view was reinforced when, in junior high, I started visiting Hawk Mountain, about an hour from our home, and met bird-watchers who'd stopped the annual autumn slaughter of hawks along the Appalachians ridges by standing up to men with loaded guns. These were not milquetoasts, but gutsy men and women. I got involved with the local bird group—the Baird Ornithological Club, named for Audubon's protégé Spencer Fullerton Baird, a local boy made good. On field trips to Brigantine or Bombay Hook, I found a fairly normal cross section of American society (at least the white, middle-class cross section).

Still, that sitcom episode gave me my first taste of the public image of birding in the middle of the twentieth century—laughable caricatures that bore no resemblance to me or my friends. I started avoiding the *Hillbillies* reruns, because the sight of Miss Jane Hathaway set my teeth on edge.

Today, I can just laugh, because that stereotype is pretty well dead and gone. Everyone knows a birder—we're hard to avoid, since there are tens of millions of us. We spend more than a billion dollars each year on feeders and birdseed, and birding festivals attract hundreds, sometimes thousands, of people to places like Cordova, Alaska, and Bisbee, Arizona. We put Sibley's guide on the bestseller list, mix oceans of sugar water for hummingbirds, and crowd places like Bosque del Apache or Garden Canyon, High Island or Cape May. We're not the fringe anymore, but the mainstream. A birder today is more likely to have body piercings than a tweed coat. The story of bird study since World War II is the tale of how birding has become (well, almost) cool.

To be honest, I sometimes miss feeling like a renegade, out there alone, pushing the envelope. But only a little; it's great to have so much company. And what the heck—after all this time, I think I can finally even forgive Miss Jane.

BEFORE WORLD WAR II, bird-watching was stuck in low gear. Sure, Peterson had given birders their first real field guide, and there were more of the "field-glass fraternity," as he called them, every year. But the economy stank, and people had more important things to worry about, like food and jobs, and the dark clouds forming over Europe and Asia.

Birding was a localized pastime, small and insular, rather cliquish; everyone knew everyone else in a particular area, and there wasn't that much interaction with birders from other regions. But change was coming, as Peterson's old Bronx County Bird Club chum Joe Hickey noted in 1943. "Bird watching is old enough to have stood the test of time, young enough to lie within the age of exploration," he said. "Bird watching today is not the groping, bewildering hobby it was only a few decades ago." People were hemmed in by wartime rationing and wartime worries, though; Peterson was drafted and ended up in the Army Corps of Engineers (his first plan, to join the Signal Corps and use seabirds to transmit messages across the Pacific Ocean, was politely declined). He designed camouflage, illustrated manuals on disarming munitions, and in a uniquely appropriate move, his "Peterson System" was adapted to help plane spotters identify aircraft.

But the years after World War II were as transformative for birding as they were for the country as a whole. There was the sudden freedom that many Americans felt—freedom to travel, freedom from the gasoline rationing and rubber shortages that kept them close to home, even the freedom to walk along the beach with a pair of binoculars again, which during the war might well have gotten one picked up by the cops on suspicion of being an enemy spy.

(It wasn't just seaside birders who had to be careful. Hawk Mountain Sanctuary, in the hills of eastern Pennsylvania, fell afoul of wartime paranoia—too many visiting cars with out-of-state license plates, too many people with foreign-sounding names staying in the guesthouse in the valley. Rumors of a huge ammunition dump on the mountain found their way to the ears of the authorities; the FBI and state police got involved, investigating the sanctuary's directors and staff. Someone saw a Nazi spy signaling with semaphore flags from a rocky outcropping—whom the police discovered to be a professor from nearby Lehigh University who'd been collecting butterflies with a net.)

One of the biggest changes was in the quality of optics available for birding. Before the war, a birder had two choices—a pair of low-magnification opera glasses, usually about three- or four-power, or much more expensive binoculars, usually imported from Germany. As prewar tensions rose, that supply dried up, but after the war, military surplus—both American- and German-made—flooded the market.

Of course, identifying a bird is the second half of the battle—first you have to find it, and that can be difficult. In the prewar years, birding was mostly a local affair; roads were poor, cars expensive, and times tough. A lot of urban birders got around by bike, train, or trolley; those in the country birded their neighborhoods, but few people traveled specifically to watch birds.

The growth of the automobile culture after World War II

With a well-dressed group of birders in tow, Farida Wiley points out a bird in New York's Central Park in the 1940s. For more than half a century Wiley, a self-taught ornithologist and educator at the American Museum of Natural History, led daily 7 A.M. bird walks in the park. *Courtesy of the American Museum of Natural History Library*

changed all that. As the interstate highway system spread across the country, with faster cars and cheap gasoline, it was possible to make a weekend swing across several states, hitting half a dozen great spots, from the mountains to the sea—that is, if you knew where to look. You could rely on tips from friends, or the occasional article in magazines like *Audubon;* you could write to national parks and national wildlife refuges, most of which had bird checklists. You could scour the old Bent series for clues to range and habitat—and if you were smart, you'd chat up the locals in diners and gas stations as you were traveling, hoping to find someone who'd take pity on a bird-watcher and point you to a good swamp or prairie. But mostly you were on your own.

For those hungry for distant birding horizons, two books appeared like a godsend in the early 1950s, written by a serious ornithologist with a delightfully goofy name: Olin Sewall Pettingill Jr., who went on to become the director of the Cornell Lab of Ornithology and a noted bird photographer. In 1945 Pettingill visited Hawk Mountain on the strength of a recommendation from friends; he had a great time, but he realized what a hit-and-miss proposition birding away from home could be. Why not create a book that highlighted the best birding spots across the country?

Using a network of local experts in every state, Pettingill assembled what quickly grew into a two-volume set: *A Guide to Bird Finding East of the Mississippi* came out in 1951, and its western companion two years later. These were big, thick books that covered the Lower 48 in exhaustive, unprecedented detail. Want to see a rare Kirtland's warbler? Head to the Grayling, Michigan, area in June. Booming lesser prairie-chickens? The grasslands around Arnett, Oklahoma, are the place to be. Find yourself in Des Moines with a morning to spare? The Water Works Park, which is good for waterfowl in the spring, may also produce winter crossbills in the conifer plantations. Planning a birding trip to Texas? Pettingill and his legion of helpers would take you by the hand in the Big Thicket, point you in the direction of the lower Rio Grande by way of the Edwards Plateau and leave you, tired but no doubt happy, your life list bulging, somewhere up in the Davis Mountains.

Pettingill painted with a broad brush, covering the entire continent, but in the mid-1960s, a fellow named Jim Lane created a series of regional birding guides, starting with southeastern Arizona— picking places with scads of hard-to-find local endemics that birders from across the continent would travel to see. Pettingill gave you the big picture; Lane told you exactly which dirt road to turn

down, and how many utility poles to count off before getting out
of the car and looking for the target bird. The Lane Guides proved
immensely popular, and the format has been copied endlessly by
other authors for other regions—though the Lane series, now
published by the American Birding Association, still sets the mark.

The quality of field guides was advancing, too—Peterson's
second edition had come out in 1947, with the Pough Audubon
guides not long thereafter—but the state of field identification was
still fairly primitive. As for truly puzzling groups, like *Empidonax*
flycatchers, Peterson advised, "Collecting has proven that it is
nearly impossible to name many individuals in the field, even in the
spring, so the wise field man usually lets most of them go as just
Empidonaxes."

A singing empid still isn't a snap to identify, but we've come
a long way since that discouraging assessment. Let that puzzling
flycatcher call, and its identity becomes clear—but learning bird
songs also posed its own suite of problems. The only practical way
to go about it was either to learn from a mentor—one of those
"wise field men" to whom Peterson was referring—or by trial and
error on one's own, tracking down each unfamiliar voice until the
singer was found. Creating a "field guide" of sorts for songs would
pose far more significant technical challenges than designing an effective identification book ever did.

In the late 1920s, Arthur A. Allen—the founder of the Cornell
Lab of Ornithology, known universally and affectionately as
"Doc" Allen—began to experiment with sound recordings of wild
birds. It was difficult, frustrating work; the equipment was so large
and cumbersome that it filled a panel truck, and the only medium
that seemed to work was nitrocellulose sound movie film, which
was not only expensive but explosively flammable. Still Allen, his

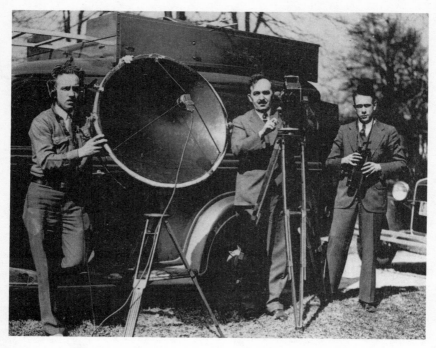

Peter Paul Kellogg, Arthur A. Allen, and James T. Tanner—parabolic microphone and movie camera at the ready—prepare to embark on a 1935 expedition across the United States to record vanishing birds, including the ivory-billed woodpecker. *Courtesy of the Cornell Laboratory of Ornithology/ Macaulay Library*

colleague Peter Paul Kellogg, and their students made remarkable strides, including two cross-country expeditions in the 1930s to record the sounds of such vanishing birds as the ivory-billed woodpecker, hauling the weighty equipment into the field in mule-drawn wagons.

A critical link in the development of field recording was a successful stockbroker named Albert R. Brand, who made quite a bit of money before leaving finance to pursue his love of ornithology at Cornell. Brand was fascinated by the idea of recording birds, and threw himself—and his checkbook—at the problem, developing new equipment and techniques; in fact, it was Brand who helped underwrite the groundbreaking Cornell expeditions. But he had another goal—to create the first audio guide to bird songs, a project on which Brand worked through the 1930s. He brought out a small book with two accompanying records in 1934, containing the voices of thirty common birds—"not whistled reproductions, such as have been made in the past . . . but actual songs of wild birds taken in their natural surroundings," noted Witmer Stone in *The Auk.*

In 1942, Cornell released a six-record set of Brand's recordings, seventy-two species that included drumming ruffed grouse, chachalacas hollering in the Texas borderlands, and wrentits singing in California. "Here are the bird song recordings that ornithologists have been waiting for," the *Wilson Bulletin* declared, calling them "a remarkable new means of facilitating bird study. No longer need the student spend years, for example, tracing for himself and attempting to remember and compare the songs of the Veery, the Olive-backed, the Hermit, and the Wood Thrush; now he need merely run the Brand record a few times and compare directly these . . . excellent renditions of all four species."

Others were following the same track. An Ohio State University entomology professor named Donald J. Borror started dragging microphones and tape recorders into the field in the late 1940s, some of it equipment that had been developed for the military during the war and had only just been declassified. Borror's work showed, among other things, that a wood thrush was able to harmonize with itself by singing two different notes at the same time, but he also produced a hugely popular series of audio field guides to bird songs that remain in use today. (Borror's recordings now form the nucleus of Ohio State's Borror Laboratory of Bioacoustics, which after Cornell's is the largest such collection in the world.)

As more attention was paid to birdsong, it became clear there were complexities there that lay beyond the visual realm. In 1828, for example, Audubon had described a brownish-green flycatcher that he named for his Scottish friend Dr. Thomas Traill. With a range stretching from Newfoundland to Alaska and Arizona, Traill's flycatcher became a taxonomic toothache for succeeding generations of ornithologists, who couldn't quite figure out whether it was one species or several, and if the latter, where the boundary should be drawn. At one point they split it into the alder flycatcher in the East and the little flycatcher in the West, then argued endlessly about where the dividing line lay, before throwing up their hands and relumping them back into Traill's (or alder—both names were used).

Peterson, in his 1947 eastern guide, warned: "Voice descriptions vary. The regular song in New York and New England is a three-syllabled *wee-be'-o* . . . [but] the Ohio bird contracts this into a sneezy *fitz-bew*. . . . Possibly collecting would prove that subspecific differences exist." In fact, as Peterson later learned, the *fitz-bew* songs were being sung by Traill's flycatchers all over the place, from the desert Southwest to New England.

And despite his hope that collecting would solve the problem, specimens proved to be of limited value—Traill's flycatchers, whether from Maine, Missouri, or Montana, all looked pretty much exactly the same. But in the late 1950s, a graduate student at Cornell named Robert Stein, who was involved in the relatively young field of recording natural sounds, began to look at those distinct song types that Peterson had mentioned. He found that the birds weren't just singing different regional dialects, as some species do—they were, in fact, two entirely separate species, identical in the field, all but indistinguishable even in the hand, but easily picked out by ear.

Follow-up research proved that even when the two forms nested close together, as they did in many areas, they used different habitats, and they never interbred. In 1973 the AOU split Traill's once again, not into eastern and western groups, but into north/south camps with wide overlap. They restored the name "alder flycatcher" for the *wee-be'-o* form that nested in swampy, northern habitats, and gave the name "willow flycatcher" to the *fitz-bew* birds of drier, generally more southerly uplands.

That was only the beginning; in the years since then, a number of so-called cryptic species have been described, birds that appear almost identical but sing very different songs, like the "western flycatcher," which was split into Pacific-slope and cordilleran flycatchers in 1989, and American and Pacific golden-plovers, split in 1993. Differences in voice suggest there may be multiple species of winter wrens, red crossbills, and Nashville warblers, among others—including the Pacific-slope flycatcher itself, since vocal and genetic differences offer evidence that those of the Channel Islands may be yet another distinct species.

One potential split is the marsh wren, which has been the subject of head-scratching among ornithologists for years; fourteen subspecies of this wide-ranging bird have been described, and based on differences in their voices, there appear to be eastern and western complexes, which may be separate species. More than a century ago, the complexities of marsh wrens—and a lot of other puzzles in western bird taxonomy—were consuming a young ornithologist named Joseph Grinnell. He was a cousin of George

Bird Grinnell's, and natural history must have been lodged deep in the family's genes, because just as George became a national force for bird conservation, Joseph became one of the leaders in avian research on the West Coast, and set the stage for the uniquely California approach to birding still later.

Born in 1877, on the Kiowa reservation in Indian Territory, and, in his early years, raised among the Sioux (to whom his father was a doctor), Joseph Grinnell pursued a love of birds when the family finally settled back in California. By age nineteen he was collecting specimens as far north as Alaska, and a few years later he had returned there to prospect for gold, but he eventually returned to California, completed a doctorate, and began to teach biology at Throop Polytechnic Institute, in Pasadena (now Cal Tech).

He was making a name for himself among naturalists and came to the attention of a remarkable woman, Annie Montague Alexander—heiress to a Hawaiian sugar fortune, an avid amateur paleontologist who was lucky enough to have the means to fund expeditions in which she then participated. (And not as a pampered hanger-on, either—Alexander did much of the cooking in the field, found and excavated fossils, and even helped pack out the heavy specimens.)

Alexander, a benefactor of the University of California, recognized that the West was changing rapidly, and she wanted to create a record of its natural state. In 1907 she offered to fund a Museum of Vertebrate Zoology at the Berkeley campus, if the university would build a structure to house it—and if she were given complete freedom over its finances and staffing, demands to which the university amazingly agreed. She also created the University of California Museum of Paleontology, single-handedly centralizing and professionalizing much of the natural history research on the

West Coast. Alexander and her longtime partner, Louise Kellogg, continued to travel themselves, collecting specimens for both of Alexander's creations.

Alexander's choice to head the MVZ was Grinnell, a position he held until his death, in 1939, succeeding in his goal of creating a West Coast research center equal to those in the East. Grinnell and his staff were indefatigable, crisscrossing California collecting specimens and recording ecosystems that were on the cusp of radical change. (So painstaking were they that now, nearly a century later, their descriptions, measurements, collections, and photographs are being used by scientists to build an extraordinarily detailed picture of how the state's natural systems have changed with time, and may permit them to predict future alterations from climate change and habitat loss.)*

Although Grinnell was a pioneer in the emerging field of ecology, birds were always a passion, especially questions of taxonomy and distribution, like the vexing problem posed by subspecies; he saw the study of the distribution of California's native birds as a lens through which evolutionary biology could be viewed. He was constantly in the field, pushing himself, his associates, and his family hard; Grinnell's wife (and former student) Hilda Wood Grinnell described a typical summer day in 1906, in which she acted as his assistant:

> There were trap lines to be visited before the rays of the
> sun struck, or ants began their day. After breakfast there

---

*Grinnell was obsessive about creating detailed field notes and demanded the same of his staff—and he was prescient about their importance. "Our field-records will be perhaps the most valuable of all our results," he said. "You can't tell in advance which observations will prove valuable. Do record them all!"

was a two-hour tramp, with notes to be taken, butterflies to be collected for a brother, grasshoppers for a friend in Philadelphia, plants for Miss [Alice] Eastwood, who had already energetically bespoken the aid of all her friends in helping to build up a collection at the California Academy of Sciences to replace the one lost in the San Francisco fire of April, 1906. After lunch came the putting up of the morning's mammal catch and of the five birds usually selected on the early walk. Any rattlesnakes found were noosed, chloroformed, and put in formalin. From four until four-thirty in the afternoon came relaxation . . . After an early supper there were traps to be re-set and baited, bats to be tried for in the twilight, lastly moths to be caught as they came toward the flicker of the little campfire.

For more than two centuries, the center of American bird study was a narrow stretch of the Eastern Seaboard, anchored by a series of academic institutions and active bird clubs stretching from Washington, DC, to Philadelphia, New York City, and Boston. That was changing, thanks to Grinnell and others. Even before Peterson's eastern field guide appeared, westerners had *Birds of the Pacific States,* a 1927 book by Ralph Hoffmann, the transplanted Yankee who had, almost three decades earlier, written the *Guide to the Birds of New England and Eastern New York,* one of the formative volumes in the evolution of modern field guides. His western book, illustrated by the noted bird artist Allan Brooks, was a combination field guide, oology manual, and distribution list, and it was an important contribution to the growth of bird study in the West. (Hoffmann, who in his later years focused more on botany than birds, fell to his death, in 1932, while trying to collect specimens on the cliffs of San Miguel Island, off southern California.)

As Grinnell grew older, he spent more and more time working to preserve California's wildlife and natural landscapes. He also continued to work on his magnum opus, a book on the state's birds that occupied almost thirty-eight years of his life. He died in 1939, the manuscript nearly finished, and *Distribution of the Birds of California* was published posthumously in 1944 by his coauthor, Alden Miller. It remains one of the most important ornithological works ever undertaken, about one of the most ornithologically rich parts of the continent. In fact, Grinnell famously predicted that with time, virtually every species of North American bird would eventually be found in California.

The West Coast also led the way in what remains one of the last real frontiers of North American bird study—pelagic seabirds. Masters of the wind, effortless travelers across the immensity of oceanic space, these birds—albatrosses, shearwaters, storm-petrels, and their relatives—may spend years without setting foot on dry land, often remaining dozens, even hundreds of miles offshore. Rarely does a year go by without one or more new species being sighted within North American waters.

What little was known about seabird distribution was largely accidental—sightings by ornithologists and birders on transoceanic journeys, ferry crossings, and fishing trips offshore. Only a handful of scientists, like Robert Cushman Murphy at the American Museum of Natural History, had made a serious study of seabirds, and much of that knowledge focused on the breeding grounds, the one time in a seabird's life when it must come to land. Where the birds went once at sea was nothing more than an endless series of question marks, scattered about the world's open seas.

Nor was there much in the way of a field guide one could use. Peterson and the other authors dealt with a smattering of predictable inshore species, including a few shearwaters and storm-petrels, but for decades, the only book that covered seabirds as a whole was *Birds of the Ocean: A Handbook for Voyagers,* by a British biologist named Wilfred B. Alexander. "It has been the privilege (or misfortune) of the writer to make a number of lengthy ocean voyages, principally in the southern hemisphere," he explained in 1928. Bored by the endless weeks spent on tramp steamers, he had no diversion except the birds, "and, with a view to the identification of the sea-birds he might meet with, filled a notebook with descriptions of birds and outlines of their distribution."

The resulting small book was nothing if not efficient, jammed with 428 pages of densely written text, broken into categories like "Small terns with gray mantle, white or pale grey underparts and black crown," or "Small auks, with upperparts dark and underparts white, or with white abdomen sharply contrasting with dark throat or breast." There were also ninety pages of photographs or paintings—all in black and white, but fortunately seabirds are a rather monochromatic lot anyway. The fairly schematic drawings, made from life, prefigured Peterson's efforts a few years later. "It is hoped that the reproductions of semi-diagrammatic sketches by the author (for which no artistic merit is claimed) will also prove useful as aids to the identification of the species represented," Alexander said modestly. He assured his readers the book would allow the identification of most seabirds, "unless it should be a species still unknown to science."

That was a very real possibility in those days—and remains an unlikely yet tantalizing prospect today—but Alexander's book, while better than nothing, was still a long way from a useful field guide. The real sticking point, though, was access; most of the rare and interesting seabirds off both coasts rarely come within fifty miles of shore, and even in a fast, modern boat, it can take twelve or more hours to reach the best areas.

Nevertheless, there were enough exciting birds close to land to encourage birders to try. Pelagic birding began slowly on the East Coast, with Murphy, Peterson, and Ludlow Griscom leading trips off New York and Massachusetts in the 1930s and 1940s, and others using existing ferry services across Long Island Sound or the Chesapeake Bay to search for inshore birds. By the 1960s, however, birders were organizing pelagic trips on chartered fishing boats and had adopted Griscom's technique (itself borrowed from fishermen) of chumming the water with bits of fish, shellfish, or meat to draw in birds—also a great way of sending those teetering on the edge of seasickness running for the rail.

It seemed that almost every trip added new species to the previously small roster of birds that could be expected. Peterson's eastern guide listed just two storm-petrels and four shearwaters along the Atlantic coast; by the 1970s, birders were recording such exotic treasures as south polar skuas and yellow-nosed albatrosses, and the 1983 publication of Peter Harrison's *Seabirds* guide—the first comprehensive treatment since Alexander's book—finally gave pelagic enthusiasts a decent field reference and the opportunity to puzzle out real mystery birds. With each new season, we add incrementally to our still-scant knowledge of oceanic species. Birders have realized that Audubon's shearwater, which the 1947 Peterson edition said was restricted to southern waters off Cape Hatteras, can be found all the way up to the southern New England coast, while the Manx shearwater, a European species Peterson didn't even include in his early guides, is routine along most of the

Atlantic seaboard these days, probably a result of better observation and an expanding population in the New World.

And if the boat can push far enough offshore, out of the chill, greenish inshore waters and into the warm, deep blue flow of the Gulf Stream, there's no telling what may turn up. The gadfly petrels—a fast-flying group that are among the least-known birds in the world, with several species whose breeding grounds remain unknown—often show up in the Gulf Stream, including black-capped petrels, a Caribbean-nesting species now known to be locally abundant in deep water off Hatteras. Fea's petrel, which breeds on a few islands off west Africa, turns out to be annual off the Atlantic coast (sometimes as far north as Nova Scotia), along with Herald petrels from the south Atlantic, white-faced and band-rumped storm-petrels from off Africa, and white-tailed and red-billed tropicbirds from the Caribbean.

In the summer of 2004, birders off North Carolina found a Cape Verde shearwater, also from west Africa, and a black-bellied storm-petrel, a species that breeds in sub-Antarctic waters. Odd-ball strays blown off course by storms, or regular visitors to North American waters? It's anyone's guess (though the sighting of another Cape Verde shearwater off Maryland two years later suggests the latter), but these rare birds are two more reasons why pelagic birding is perhaps the most exciting frontier in the hobby.

The summer of 2006, a yellow-nosed albatross from the sub-Antarctic showed up along the coast of Maine, hanging out with nesting terns on Stratton Island and surprising a lot of people—but not, perhaps, Mark Libby.

Not everyone who watches birds at sea does so just for fun. A lean man now in his mid-eighties, Mark Libby grew up near Pemaquid, the dramatic, rocky point anchored by one of the most photogenic lighthouses on the Maine coast, and still lives nearby. He was enrolled at Amherst College when World War II broke out, dropped out to enlist in the navy, and never went back. Instead, he returned to fishing the Gulf of Maine, dragging trawls for ground-fish and shrimp, and keeping an eye on the seabirds that had first enthralled him in the Pacific in his navy days.

"It was the best way I knew of to make a good living and watch seabirds at the same time," Libby says now. But he didn't just watch—he kept meticulous notes on what he saw, and his observations flew in the face of what many ornithologists thought they knew about pelagic seabirds. He found, for instance, that pomarine and parasitic jaegers were more common along the New England coast than anyone had suspected, and he was among the first to document the expanding numbers of Manx shearwaters. He helped William Drury of Massachusetts Audubon conduct seabird counts along the Maine coast, and was a regular with Dr. Drury at the Nuttall Ornithological Club in Massachusetts.

In late March 1960, Libby was sixteen miles southeast of Monhegan Island when an enormous bird hove into view, dwarfing the gulls that surrounded his boat. Libby threw chum over the side, drawing the huge bird close, where it scattered the black-backed gulls. He calmly sketched it, capturing the pearly gray head and neck, the dark brown mantle and stripe of orangey-yellow along the top of the immense bill. As if that weren't remarkable enough, four years later another yellow-nosed albatross (perhaps the same bird, since these huge creatures of the sub-Antarctic may live thirty to fifty years) appeared again around his boat near Monhegan. It was just another astounding sighting for an equally remarkable sea-going birder.

On the West Coast, one of the first ornithologists to give serious attention to pelagic birds was a Californian named Rollo Beck, who started as a teenaged oologist in the 1880s and who, despite only an eighth-grade education, became a respected professional collector for a variety of museums, including the Museum of Vertebrate Zoology at Berkeley and the American Museum of Natural History in New York.

Beck specialized in seabirds, and collected across the Pacific, spending years at a time in the South Sea islands and New Guinea. He appears to have been fearless as a young man, rowing out into Monterey Bay in a small, open boat and staying there for a week or more at a time, shooting seabirds, skinning them, and cooking the carcasses over an open fire built on a box of sand in the middle of the boat. (On a less savory note, Beck is also credited—if that is the right word—with collecting nine of the last eleven Guadalupe caracaras, a now-extinct endemic subspecies of this odd raptor found only on Guadalupe Island off western Mexico, as well as hunting down and collecting the very last giant tortoise from Fernandina Island in the Galapagos.)

Other scientists were exploring the Pacific coastal waters as well, including Dr. Ira Gabrielson—who later became the first director of the U.S. Fish and Wildlife Service—in the 1920s in Oregon. But birding trips didn't really start until the early 1950s. As on the East Coast, birders would often charter fishing boats, or join bemused tuna fishermen on party boats heading forty or fifty miles offshore, into waters no one had ever really explored.

The payoff was huge. The cast of characters is considerably more diverse in the Pacific anyway, and by happy geologic accident, there are very deep, bird-rich waters relatively close to shore in several places, most notably Monterey Bay, where a submarine canyon ten thousand feet deep runs within a few miles of shore, bringing seabirds and marine mammals within sight of land. The Farallon Islands off San Francisco, and the Fort Bragg peninsula to the north, also provided destinations and jumping-off points for pelagic trips, as did parts of the Oregon and Washington coasts.

The Pacific pelagic birding scene blossomed, with pioneers like Terry Wahl exploring the region in the 1960s and 1970s. A young woman from back east named Debi Robinson, who'd been birding heavily in Texas, arrived in California in 1976 and took a pelagic trip onto Monterey Bay that changed her life—and, eventually, her name. Before long, she was organizing birding trips of her own, mostly as an excuse to get herself out into the deep, largely unknown waters, and she fell so hard for seabirds and marine mammals that she legally changed her name to Debra Love Shearwater. Her Shearwater Journeys remains one of the best pelagic companies in the country, and Debi and her West Coast colleagues keep adding breathtaking rarities to the region's bird list, including the great-winged petrel—only the second time this denizen of the "Roaring Forties," the storm-tossed latitudes below New Zealand and Australia, had been seen in the northern hemisphere.

One of the youngest birders on the early pelagic trips to the Farallon Islands, sponsored by the Golden Gate Audubon Society in the late 1950s, was a kid named Rich Stallcup, from Oakland, who was always messing around with birds—banding them, stuffing them, playing hooky from school so he could chase them. He earned an early reputation as a crack birder, and by the 1960s Stallcup, then in his late teens, began birding with a young Scottish immigrant named Guy McCaskie.

Coming to California as a boy, in 1957, McCaskie had an impact on birding in that state—and across North America—that is hard to overstate. Even though California has one of the most diverse avifaunas in the country, McCaskie wasn't satisfied with looking for the same predictable birds each time he went out; instead, he specialized in finding mind-bending rarities over and over again, until it seemed as much a function of necromancy as ornithology. Stallcup had much the same talent and drive, and together they turned California birding on its head.

"Mentor is not the right word, even though we learned an awful lot from him," Rich Stallcup said of McCaskie. "Guy was a hard master." They would make the eight-hundred-mile drive from Oakland to the Chiricahua Mountains in southeastern Arizona and back in a weekend. "We would leave on Friday at noon and Guy would drive till maybe nine o'clock, then sleep in his bed in the back of the station wagon while I drove the next seven hours, arriving at four a.m., falling from the car into my sleeping bag, exhausted. Then at dawn, maybe around 5:30, Guy would be standing there next to me, kicking me in my sleeping bag, saying, "'Fer Chrissakes, are you going to sleep all day? You've already missed an olive warbler!'"

McCaskie also provided a figurative kick to the western birding community, shaking them out of their complacency. Years earlier, old Joe Grinnell had said that every species of North American bird would eventually show up in California. Grinnell might have meant that facetiously, but in the 1960s and 1970s, McCaskie, Stallcup, and others started proving that he wasn't far wrong. They found that by seeking out little islands of habitat—an oasis in the middle of high desert near the Nevada border, a thicket of cypress and pines and a few small ponds on a peninsula like Point Pinos at Monterey—one could reliably find the most remarkable strays and rarities. Sometimes, the best spots were literal islands, like the Farallons, about thirty miles off San Francisco; others were man-made, like the Salton Sea in the Imperial Valley, created by a rup-tured irrigation canal and an unlikely inland hot spot for seabirds.

All of these were classic "migrant traps," life rafts to birds that had been flying all night, only to find, at dawn, that they were in a vast and often inhospitable landscape. In the early 1960s, McCaskie haunted the Tijuana River valley near San Diego, finding one new rare species after another, from Asian strays like red-throated pip-its to a variety of eastern warblers. Meanwhile, Stallcup and his buddy C. J. Ralph found a similar phenomenon at Point Reyes, an enormous peninsula of grassy hillsides, brushlands, and forested pockets north of San Francisco, where on a good morning, a single clump of cypresses might have half a dozen species of eastern warblers, vireos, or flycatchers flitting among their branches.

Point Reyes, now a national seashore, has proven to be one of the greatest migrant traps on the continent. But at the time, a lot of the land on the point was still privately owned, and as talk of a na-tional park grew, ranchers increasingly felt their backs were against the wall. Armed patrols gave short shrift to any birders they found skulking around posted property. "So we did a lot of sneaking through the bush lupine out there," Stallcup recalled. "It was real guerilla birding." The risk of arrest didn't stop him from spending days at a time on the point, ferreting out its birding secrets.

Since Stallcup and others began birding it regularly, more than half of all North American birds—490 species so far—have been seen on Point Reyes, making this the birdiest unit of the entire na-tional park system. Maybe Grinnell wasn't giving California enough credit; at this rate, every species on the continent may show up not just in California, but in this one surpassingly beautiful place.

In the spring of 1965, less then three years after the national seashore was created, Stallcup, Ralph, and several others formed the Point Reyes Bird Observatory, which began regular netting and banding in an effort to study resident and migrant birds. The observatory concept, almost always focused on locales with heavy migration, dates back to the mid-nineteenth century in Europe, spreading to Great Britain in the 1930s. Long Point Bird Observatory, on the Canadian shore of Lake Erie, opened in 1960 and was the first in North America. PRBO, which came into being with the National Park Service's blessing, was the first of its kind in the United States. Stallcup was quickly hired as biologist, and it seemed like a dream come true for the kid from Oakland. "I thought it would be great that someone could pay me to run around and look at rare birds; that was just such a deal. And, you know, to live away from the city; it was really such a beautiful spot."

It's certainly beautiful, but it was less than a paradise in some respects. The field crew worked out of a once-abandoned bunkhouse, trying not to lose their expensive mist nets to cows that still wandered the national seashore.

"There were almost no visitors," Stallcup recalls. "Dick Mewaldt [an ornithologist at San Jose State, and one of the PRBO founders] would show up once in a while and tell me to sweep the nine bedrooms and clean the one stove that I always made my macaroni and cheese on—that was all I ate—and a couple of people would drop by every once and awhile with something like a care package. But most of the time, it was just me and my bicycle."

With time, however, the operation grew dramatically. Stallcup was fascinated by old reports in the literature about rarities on the Farallon Islands, and as early as 1958 had gone out to the remote island cluster to see what was there. In 1967 PRBO began annual

monitoring, not only of migrant land birds but the Farallon's teeming seabird and marine mammal colonies. The observatory was instrumental in having the islands protected as a national wildlife
refuge, and after two oil tankers collided in 1971 near the Golden
Gate, creating one of the most infamous spills on record, PRBO
became a leader in oil-spill response along the California coast.

While Long Point and Point Reyes may have been the first bird
observatories in North America, they have certainly not been the
last to appear; there are now dozens, with more being formed almost every year. Many have remained small, shoestring operations,
run mostly by volunteers, while others have grown tremendously,
like New Jersey Audubon's Cape May Bird Observatory. Some
have expanded so far beyond bird monitoring that they have
changed their names, like Manomet Bird Observatory in Massachusetts, which started as a small banding operation in 1969 and is
now active in areas as diverse as tropical forest management and
ground-fisheries research along the Northeast coast. It has since
morphed into Manomet Conservation Science to reflect this but remains committed to birds, especially shorebirds, serving as the administrative home for the Western Hemisphere Shorebird Reserve
Network, which operates in eight countries from Tierra del Fuego
to Alaska.

Point Reyes Bird Observatory has experienced similar growth
and change over the years. The organization now has a research
staff of nearly seventy, a large new headquarters, and wide-
ranging research projects in terrestrial, wetlands, and marine ecology. Their main focus remains birds, from passerines to spotted
owls, but PRBO's scientists also study marine fisheries, seals, and
even the great white sharks that gather in awesome numbers
around the Farallons each year.

In May 2005 the Point Reyes Bird Observatory (itself now known as PRBO Conservation Science, a nod to its far more sweeping vision these days) celebrated its fortieth anniversary and asked me to come out to speak at their celebration. It was my first visit to the storied point, and I was stunned by the raw drama of the landscape—foggy redwood stands in the high hills, flower-spangled grasslands, the surf thudding and crashing along the jagged coast.

But for me, the central memory of the weekend will always be the chance to have tagged along with Rich Stallcup one morning as he led an overly large group birding in the hills of Point Reyes. Stallcup is a quiet, burly guy with a genial manner, but while the shock of curly black hair and bushy beard that gave him the nickname "Great Curassow" years ago has gone gray, he still becomes as genuinely excited about the birds of the northern California hills as he was back in the 1950s and 1960s, when he was a guerilla birder.*

For a legend, he's a soft-spoken man, but that doesn't lessen the impact Rich Stallcup and Guy McCaskie had on California birding—and the rest of North America. At a time when birding's engine was idling, they hit the gas—propelling it along a very particular road, one focused on ever-more virtuosic feats of field identification, combined with an emphasis on rarity-chasing. The journal *Western Birds*, published since 1970 by the Western Field Ornithologists (with McCaskie serving as its inaugural editor),

---

*The great curassow, a turkeylike cracid of the neotropics, has a black, shaggy crest, hence the fancied resemblance. This habit of bestowing bird nicknames apparently started in Texas with Edgar Kincaid, a dispeptic ornithologist from Austin who called himself the "World's Oldest Cassowary," referring to the huge flightless bird of Australia and New Guinea reputed to disembowel humans with a single kick. Kincaid picked names that hinted at a birder's personality; quiet Victor Emanuel was the Hooded Warbler, while Roger Tory Peterson was the King Penguin, doubly appropriate because of Peterson's fascination with that family of birds. The nickname fad was picked up by California birders in the 1970s, although they were chosen by a self-appointed committee instead of individual whim; McCaskie, for example, was the Magnificent Frigatebird.

has, since its beginning, focused on field science, with an emphasis on distribution and identification—the kind of descriptive ornithology at which amateurs had always excelled, and which was disappearing from the more academic journals.

And they gained converts in a hurry. "The way it was before, there were so few young field ornithologists," Stallcup said. "When I would find a Cape May Warbler out on the point I would call all my birder friends—like, six of them. And they would come from San Diego and Humboldt, and that was all the bird chasers there were. But at the turn of the [1970s] there were thousands. That was the big change [in] the late sixties and early seventies."

The California approach spread nationally, as younger men and women inspired by McCaskie carried his techniques and enthusiasms across the continent. "No one can see him objectively," Susan Roney Drennan wrote of McCaskie in *American Birds* in 1992. "He is one of the most original, colorful, insightful and influential people in the field of modern day birding." Pete Dunne, the director of the Cape May Bird Observatory (and himself one of birding's current leaders) wondered aloud to me one day whether American birding would have developed the way it has in the past half-century, had McCaskie stayed in Great Britain. Instead of the British-like focus on ever-finer levels of field ID and rarity chasing, Pete wondered, would birders have pursued a different course, perhaps a more scholarly appreciation of bird ecology and life history, instead of distribution and identification?

Who knows? Birding had grown up in the urban corridor of the East Coast, began maturing in dozens of isolates around the country—in Chicago, in Florida, in Texas—but it came of age in the West, and the California style of birding spread rapidly. The die was cast, and a lot of birders who were serious—one could say manic—about their hobby were looking for a way to harness this newfound sense of enthusiasm and increasingly national camaraderie.

The first hint of a new era for birding appeared just before Christmas 1968. It was four or five stapled pages, still smelling of purple mimeograph fluid, called *The Birdwatcher's Digest*.

JIM TUCKER HAD GROWN UP birding, in a bird-happy household—he often said he'd taken his first bird walk in his mother's womb, and his earliest memory was a white-breasted nuthatch outside the family's kitchen window. By the time he was old enough to vote, Tucker had become a bander, a member of the Tennessee Ornithological Society and president of its Chattanooga chapter. When he looked for a job teaching biology, he picked Florida because of the birds.

In Florida in the 1960s, he'd been the president of the local Audubon chapter and regional editor for *Audubon Field Notes*, the journal of the National Audubon Society, which took a rather scholarly approach to birds. But like a growing number of birders, Tucker was snagged early on by the thrill of birding's more competitive side, the challenge of building up a variety of lists—life lists, country lists, state lists. The same bird, spotted just once, could count as a point in a variety of listing games, depending on how one chose to approach it. You could compete against yourself, or against others.

One of the people he met through his Audubon work was Stuart Keith, a Brit who'd made a name for himself by beating Roger Tory Peterson's Big Year record in the 1950s, and who was by then a research associate of the American Museum of Natural History.

He and Tucker hit it off and engaged in a friendly competition to see who could beat the other with the most birds seen in a year.

But when Tucker moved to Texas in the late 1960s to do post-doctoral work in child psychology, he found himself cut off from the birding world he'd known, even though he got involved with the Austin Audubon chapter. By the 1960s—with the environmental movement rapidly gathering steam—Audubon was moving away from being primarily a bird organization and was focusing even more of its energy on conservation issues. Scientists had a variety of academic journals; conservationists held sway at Audubon—why wasn't there a publication aimed specifically at bird-watchers? Tucker wondered.

So he decided to fill the void himself. In December 1968, Tucker typed up a simple little newsletter that he called *The Bird-watcher's Digest*, describing it as "a journal devoted to the hobby of birdwatching," which he puckishly identified as "volume 0, number 0." Then he mailed it to about ten or eleven friends—people like Stuart Keith and Marjorie Valentine Adams, who wrote a syndicated column about Texas birds.

The first issue had an editorial about what makes a bird-watcher and promised "the latest statistics on the various games that members are playing and how they rank on the overall basis," which it described in some detail. There were lists of who was ahead in those statistics, but it was a scant roster—the Top Ten Life Lists had only nine entries, for example. There were a few short items about rare birds in Texas and an invitation to join Tucker's new "American Birdwatcher's Association" for three dollars a year.

But Jim Tucker had hit on something, and he got an excited response from the small group to whom he mailed his newsletter.

When Keith recommended dropping the references to bird-watchers in favor of "birders," the name of the publication was quickly changed to *Birding*,* and the group changed to the American Birding Association. The core of the new organization soon gelled, with people like Guy McCaskie, Arnold Small, and Olga Clark—all central to the California birding scene—as well as eastern birders like Bob Smart, and midwesterners like David Easterla and Charlie Clark, signing on as officers or members.

The ABA's founders saw a fairly narrow mission for their new organization. "It would be nice if *Birding* could be 'all things to all men' but it cannot," Tucker wrote in an editorial in 1970. "There are those who would like to see it emphasize the competitive aspects of birding, and then there are those who shudder at the thought of birding being in any way related to competition." He saw no reason to apologize for focusing on lists and competition, but he also put his finger on what would be a long-running bone of contention within the organization.

"Sooner or later someone is bound to ask where the American Birding Association stands on the issue of conservation," Tucker wrote in an early issue of *Birding*. Every member of the ABA was no doubt keenly interested in the subject, he said, and most were active as conservationists, but that wasn't the purpose of *Birding*. "It has been obvious in recent years that the trend of most (if not all) national publications in natural history and related fields is leaning more and more toward conservation issues . . . So there

---

*Coincidentally, in 1978 a small magazine also called *Bird Watcher's Digest* began publication in Marietta, Ohio, the brainchild of Bill and Elsa Thompson. Unaware of Tucker's title, they picked the name because they originally planned a *Reader's Digest*–style compilation of previously published material, although they soon shifted to publishing original material, including popular columns by Roger Tory Peterson. Today, *BWD* (as it is widely known) is one of the most popular birding magazines on the market.

seems to be little if any reason to take up space in *Birding* to harp further on items which are receiving adequate coverage in the major conservation journals."

By the early 1970s, the ABA was gathering a little speed. The newsletter had graduated from four or five stapled pages to a trim little magazine. For treasurer, they'd signed up Joe Taylor from Rochester, New York, who had just retired as corporate treasurer of Bausch & Lomb; Taylor had been birding since childhood, learning from his father, Tom, who had also been Bausch & Lomb's treasurer and a birder, as well as the first to note a difference between alder and willow flycatcher songs. Joe Taylor was a trailblazer among the newly competitive, list-oriented birders rising to national prominence in the 1960s and early 1970s—the first, for example, to prospect for Asian strays during spring migration on the remote Aleutian island of Attu, and the first birder to break the seven-hundred-species ceiling in North America.

By 1973, the membership of the ABA had risen to two thousand, and Stuart Keith suggested they hold a conference. Not in some cushy resort or bucolic island getaway, like most organizations; no, the ABA zeroed in on Kenmare, in northwestern North Dakota, a little prairie hamlet between Minot and the Canadian border, the living embodiment of the middle of nowhere. Why? The reasons were all around—chestnut-collared and McCown's longspurs, Sprague's pipits, LeConte's sparrows, sharp-tailed grouse, several large national wildlife refuges, prairie pothole marshes full of waterfowl, including a colony of western grebes in the middle of town.

Kenmare had all the elusive grassland birds a lister could want; what it didn't have was much in the way of tourist infrastructure beyond a motel and a hotel, both small, both overwhelmed. That stopped neither the ABA nor the community. "My God, nothing like this had ever even been *conceived* of in Kenmare," Joe Taylor told me years later. "The whole town was decorated with red, white, and blue, and big 'Welcome ABA' signs. They stopped us on the street and wanted to know about birding, [asked] if we were having a good time—it was a joy." It was a homespun convention; locals made room in their houses for the overflow crowd (those who didn't simply camp, that is), the high school served as the conference center, and the ladies of Kenmare handled all the cooking.

They wound up cooking plenty. The ABA leadership had expected about fifty people to show up; instead, somewhere between two hundred and two hundred and fifty (depending on who was counting) made the trek. At daybreak, birders packed six yellow school buses, decorated with KENMARE HONKERS signs, and rolled out to find local specialities like Baird's sparrow. In fact, the whole affair was so successful that National Audubon, which was holding its biennial convention at about the same time, griped about the competition.

The conference keynote address was given by Roger Tory Peterson, who praised the ABA as an antidote for the "professional snobbery" that was increasing among academic ornithologists who "insist that our brand of birdwatching isn't really scientific. Well, I don't know why it isn't valid—just the pleasure of watching these exciting creatures . . . If we have fun, that's reason enough," he told the crowd. (Besides lending his prestige to the conference, Peterson refereed at least one family dispute; Keith overheard a man, seated near the head table, arguing with his sons about their dinner. Exasperated, he called upon a higher authority: "Dr. Peterson, will you please tell my boys to drink their tomato juice?")

For a while, the ABA seemed to go off like a bottle rocket. "It filled a niche that needed filling," Joe Taylor told me, not long before his death in 1992. "Audubon had kind of been like that in the old days, when *Audubon* magazine was still *Bird-Lore*, but they had drifted away from that, and [ABA] was just stepping in and filling the niche." It continued to grow through the rest of the 1970s and into the early 1980s, with membership at six or seven thousand. When National Geographic brought out their bestselling field guide, ABA's new sales division was its sole distributor.

But there were problems, too; money was perennially tight, the magazine fell further and further behind schedule, and the membership flattened and stagnated. The organization was still overseen by a small group of 150 elective members, a holdover from the its earliest days—a self-selected clique of top listers who were approved by the ABA's officers; the elective members, not the general membership, made the decisions that really mattered at the ABA, including picking the board of directors or altering the bylaws.

In 1986, though, the ABA board moved to modernize the operation, eliminating the elective-member category and agreeing it was time to hire a full-time director.

But to their shock, an audit in September of that year revealed that the ABA was nearly a quarter-million dollars in debt, much of that from unpaid bills to National Geographic for the field guides.

"It added up that ABA was broke," Joe Taylor said. "I mean literally, by whatever definition of insolvency, we were insolvent." It was the winter of 1991, and I was interviewing him for a magazine profile; as he recalled those days, he pushed one hand back through the big receding wave of gray hair that crested over his head, which with his bushy sideburns were his trademark.

To most observers, including a lot of the members, it appeared the ABA was doomed. But several board members (most notably Taylor) loaned the ABA eighty thousand dollars to keep it afloat, and although few thought they'd ever see their money again, after a few shaky years, the organization righted itself, repaid the loans, and has been a going concern ever since.

In the twenty years since then, the ABA cemented its place as the standard-bearer for serious birding in North America. *Birding,* now a large glossy magazine, has continued to set the mark on issues of identification and bird-finding (though much of the latter information now appears in its newsletter *Winging It*), and the ABA also publishes *American Birds,* originally the quarterly ornithological journal of the National Audubon Society, renaming it *North American Birds.* ABA activities include workshops and tours; ABA Sales (which grew out of the field guide sales); the Birders' Exchange program to get optics, field guides, and other equipment to ornithologists in the developing world; and a variety of resources and events for young birders, including conferences and camps in bird-rich places.

One issue has remained contentious over the years, though— bird conservation. Jim Tucker had laid out the reasons why the ABA wasn't going to reinvent that particular wheel, despite the deep commitment he and many other ABA founders had to the idea, and in one of the very first issues, Tucker predicted, "This may well be the last time the subject of conservation will be dealt with in *Birding.*" Well, hardly; it's bubbled up again and again over the years, in editorials and letters to the editor, pro and con, and the organization still wrestles with how much space and attention to give to a topic that other groups make their central focus. (Birders' Ex-

change is one example of an ABA program with a very clear conservation aim.)

But are serious listing and bird conservation mutually incom-
patible? Even Tucker would have said no; the ABA approach was
to put fun first—to create a place for listers to be listers. Others
have seen a way to marry enjoyment, competition, and conservation—and thus was the World Series of Birding born.

In the beginning, there was the "birdathon." The idea, like a
walkathon or other fund-raiser, is to cajole pledges from your family and friends, so many dollars or cents per bird, and then on a day
at the peak of migration, comb the woods and fields and see how
many species you and a small band of friends can find. A lot of bird
clubs and Audubon chapters raise most of their operating funds
this way—a birdathon in the spring and a birdseed sale in the fall,
generating enough to keep the chapter in newsletter postage and
monthly guest speakers, or to send a half-dozen kids to ecology
camp the next summer.

Others have taken it to a higher plane. More than thirty years
ago, Bird Studies Canada started the Baillie Birdathon, the oldest
sponsored event of its kind in North America, which has raised
more than half a million dollars for bird conservation in Canada.
There is obvious potential to do some serious good for birds, if a
birdathon can be scaled up beyond the local level.

But leave it to Pete Dunne, the director of New Jersey
Audubon's Cape May Bird Observatory, to push the birdathon idea
to its (perhaps illogical) extreme. Pete has a flair for the dramatic
that dates back to his first fall at Cape May in 1976, when he turned
his back on a career in political science to work as a hawk counter,
stunning the birding world with news that almost fifty thousand

raptors had passed over the little count platform he'd cobbled together at the point. Balderdash, a lot of people said; that's twice as many birds as a famous migration choke point like Hawk Mountain records. The next year, Dunne calmly reported that he and the other hawk-watchers had counted *eighty-one* thousand raptors. The doubters started coming to see for themselves, and Cape May was on the map.

Cape May, in fact, may be the single best place in North America—perhaps the world—for birding. In addition to raptors, it boasts annual counts of more than a million seabirds, close to a million and a half shorebirds, and passerine flights that beggar belief; when a big cold front pushes through in the fall, it's possible to see a quarter-million songbirds at Higbee Beach alone.

And New Jersey as a whole is a singularly fertile state for birds. Forget urbanized Newark and snide jokes about how funny the Jersey air smells; with habitat ranging from high Appalachian ridges in the north to the vast and still-empty Pine Barrens, miles of ocean beach and barrier islands, and the tidal marshes of Delaware Bay, New Jersey is a birder's dream. Having grown up in rural north Jersey, Dunne knew that on a good day in spring migration it would be theoretically possible to see two hundred species within the state's boundaries—but no one had come close, despite decades of Big Day attempts. During the 1982 New Jersey Audubon birdathon, he and some friends, calling themselves the Guerrilla Birding Team, hit 185 species and raised about six thousand dollars for the organization; the next year—having persuaded Saab to loan them a brand-new 900 Turbo, which they drove like lunatics through pine scrub, farmland, and beach sand—they managed to reach 196 species.

But Dunne realized there could be more to this than just a good time, an abused loaner car, and a few thousand bucks for the home

office. In 1984 he announced the first "World Series of Birding"—
a twenty-four-hour, high-profile marathon within the state lines,
featuring sponsored teams and the promise that whatever money
each team raised would go to the conservation charity of their
choice; New Jersey Audubon would take nothing, beyond a modest entry fee. The top prize, for the highest number of species, was
the Urner-Stone Cup, a big silver-plated affair on a pedestal, but
the trophy for best out-of-state team would be a pair of expensive
binoculars partially embedded in a block of concrete—it's that
kind of competition. The motto of the event was "For Fun, Birds
and Conservation (But Mostly for the Fun)".

The ABA and *Bird Watcher's Digest* got behind it, and Roger
Tory Peterson, the King Penguin himself, joined Dunne, David
Sibley, and two companions to beat twelve other teams for the cup,
racking up 201 species, including Peterson's 697th North American
bird, a South American fork-tailed flycatcher that showed up just
before the event. Every year since then, the World Series has
grown, the number of participating teams multiplying. The pre-
season scouting and logistical planning have reached D-Day intensity, with teams of tight-lipped überbirders from around the world
sketching out the most efficient way to get from, say, High Point
and Black Spruce Bog up near the New York border, with their
ruffed grouse and purple finches, to Turkey Point on the Delaware
Bay near Fortescue, with its black rails and marsh wrens, by way of
Featherbed Lane near Woodstown for eastern meadowlarks and
upland sandpipers. Some of the teams even hold "swap meets" the
night before the big event, sharing their scouting information—
because that raises everyone's totals, and in the end means even
more money for conservation.

At the stroke of midnight on the middle Saturday in May,

they'll be deep in the woods, listening for owls or nightjars (many of them at Great Swamp National Wildlife Refuge, a traditional jump-off point), or on the edge of a tidal marsh, hoping for rails; one birder found that singing an opera aria can provoke a king rail to call back. Then the sprint is on, from hot spot to hot spot, careening around the state like pinballs, most winding up in the late hours before the next midnight far down the peninsula near Cape May. Participants have kept on birding despite hurricane-force winds, flat tires, sleep deprivation, serious traffic accidents, and virulent food poisoning.

The rules are simple; like most things in birding, it's the honor system. All birds counted must be seen by at least two team members, and ninety-five percent of the birds on the final list must have been seen by everyone on the team. When cynical reporters ask why participants wouldn't just lie in order to win, Pete Dunne always looks pained. "Because we're birders. Birders don't do that."

Being human, of course, sometimes they do, though that's rare. The team has to agree on the identification—though there does not have to be agreement *between* teams. Pete recalls a year when his team and two others all stopped to find the same scaup, which had been staked out on a lake days before the event. "Two of the teams, including ours, thought it was a greater scaup, but the other team called it a lesser. Doesn't matter. The rules don't say a bird has to be identified correctly," Pete said, "only that it has to be identified *unanimously*."

Of course, ricocheting around the Garden State in the middle of the night has attracted more than one cop's attention (one trooper, pulling over a team for speeding in daytime, listened to their explanation, then pointed them in the direction of a bald eagle he'd just seen). And occasionally, it causes a run-in with the other side of the law.

"One year not long after the World Series started, the Bushnell team was taking a midnight shortcut on this one-lane dirt road through the Pine Barrens," Pete likes to recall. "They round a bend a little too fast in this old beater station wagon they're driving, and here come headlights. A big Cadillac. The Bushnell guys swerve, the branches are scraping the side of the car, but their fender catches and—*Rip!*—right down the side of the Caddy.

"They stop, the Cadillac stops, and the leader thinks, Oh God, there goes two hours, at least, to deal with all this. There isn't a mark on the old station wagon, but there's this huge gash down the side of the Cadillac.

"Out of the Caddy comes what he later described as a 'short, swarthy man with a Mediterranean complexion,' dressed in an expensive suit but somewhat disheveled, and dirt on the cuffs of his slacks. There's another guy sitting in the car, but he keeps his head turned away from the light. Before the Bushnell team can start to apologize, the guy in the suit looks at the Cadillac and says, 'Hey, it's just a scratch—no problem, no problem!' He looks at the Bushnell car. 'See? Nothing at all. Here's fifty bucks—let's call it even, okay?' And gets back in the Cadillac and goes roaring off."

Despite the odd run-in with the Mob, the popularity of the World Series has ballooned, attracting more and more teams— more than sixty in 2006, including the Cornell Lab of Ornithology's Sapsuckers, which took the cup with a near-record 229 species. The Sandy Hook Bird Observatory had just half that total—but they got their 114 species by sitting on the observatory's observation platform all day, winning the "big stay" division.

There were seventeen youth teams as well, ranging from the senior-high Space Coast Cuckoos, with 212 species, to the elementary school–level Merlins, with 111.

And the money? The winning Cornell team alone raised more than $180,000, money they directed toward bird conservation in Central and South America. Overall, the event has brought in something like $10 million for birds through the years.

The success of the World Series has spawned others. There is a Superbowl of Birding (of course) held each January in Massachusetts, while the Great Texas Birding Classic is a weeklong team competition every April along the Gulf coast that has raised half a million dollars in its first decade. The model here is different from the World Series; the money comes from large corporate donations, and the winning teams get to decide how to spend it, choosing from a variety of Texas projects, like habitat restoration or acquisition, recommended in advance by bird conservation groups across the state.

The Texas competition takes place along the Great Texas Coastal Birding Trail, the first of its kind in the country—an auto route that traces twenty-one hundred miles through forty-three counties, hitting more than three hundred good birding spots. In the decade or so since the Texas trail was completed, similar routes have popped up all over North America—in more than thirty states and provinces, at last count, with more in the pipeline, one sign of how commonplace birding has become.

Birding continues to grow rapidly, by some measures outstripping every other form of outdoor recreation in terms of its expansion—something that even its most ardent popularizers never foresaw. Just a few months before he died, in 1992, I asked Joe Taylor—who did so much to solidify the modern popularity of birding—where he saw his beloved hobby going.

"I don't think it will go much beyond where it is today," Joe said. "I don't see how it can. There's too much competition with other things—there's so much to do, and birding isn't something you do in a hurry. I don't think that a lot of people are going to want to take the time to really get into it. I think it will grow some, but I think we're close to the saturation point."

Which just goes to show that even visionaries get it wrong sometimes. But beneath the simple question—Where is birding going?—lies a much bigger one, a question that speaks to birding's soul in the new century.

Without doubt, technology has revolutionized birding, and will continue to do so—breathtaking optics (with equally breathtaking prices), iPods and similar devices that put a continent's worth of birdsong at your fingertips, digital cameras that have democratized bird photography by making any good scope a telephoto lens. You don't even need a camera, really; you can find a rare bird, "phonescope" it by holding your cell phone's camera to a spotting scope, send the image instantly to a friend who will post the photo on the Internet, so that in minutes birders in every corner of the world can know about your discovery. And to think we were once jazzed by a telephone hotline updated once a week.

Most of the predictions one reads about what life will be like in the future are laughably wrong, but birding may be the exception; a lot of the predictions I've heard in the past twenty-five years have largely come true. Chan Robbins, speaking at Hawk Mountain's fiftieth anniversary celebration, in 1984, forecast binoculars with little built-in computers that would scan the image of a distant raptor and offer an identification. And if we're not quite there yet, no one will be surprised when such a gizmo hits the market, probably week after next.

In *Birding*'s twenty-fifth-anniversary issue in 1994, the late Rick Blom imagined a day of gull-watching in 2015: "One of your friends pulls from her pocket one of the new electronic field guides and has at her fingertips immediate access to the complete text and plates of over two hundred bird books." With eight years still to go, I think Rick lowballed that one, and he didn't even mention audio or video files. PDA, anyone? (One big miss, however, was a NASA prediction, from the late 1970s, that suborbital flight would soon be so cheap and commonplace that anyone would be able to fly to any city on Earth in an hour—a prediction *Birding* noted with gusto because of the possibilities for truly global listing.)

No, the question that I wonder about isn't how birding will change technologically; the real issue is whether and how it will change philosophically.

American bird study has gone through many phases in its four centuries, from halting discovery through stuffy academia and the frenzy of postwar birding, to a time today when birding's not just normal, but is (almost) cool. This has been the democratization of birds: to make them the province of anyone with the curiosity to observe their surroundings. As a result, today there are millions of people outside, watching, beating the bushes, and scouring the marshes, electrified by the sight of a bird. Which is a good thing, right?

Well, yes and no. Our ranks have grown beyond anything that Frank Chapman or Ludlow Griscom could have imagined, and I think that even Joe Taylor would be surprised by how far we've come beyond his imagined saturation point just fifteen years ago.

And yet, I would argue that birding itself has become a decidedly more superficial activity than it was in the days of Wilson or Coues, of Florence Merriam and Mabel Osgood Wright, or even

Roger Peterson and the lads of the Bronx County Bird Club. It's true that we know far more about birds, as ornithology probes deep into genes and stable isotopes, ferreting out the secrets of metabolism or migration. But where the public's interest was once driven by a fundamental curiosity about birds, and a basic joy at their existence, today it seems (for many of its practitioners) that birding is simply another outlet for frenzied hyperactivity. I don't see that our concern for birds has kept pace with our involvement with them as objects; we depend upon them for our amusement and our excitement, but for many birders, the sense of reciprocity, of obligation to the birds themselves, is missing.

For many years, I've harbored a growing unease and frustration at the disconnect between the burgeoning enthusiasm for birding and a pervasive apathy about the birds themselves, as organisms in their own right, whose protection and preservation should be among our highest priorities. As the World Series shows, hot-shot birding and conservation needn't be mutually exclusive—and yet a lot of birders seem to treat the latter as a distraction, honored more in the breach than in daily practice. They seem to forget that without a commitment to avian conservation, birding is a dead-end street.

There are two paths that birding can take. One is an acceleration of the course we've been on since the 1960s, a greater and greater emphasis on the sporting aspect, on competition, listing, and the march of progress on identification. Lists are fine things, as far as they go, but for a lot of birders, the list has become the whole shooting match, the alpha and omega. It needn't exclude conservation, but for too many birders, it does.

Is that the path we will we take? If one were looking at recent history, that's where you'd find the smart money. But there are signs—hints, perhaps, nothing more—to suggest the pendulum may be starting to swing the other way. Back to birding's roots, to bird-*watching* in the original sense of the word, where the bird exists not as a symbol or a tick mark or a challenge, not as a state record or a can-you-top-this vagrant—or at least, not solely as these things. A path in which the thrill of the sport is tempered by a celebration of the creature that makes it all possible—the small, contained miracle that is a bird.

8

Beyond the List

A FRIGID WIND was keening in the superstructure of the *MV Tiglax* as it pitched in heavy seas, its bow digging deep into the waves and kicking up spume and spray that was whipped off to port. For several hours David Sibley and I had been on the wheelhouse roof of the 120-foot ship, swaying with the increasing roll, hands jammed in our pockets for warmth between bouts with binoculars.

We were in one of the most remote parts of North America—one of the most remote parts of the world, for that matter—plowing through the North Pacific two-thirds of the way out the Aleutian Island chain. All day the ship had been threading its way among rugged volcanic islands, with names like Kagalska, Little Tanaga, and Umak, beneath heavy clouds pierced by rare shafts of sunlight. From time to time a Laysan albatross would slide across our wake and tack up to the ship on slender wings six and a half feet wide, effortlessly matching our speed. The rough waters around us were alive with other seabirds—horned puffins and ancient murrelets riding the wind-torn whitecaps, fulmars and short-tailed shearwaters coursing back and forth inches above the water.

Then we turned into Fenimore Pass, a turbulent gap in the archipelago twenty miles wide, where the Pacific and the Bering Sea wrestle twice a day as the tides turn—a churning, chaotic seascape. We had to brace ourselves now, hanging on to a stanchion or a railing as the ship lurched among the uneven waves. Soon the surface of the ocean was seething with yet more birds: crested auklets and parakeet auklets in close-packed rafts, or swift-flying flocks whose bumblebee wings blurred as they flew. But as astonishing as the sight was, Sibley was searching for something else—a tiny bird found nowhere else but this far-flung corner of the world, where it revels in the tidal violence of places like Fenimore Pass.

The *Tiglax* (pronounced TEK-lah, it is an Aleut word meaning "eagle") is the research vessel of the Alaska Maritime National Wildlife Refuge, which encompasses virtually all of the Aleutians. We were hitching a ride for a few days, hoping to reach the home waters of the whiskered auklet, a creature that had haunted Sibley's birding dreams since childhood. Barely eight inches long, the auklet is sooty gray, with a small blood-red bill, a slender crest of dark feathers curling over the forehead, and thin white plumes that angle back over the face like some kind of warbonnet, framing a pair of white shirt-button eyes.

"The whiskered auklet has been at the top of my wish list since I was a teenager," Sibley had told me some days earlier. "It's so little-known, and lives in such a remote, exciting place, that I've always wanted to see it."

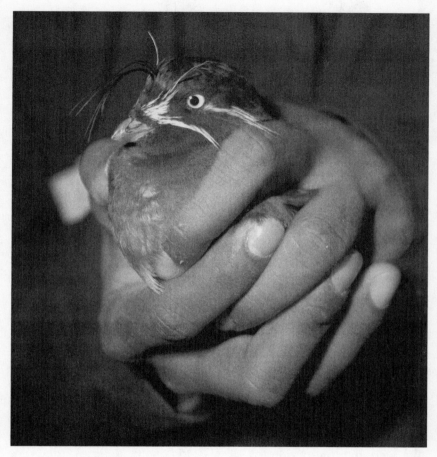

Found only in the lonely, chaotic seas of the western Aleutian Islands, the whiskered auklet is one of the least-known species of seabirds and a prize for avid listers willing to travel that far. *Photo by Scott Weidensaul*

In the years when he was developing his field guide, David crisscrossed North America repeatedly; by the time he'd finished his book, he'd observed almost every one of the 810 species of birds routinely found north of the U.S.–Mexico border. Only a few of the regular breeding species had eluded him; to illustrate these, he was forced to rely on museum skins and photographs, not his own eyes, ears, and sketches. One was Gunnison's sage grouse, from a corner of Colorado and Utah—a bird not even described for science until 2000; another was an endemic scrub-jay found only on Santa Cruz Island off the coast of southern California, which he finally saw in 2004.

But the whiskered auklet inhabits some of the roughest, loneliest, most forbidding waters on the planet, and until now, it had evaded him. It was easy to see why; just getting all the way out here had been a challenge that stretched over many days. (I was tagging along to write an article for *Nature Conservancy* magazine about Sibley's quest, which would also bring needed attention to the risk facing Aleutian seabirds from introduced rats and foxes that have decimated some colonies.)

First we took a chartered plane heading for Shemya, almost the very last island in the Aleutians, where the *Tiglax* was to meet us; the eighteen-hundred-mile flight from Anchorage was the equivalent of flying from Nashville to Los Angeles—only in a small, twin-engine plane over empty ocean and uninhabited islands. And through bad weather; a huge low-pressure system had blanketed the region in clouds, rain, and fog, and conditions on the ground at our second refueling stop, Adak Island, were deteriorating. We needed the gas at Adak; without it, we couldn't go on. The pilot, chewing his lip for long minutes, watched the fuel gauges dropping, then barked an announcement that he was aborting, pulling us in a tight 180-degree turn.

So much for Shemya; the only place to land was far back to the east, at Dutch Harbor on Unalaska Island. We cooled our heels there for several days before catching another flight west, making it to Adak this time. Shemya was no longer an option, but all this time the *Tiglax* had been steaming east and would meet us that night in Adak's harbor.

Adak, a rugged, treeless island twenty-eight miles long, used to boast Alaska's sixth-largest city, a bustling naval base that was home to five thousand people. But in 1997 the military pulled out, leaving the place a ghost town, and today, about the only reason to come to this island is for the birds. As close to Siberian Kamchatka as it is to Anchorage, Adak—like most of the islands of the western Aleutians—attracts a host of vagrant Asian species in spring and fall migration, birds that dedicated listers can add to his or her North American totals only if they make the long, expensive trip out here, to the middle of nowhere; birds that are, to a hard-core lister, worth their weight in gold.

Listing is at once the easiest and hardest part of birding to explain to a nonbirder. Most people have at least a little competitive spirit in them, and so the idea of birding as a game, with the species count forming the score, is a concept that anyone can grasp. Whether it's a Christmas Bird Count, where the goal is to amass a big tally for a single day, or a birder's cumulative life list, it makes intuitive sense that birders would enjoy keeping track of what they've found.

But *serious* listing, the kind that empties bank accounts, ruins marriages, and borders on the pathologically compulsive, is another critter altogether. How normal is it to keep a travel bag packed and always ready in the closet, so that you can snatch it up and catch a plane across the country on a moment's notice at news of a rare sighting? How normal is it to abandon your career and family for a year, ricocheting from one end of the continent to the other as you try to rack up a record-breaking list of birds seen in one twelve-month period? But then, how normal is it to pay sixty or seventy thousand dollars to risk death climbing Mount Everest? Every pastime, if pushed to its logical bounds, becomes peculiar;

push it well beyond those limits, and it becomes bizarre. Somewhere, I'm sure, there are extreme bowlers or gonzo stamp collectors who would make the rest of us shake our collective heads as well.

For years the ultimate listing destination was Attu, at the far end of the Aleutian chain, so far west that the international date line has to make a big zigzag around it. The only inhabitants are a few coast guard personnel manning a loran station. In 1972 Joe Taylor became the first birder to spend any time on Attu in the spring, looking for his seven-hundredth species of North American bird.

"It was as close to wilderness as there was in this world," Taylor told me twenty years later. "There was the loran station with thirty-eight guys and one dog. Most of the guys never left the building unless they absolutely had to. I was totally on my own.

"You look at Attu on a map, and it's a pinpoint, but when you get there, it's forty miles long and thirty wide, all mountains and cliffs." Every morning at five, Taylor made himself breakfast in the station's mess hall, slipped a sandwich into his coat pocket, and headed out, averaging fifteen or twenty miles a day on foot.

"I got my seven-hundredth species, a gray-spotted flycatcher. I got a couple of smews, a greenshank, common sandpipers, and wood sandpipers," all Asian birds that were priceless to a lister. The word got out quickly, and Attu became the must-see spot for serious listers. Six years later, when Taylor came back, he and his wife found three birding groups on the island, and people everywhere. "It was nowhere near as much fun, even though I did see more birds," he complained. Nor was it a holiday for the birders; for a steep fee they got to hunker down in abandoned, leaky old military buildings (birders could no longer stay in the active base housing) with sporadic electricity and limited hot water, hiking, or riding decrepit bicycles around the perpetually rainy, perpetually windy island, looking for such treasures as Oriental greenfinch and narcissus flycatcher.

Since 2000, however, because of changes in military regulations, Attu has been accessible only to those who charter an ocean-going boat from Siberia, as one or two bird tour operators have done. Adak has become the fallback choice these days for Aleutian birding, although it has seen better days, too. When the military left, it abandoned more than a thousand homes, offices, and businesses; it is the only place in the world where I've ever seen a boarded-up McDonald's restaurant, the golden arches crumbling. A handful of residents remain, many working for the local Native corporation, which is trying to build a tourist industry based in part on hunting for introduced caribou, although the recent arrival of a ballistic missile–defense radar unit promises a few more government jobs.

A spotting scope on his shoulder, Sibley walked through an abandoned neighborhood on Adak, heading for the beach. In the distance loomed the hulking white cone of the Great Sitkin volcano. The windows on many of the oddly angular modular houses were broken, the siding peeling away in the constant wind, tufts of pink insulation strewn for miles across the surrounding tundra. The front yards were rank with high grass and dandelions, grown enormous in the mild, damp climate, on whose seeds flocks of gray-crowned rosy-finches fed.

"Well, that completes the twilight-zone effect," Sibley said. "Rosy-finches feeding on giant dandelions in a ghost town near a boarded-up McDonald's." Actually, it felt disquietingly like a scene from one of those postapocalyptic movies, like *On the Beach*.

It was early June—late for Asian migrants and, in fact, that morning in the tiny airport, we'd passed the last birding group leaving as we arrived. We did soon locate a terrific find—a Far Eastern curlew, a shorebird with an astoundingly long, deeply decurved bill, one of only a few dozen that have been seen in North America and a first for David, who filled page after page in his sketchbook. Later we had dinner in the smoky VFW post, where a bunch of hard-looking guys—maybe a quarter of the island's population—cracked pool balls and drank, and by midnight, we were down at the harbor, watching the *Tiglax* ease up to the dock.

The following day was a long and fruitful one, accompanying refuge biologists in inflatable Zodiacs, to explore neighboring islands and hidden coves, and discussing their work removing foxes and rats from some of the Aleutians. But now, as we moved into the maelstrom of Fenimore Pass, we were looking sharp for the auklets that had brought David all this way.

And we found them—at first hundreds, then thousands of whiskered auklets, sliding up and down the steep-sided waves in flocks so tightly packed they looked like black carpets thrown on the water. "I've seen a few parakeet auklets, and some crested auklets a little while ago, but otherwise, it's just been thousands and thousands of whiskereds," David said. "Maybe tens of thousands. I've never seen anything quite like this."

Exciting as all this was, that stormy evening on the *Tiglax* wasn't actually the first time Sibley found his long-sought auklet. A few days earlier, during our forced layover in Dutch Harbor, we'd managed to hire a boat to take us out to the Baby Islands, just north of Dutch Harbor. There we found a few small flocks at the easternmost edge of the species' range.

Months after we got home, I was telling the story of Sibley's auklet hunt to an acquaintance of mine who's a fairly enthusiastic lister. He heard me out, cocked his head, and asked, "Why?"

Not, why would someone travel to a remote and frozen part of the world to find a single small gray bird; he understood that part perfectly well and would do it himself in a heartbeat if he had the chance. No; he meant, why go looking for a bird we'd already found, instead of focusing on finding something new? "I mean, getting that Far Eastern curlew was great, but that was the only new bird you had there. If you'd spent your time on Adak instead of out on the boat looking for auklets, I'm sure you could have scraped up a few more species. There had to be a couple more Asian strays left on the island."

Here, in a nutshell, are the twin polarities of modern birding. At one extreme you have birds as a source of inspiration and awe, as objects of curiosity, whether intensely scientific or at the layman's more general level. At the other extreme, you have birds as tick marks on a list, as inventory, treasures in a scavenger hunt that may encompass one's backyard or the planet, a single day or a lifetime.

Roger Tory Peterson was only the most famous writer to observe that birding can be many things to many people, and for most of us, the lure of birds lies somewhere between these two poles, incorporating elements of each. But there's no denying that, just as bird study in the nineteenth century focused almost exclusively on the ornithological—taxonomy, field studies, life history—the twentieth (and now, the twenty-first) have been dominated by birding as a competitive pastime, one that places a premium on challenge rather than knowledge.

I'll confess that I've always been uncomfortable with this modern approach. I like the rush of a good CBC as much as the next birder, but there is a shallowness about list-mania that I find off-putting. So, I suspect, does David Sibley; for him, finding the whiskered auklet represented more than just a penultimate notch on his belt; the real attraction was seeing an almost legendary bird in its wild and beautiful habitat, and the more (and more often) the better.

Stories abound of hard-core listers who spend a small fortune tracking down a single species they need to flesh out their North American list, only to ignore it mere moments after they've seen and identified it. Every field trip leader knows the type, the person who sees nothing but fresh numbers in each new excursion, whose acquisitive streak seems to blot out all other pleasures afield. To such birders, everything else—the ability to assess field marks, recognize songs or "read" habitat, among much else—exists merely to service the list, and a bird, once ID'd, has no more value.

Sometimes, even this minimal hurdle—identifying the bird yourself—is ignored. Leading a trip once in Central America, I was tailed for days through the forest and savannahs by a tour member who scarcely raised his binoculars to look at the birds we found. Instead, he was forever scribbling in his notebook, asking me to spell the names of birds I'd found, which he hadn't bothered studying in his field guide; in fact, I'm not sure he'd even brought his own copy. After all, why else would you pay for a guide? At the end of each morning's excursion, he'd run through his tally and ask if there'd been anything else we'd seen. Of course, "we" hadn't seen much of anything, because he hadn't been looking.

One day we found a male violaceous trogon, an eyepopper of a bird with an iridescent green back, brilliant yellow belly, and a chest of stunning purple-blue, lit up like neon by a shaft of sunlight. We got a scope on it, and the sight left everyone breathless.

Almost everyone. "But we've *seen* this one already!" the lister kept whining. "Why are we messing around with a bird we've already seen?" Where's a hungry jaguar when you need one?

But it's easy to beat up on such boors. There are plenty of other listers who never incite homicidal thoughts. Lists can be a tool, a means as well as an end, and the well-balanced birder uses them as such. If nothing else, they are a wonderful memory prod; leafing through the stacks of old checklists I've amassed over the years, I find myself transported back—to Hawk Mountain on a humid late-August day in the early 1970s, when I was in high school, the single immature bald eagle we saw a sight worth celebrating in those DDT-era years when the entire fall count might be only a dozen and a half eagles. Or my first trip to Monterey Bay, where the wealth of seabirds (and sea mammals) left me openmouthed. Or a trip up the Maine coast during college, catching the late-May migrants as they streamed into the spruce forests.

But it's also undeniable that listing is a slippery slope, something that birding's pioneers sensed very early on. Competitive listing seems to have gotten its start in the urban East, where both the Christmas Bird Count and what's become known as the Big Day began. As early as 1898, bird-watchers in Ohio were recording up to one hundred species in grueling full-day hunts. "This all-out May-day tournament was something I had never heard of before I came in contact with the birdmen of the big cities along the East coast," Roger Tory Peterson wrote in his 1948 book, *Birds Across America*. "New Yorkers and Bostonians call it the 'Big Day'; the New Jerseyites the 'Lethal Tour'; Philadelphians the 'Century Run,' and Washingtonians the 'Grim Grind.' One museum man, with a note of scorn, dubbed it 'ornithogolfing.'"

That unnamed scoffer might well have been Witmer Stone, the editor of *The Auk*, who in 1936 lambasted the idea of competition and listing, from CBCs on down.

The really unfortunate feature of the "Christmas Lists" is the element of competition which naturally creeps in. Even the most careful individual observer will, more or less unconsciously, give a record the benefit of a doubt if it adds one more species to his team score. Such lists if confined to a limited area and repeated for a number of years with counts of individuals as well as species have a definite value but we have absolutely no sympathy with the so-called "century runs" extending from 3 A.M. to 10 P.M. and covering a hundred miles or more. They are purely endurance tests for the participants.

Peterson's old mentor, Ludlow Griscom, did much to cement the popularity of listing—which was, ironically, known as "birding" in the old days, as distinct from the more serious, scholarly approach known as bird-watching. (The evolution of these terms is interesting; Florence Merriam's *A-Birding on a Bronco* first used the word in its modern sense, but then it faded away as "bird-watcher" gained ascendancy. Today, of course, many serious birders cringe if they're described as "bird-watchers," that term being most often associated with beginners and the old-lady-in-tennis-shoes stereotype. "Are you a bird watcher, an ornithologist, an ornithophile, an aviphile, a bird lover, bird fancier, bird bander, birder, bird spotter, lister, ticker, twitcher—or what?" Peterson asked rhetorically in a 1984 article.)

Griscom was sensitive to the criticisms of listing, especially the purported inaccuracies of sight records versus collecting, and did whatever he could to keep the results above reproach. One older chap who was a regular on Griscom's Christmas count had a habit of going off by himself and then reporting the most improbable birds. So one year Griscom assigned a young man to shadow the gent and keep him under constant observation—but the old fellow slipped his leash for just a moment, and that night at the compilation dinner (to Griscom's frustration and his young keeper's chagrin) he announced yet another unlikely discovery.

Griscom also casts a long and formative shadow among those who keep life lists, as almost every birder does to one degree or another. Some of us simply put a little checkmark (along, perhaps, with the date) beside the species in the index of our field guides, then forget about it; I'm one of these lackadaisical listers and probably couldn't say within fifty or a hundred species how many are on my North American list. (By custom, such lists include only birds seen north of the Mexican border.) Others, not surprisingly, obsess about their totals, using sophisticated computer programs to track them, and keep a keen eye on those birders whose North American lists place them at the top of the standings, published annually by the ABA.

Keeping track of one's list is made more complicated by the ever-evolving state of ornithological science, and the fluid concept of what constitutes a species. When I started birding, in the 1960s, one of the common late-fall songbirds was the myrtle warbler, so named for its fondness for wax-myrtle berries. Its western counterpart, the Audubon's warbler, was similar except for possessing a yellow, not white, throat. All well and good, except that in a narrow zone in British Columbia, where the two species' ranges overlapped, they sometimes hybridized—something that well-behaved species aren't supposed to do.

Nor were they the only ones coloring outside the lines; hybrids could be found in the overlap zone between pairs of oriole species, flickers, and other birds. In April 1973 the AOU lumped many of these formerly separate species; myrtle and Audubon's became the yellow-rumped warbler, Baltimore and Bullock's orioles were con-joined in the northern oriole, and no fewer than three species of juncos were subsumed into the newly minted "dark-eyed junco." Gone were the yellow-shafted and red-shafted flickers, now merged into the colorlessly named "northern flicker." Likewise lost were the great white heron and the blue goose, the American green-winged teal and Harlan's hawk, to say nothing of the black-eared and common bushtit, and the Ipswich, dusky seaside and Cape Sable sparrows.

There were a few splits—alder and willow flycatchers from the old Traill's, great-tailed grackle separated from the boat-tailed, and Thayer's gull from the herring gull, but it was a pretty lopsided affair, with lumps far in the lead. There was general confusion among birders, whose field guides were now hopelessly out of date, but real anger and consternation among zealous listers, some of whom were set back to a considerable degree by the net loss of countable birds. Some talked without irony about "the great April massacre." (Ironically, with the rise of DNA and song analysis in the last twenty years, the pendulum has lurched back the other way, and splitting rather than lumping is now in vogue—to consider-ably less nay-saying from the listers, as you can imagine. Towhees, plovers, sparrows, vireos, flycatchers, jays, and thrushes are just some of the groups where wholesale splits have occurred; it now appears that the red crossbill alone may comprise as many as nine species in North America [and more in Eurasia], identifiable only by call note and minute differences in bill size. Even some of the 1970s lumps, including the Baltimore and Bullock's orioles, have been reversed, and rumors of further resplitting abound.)

In Griscom's day, it was customary to count both species and subspecies, which accounts for his amazing life list of 980 birds seen north of Mexico. Because of the difficulty in separating sub-species, Griscom himself later advocated counting only full species, but even shorn of these, his list was still a remarkable 650. His company at the top was limited. By the 1960s *Audubon* magazine profiled what Stuart Keith had dubbed "the 600 Club," the small group of birders like him who'd seen more than six hundred species. As late as 1970 Joe Taylor was wondering whether it was possible to see seven hundred species in North America, but only two years later, Taylor himself proved that it was, becoming the first member of what inevitably became known as "the 700 Club." Since then, only a few hundred of the most ardent, zealous birders have broken that ceiling, and an elite handful have cracked the eight hundred mark. In 2005 the ABA's top lister—a Michigan birder, poet, and university prof named Macklin Smith—had seen 873 species, and people were taking bets on when someone would break nine hundred.*

Globally there are about ten thousand species of birds—a fertile field for listing if one has the time and means to travel. The yardstick here isn't seven hundred species, but seven *thousand*, a total that fewer than a dozen people have achieved. Interestingly—given that

*The ABA actually tracks lists in several overlapping regions. Smith's record is for what's known as the ABA Checklist Area, which encompasses the continental United States, including Alaska, Canada (including the French-owned islands of St. Pierre et Miquelon) "and adjacent waters to a distance of 200 miles from land or half the distance to a neighboring country, whichever is less." Bermuda, the Bahamas, Greenland, and Hawaii are not included. Some listers prefer to use the much broader AOU area, which includes North and Central America to the Colombian border, along with Hawaii and the West Indies, but not Greenland; the leader here in 2005 was Dan Canterbury of Florida, with 2,037 species. The ABA also tracks its members' rankings at the country level in Canada, the United States, and Mexico, along with nine global areas that divide the world into manageable chunks (including major ocean regions) and individually in all fifty states and twelve Canadian provinces and territories (both annually and cumulatively), *not to mention* a millennium list (birds seen since Jan. 1, 2001) and a list of birds not only seen but also photographed. Understandably, the annual list report runs to almost one hundred pages of ridiculously fine print.

big-time listing is an overwhelmingly male pursuit—the all-time champ remains a midwestern housewife named Phoebe Snetsinger, who started birding in 1965, at age thirty-four, and who had, by 1981, seen more than two thousand species around the world. That year, however, Snetsinger's doctor found that a malignant melanoma she'd been treated for five years earlier had recurred; the cancer was removed, but the prognosis was for three months of fairly good health, then a rapid spiral to death within the year.

"I never doubted I would die, but I wasn't actually sick, and I was determined to make good use of the time available," she wrote later. She threw herself into birding, first in Alaska, then, as her health seemed to be holding, ranging much farther afield. She saw her three-thousandth bird, a diademed sandpiper-plover, in Peru, about the time doctors had predicted she would die; a bit more than a year later, she broke four thousand in India. The cancer had gone into remission again, but by now, Phoebe Snetsinger had found her calling, and nothing—not a confrontation with machete-armed villagers on the South Pacific island of New Britain, not the sinking of the outrigger she was on in Indonesia, not even a brutal gang rape in Papua New Guinea—seemed to deter her. She eclipsed eight thousand in 1995 and kept traveling (and listing, although she stopped publishing her totals after reaching eight thousand) until her death in a bus crash on Madagascar in 1999.

But life lists are only one variant—call them a subspecies—of what Peterson termed "the lure of the list." There are trip lists, county lists, state lists, park lists, and yard lists. Friends of mine are mad for a tradition known as the Big Sit!*: one counts all the birds

---

*Although people have been doing "big sits" for years, in 1990 the New Haven, Connecticut, Bird Club codified the rules and registered the trademark, including the tiresome exclamation point.

seen in a single day from a circle seventeen feet in diameter; it is the ultimate in sedentary birding, a sort of tailgate party for birders. If you think that's odd, I'll introduce you to another birder I know, who kept a list of all the birds she'd seen copulating.

Then there's the notion of seeing how many species one can identify in a calendar year—a Big Year, akin to the Big Day that Peterson encountered when he moved to New York. Here again, Griscom was a motive force behind the idea. Having once declared that it was impossible for even the best birder to see two hundred and fifty species in the New York City area in a year, he went on to rack up annual totals far in excess of that mark, inspiring others to set local records of their own.

Inevitably, some birders tried this game on a grander scale. A New York banker named Guy Emerson—a birding companion of Peterson's, and a longtime board member of National Audubon—combined his business travels with his hobby and, in 1939, chalked up a continental Big Year total of 497 species. Through the war years, no one was able to touch it, but in 1952 an up-and-coming birder named Bob Smart (later an ABA founder) bumped the mark up to 510 species.

The following year, Peterson and his friend the English ornithologist James Fisher were preparing a three-and-a-half-month expedition across North America, a journey they described in their book *Wild America*. That old benchmark of Emerson's and Smart's beckoned.

"It occurred to me that we might as well do things up brown and try for a record," Peterson wrote—this despite Fisher's initial distaste for mere listing, a sport once known as "tally hunting" in Britain. But as the pair got underway—starting in Newfoundland and, largely hugging the coast, traveling to western Alaska by way of central Mexico—Fisher caught the spirit of the enterprise, shouting "Tally ho!" at each new bird. Not including Mexican species, they trounced Smart's total, with Fisher winding up with 536 species—a few more than Peterson, who missed two days of birding in Alaska. But it was only July when they finished, and naturally, Peterson kept birding for the rest of the year, long after his friend had returned home. By December 31, 1953, he'd seen 572 species.

Peterson and Fisher triggered something among the newly active birding community. The year after their book came out, a young Englishman named Stuart Keith and his brother Anthony came to the United States and did their own Big Year. They had the advantage of Peterson's and Fisher's advance work—scouting, if you will—and the newly published Pettingill bird-finding books, and they were able to beat Peterson's total by twenty-seven species. (Keith, of course, went on to help found the ABA.) In 1971 Ted Parker, a college freshman from Pennsylvania, had trumped that with an astounding 626.* Lists that had once taken a lifetime to accumulate were now the work of a single, frenzied year.

But perhaps the strangest Big Year of all began in 1973, when a Kansas teenager named Kenn Kaufman stuck out his thumb and started hitchhiking across the country, a pair of binoculars in his pack. Two and a half years earlier, at sixteen, he'd dropped out of

---

*Ted Parker was perhaps American bird study's greatest prodigy; his record-breaking year had actually begun while he was still in high school. A few years after his Big Year feat, Parker dropped out of college for a while to join his first of many scientific expeditions to South America. Despite the lack of an advanced degree, Parker went on to become one of the greatest neotropical ornithologists ever, able to identify—by sound alone—several thousand species of birds. He added immeasurably to our understanding of tropical birds until he died, tragically, along with several equally skilled colleagues, in a plane crash in Ecuador in 1993 while conducting a biological survey.

high school despite good grades, and—with his parents' under-standably agonized permission—hitchhiked across the country to chase birds. Picked up as an unsupervised minor in California and shipped home, he sold his blood for money and took temp jobs until he had enough cash to head out again; about fifty dollars a month was all he needed, sleeping outside and eating the cheapest food (including dried cat food) that the grocery stores carried.

His ramblings were at first aimless, propelled only by his desire to find the birds and places he'd been reading about, but in late 1972, Kaufman decided to break Ted Parker's record, a story he tells eloquently in his memoir *The Kingbird Highway.* He began New Year's Day 1973, in the Chiricahua Mountains of southeastern Arizona, and hitched maniacally back and forth across the country, finding cave swallow in the Dry Tortugas in Florida, great cor-morant in New Hampshire, and gyrfalcon in Vancouver. Picked up by a driver who offered him the wheel, Kenn almost wrecked the car trying to avoid a rabbit; another vehicle in which he was riding caught fire. He tagged along on a Big Day in Texas with Stuart Keith, Joe Taylor, and Jim Tucker, and caught up with Roger Tory Peterson at the first ABA convention in North Dakota. (A photo of the two of them—Peterson looking patrician, Kaufman with a thick beard and hair halfway to his shoulders—appeared on the cover of *Birding*'s next issue.)

Kaufman hitched all the way to Fairbanks, then used his care-fully hoarded cash to fly to Nome and Gambell Island, where he found rare seabirds and gulls. When he heard that a Eurasian spotted redshank had appeared in New Jersey, he thumbed for five rainy days from Arizona, only to discover, upon arriving, that it was just a greater yellowlegs with oil on its feathers. A friendly game

At the 1973 ABA conference in Kenmare, North Dakota, Roger Tory Peterson hunts for a bird with Kenn Kaufman, who was halfway through his yearlong hitchhiking attempt to set a new Big Year record. *Courtesy of the Stuart Keith estate*

warden in Oklahoma, responding to calls about a suspicious-looking character, gave him a tip on finding prairie-chickens. Toward the end of the trip, he was washed off a frigid winter jetty by storm waves, losing a borrowed spotting scope and only just escaping with his life.

When the year ended, Kaufman had broken Parker's record— but he was nudged out by a grad student from Michigan named

Floyd Murdoch, who had been doing his own Big Year and wound up with 669 birds, three more than the young hitchhiker. In the end, for both men, it was the process and not the results that counted. "The Big Year had been a great excuse to go birding," Kaufman later wrote. "To both Floyd Murdoch and me, that had mattered more than the numerical outcome. All along, Floyd had been more interested in the protection of birds and their habitats than in the accumulation of checkmarks. As for me, my own passion for list-chasing was dwindling fast, while my interest in the birds themselves was becoming ever stronger. So the contest was coming to matter least of all to the contestants."

Others have continued to set new Big Year records, but as the mark climbs higher and higher, the only way to best it has been by relying on increasingly hefty bank accounts. In 1979 a Mississippi forest manager and self-confessed "routine" birder named Jim Vardaman performed the equivalent of engaging a guide to carry him up a mountain—he hired a number of top birders (including Kaufman) to create a Big Year plan, contacted hundreds of other birders across the country for tips, and spent lavishly to see 699 species, most of which he was led to by others who had staked out the birds. His visits were sometimes measured in minutes, if that. He figured that the publicity—and there was plenty—could only help his business. Birders were aghast; Vardaman was unrepentant. "I didn't need anybody to like my project," he told *Birding*. "If someone was interested, fine; if not, well, I'm not going to poll the delegation to find out if there's sufficient support."

Kenn Kaufman, on the other hand, went on to become one of the most respected birders in the country, a teacher and prolific writer I'm grateful to call a friend. But Kenn is no longer a lister; he doesn't even keep a life list anymore. That long-ago Big Year refocused his attention on the joy of birds for their own sake, not as inventory. But he's also keenly proud of his youthful accomplishment, especially the one record that I'm sure will never be broken. Kenn spent less than a thousand dollars on his yearlong journey (and most of that getting to and from northern Alaska). This works out to about a buck and a half per species. I'd like to see some hotshot break *that* one.

AMID ALL THE HUBBUB that surrounded the publication of David Sibley's guide in 2000, many birders overlooked the fact that it was actually one of two important field guides released almost simultaneously that autumn. The other was an intentionally slender book, about half the size and a quarter of the weight of Sibley's—the *Focus Guide to Birds of North America*, by Kenn Kaufman.

In the years after his teenaged adventure, Kenn's star continued to rise as one of the premier birders in North America. He guided for WINGS and Victor Emanuel Nature Tours, two of the best birding-tour companies in the world. A prolific writer, he became an associate editor of *American Birds,* then the scholarly journal of the National Audubon Society, and was a frequent contributor to *Birding* and virtually every other bird magazine, always pushing the envelope of what was possible in terms of field identification. In 1990 he broke into the big time in a big way, authoring a guide in the Peterson series on advanced birding—how to distinguish immature accipiters, confusing peeps, and diabolical *Empidonax* flycatchers, among other feathered puzzles.

After *Advanced Birding* was published, though, Kenn had a change of heart. "I decided we didn't need more serious birders who could discuss the molt sequences of third-year Thayer's gulls," he said. "Instead, we needed a lot more people who had maybe seen a yellow warbler and who understood that there was a connection between this attractive bird and its need for habitat."

That's when he turned from creating guides for ever-more-skilled birders whose main focus is field identification to ways of popularizing bird study. Surveying the guidebooks on the market, he saw an increasing specialization, a rising technicality that made the hobby less and less accessible for newcomers. The original Peterson guides—first for birds, then for so many other facets of the natural world—had been an entry point for millions to whom nature had once been unknown; they were detailed enough to be useful, but not so Gordian as to be intimidating. Today, the sight of a thick, complex field guide—like the one he'd just written—was more likely to befuddle beginners than to inspire them.

So Kenn set about creating a guide specifically for new and intermediate birders—a basic field guide in the classic Peterson mold, one designed to help people having trouble telling a warbler from a finch, instead of those trying to distinguish the relative width of the wing stripe between eastern and western willets. One way to simplify, of course, is to leave out some of the birds; Peterson himself did this with the eastern and western versions of his guides, but omissions inevitably frustrate users when they find a species not in the guide. Kenn covered all the North American species, but he pared everything down to the minimum; instead of the dozen or so song sparrows in Sibley's guide, for instance, there were just four of the most widespread or distinctive forms.

Kaufman accomplished this back-to-basics guide, however, in a decidedly high-tech way. Although he's an accomplished artist, he opted to use photos instead of paintings—but he sought to overcome the drawbacks that had plagued photographic guides for decades, by applying digital technology. Taking a photograph of a bird, Kenn first isolated it from its background, then tweaked the colors, corrected shadows and highlights, sharpened contrast, and accentuated certain field marks—thus making it look like the idealized image of that species. Then correcting for scale, he arranged the enhanced photographs for easy comparison in groupings like "brown ground warblers" or "huge aerial waterbirds."

The response from birding's elite? Surprisingly vicious; many of them treated Kaufman like a traitor to the cause for "wasting" his time on beginning birders, instead of applying his considerable skills to thorny identification issues. Others sniped at the book, dismissing the way he grouped similar but unrelated birds, like hawks and owls, instead of following the dictates of taxonomy (even though avian taxonomy is a confusing mystery to newly minted birders, who don't care a fig that owls are more closely related to nightjars than to hawks and just want to find a bird without a lot of paging back and forth). Still others berated him for digitally altering photographs, implying that this was somehow inherently dishonest—as if he'd been doctoring the Zapruder film instead of simply crafting identification plates.

It was a strange and inexplicable reaction to a man who was just trying to make a good, basic field guide. It must have hurt, but Kenn shrugged it off as small-minded and kept his eye on what he'd realized was important—bringing new people into birding, as a portal not to competition, but to appreciation.

On the face of it, birding would hardly seem to need the help. Surveys routinely show it as one of the fastest-growing outdoor activities, and depending on who's counting, the number of birders has been pegged as high as 67.8 million Americans—which is almost certainly bogus, given that such surveys count as a birder anyone who tosses sunflower seeds for the juncos. The U.S. Fish and Wildlife Service, which also takes a liberal definition of "birder," put the number at 46 million, with 24 million making trips away from home to watch wild birds.

If you look at just those who can identify more than twenty species of birds, however—itself a pretty generous definition of a birder—that figure drops to just 6 million, and those able to ID one hundred species number a few hundred thousand at best. That's a lot of people, but not when viewed through the lens of 300 million Americans. While one national survey found that participation in birding had jumped 232 percent between 1983 and 2001, other studies have shown the growth curve for birding flattening out or even falling in recent years. (The same survey showing such dramatic growth in birding is also the one that put the number of birders at nearly 70 million, or almost a quarter of the nation's population, so I take their conclusions with a grain of salt.)

Other measures continue to show upward signs; the number of participants in Christmas Bird Counts has risen steadily, for example, from 15,000 in 1970 to more than 57,000 in 2005, and those are generally reflective of the most serious slice of the hobby. But birding festivals, which tend to attract beginners, have exploded in number and popularity, from just 12 in 1993 to 140 in 1999 and more than 260 in 2005, ranging from the Sandhill Crane Festival in Fairbanks, Alaska, to the Yucatan Bird Festival in Mexico, with the number continuing to grow so rapidly that it's impossible to find a truly comprehensive list.

Who are birders, for the most part? The majority of them are middle-aged, economically comfortable, and have higher-than-average education. They are also overwhelmingly white; there are surveys to document this last point, but if you simply look around the hawk-watch or refuge-loop road, it's starkly obvious.

It's also a sore issue. In 1999 a transplanted Brit and ABA member named Martin Reid started a firestorm in the pages of *Birding* with a letter to the editor. "Why Are We So White?" Reid asked, wondering if birders, by their inaction and their comfort with the status quo, were allowing birding to become what he called a "White Preserve." Reid said he wanted to encourage debate—and boy, did he ever. The magazine ran a lengthy string of responses, many of them expressing anger at the implication of at least passive racism. The respondents ranged from a young black birder recounting his experiences, good and bad, as a minority in the sport, to those who compared Reid and his supporters with "race-obsessed, guilt-ridden, high priests of liberalism." One letter writer who agreed with Reid said part of the problem stemmed from what readers of magazines like *Birding* see—"white Americans writing about white American topics in a white American language . . . you will see white Americans modeling the latest in birding fashion, and white Americans demonstrating the more recent developments in optical equipment."

Interestingly, among those who reacted favorably to the letter were prominent borderlands birders like Father Tom Pincelli, who started the Rio Grande Birding Festival in Harlingen, Texas—an event that includes beginning birding sessions in both English and Spanish. Kenn Kaufman, who lived for years in Tucson, called the subject of ethnic homogeneity an "obviously real one," and suggested that the solution lay mostly at the local level, through the work of nature centers and environmental educators already connected to minority communities.

But though he didn't say so in his letter, Kenn also believed there was a more direct solution. More than 28 million people in the United States speak Spanish at home; of those, only half speak English "very well," according to the U.S. Census Bureau—so even if the rest have an interest in birds, navigating through an English field guide presents a fundamental obstacle. So why not, Kenn wondered, create a Spanish-language version of his new guide?

Easier said than done; the publisher was decidedly cool to the idea, worried that the market wasn't large enough, the demographic not attuned enough to nature to make it worth the financial gamble. Kenn kept making expensive concessions. He agreed to pay for the translation costs, including recruiting Mexican ornithologist Héctor Gómez de Silva to create Spanish transliterations of bird voices (since, for example, *Oh dear me*, the usual description of a golden-crowned sparrow's song, doesn't work in Spanish). He agreed to pay another round of copyright fees to all the photographers *and* to do all the pre-printing preparation work himself—an exorbitant expense for any author to shoulder.

In late summer 2004, I was birding in southeastern Arizona with Kenn and a couple of mutual friends. After a morning up in the Huachuca Mountains, with the Mexican border just a few miles away, we were eating lunch and rehydrating ourselves with huge lemonades when Kenn quietly mentioned that he'd finally won his long, expensive struggle; the Spanish guide would soon be released, and we offered our heartfelt congratulations.

There are other glimmers of growing diversity as well. A National Survey on Recreation and the Environment conducted in 2000–2001 found that Hispanics were the fastest-growing ethnic group among birders, making up almost 40 percent of the growth in birding since 1995. The hobby is getting less middle-aged, with a big jump in the number of teenagers and twenty-somethings entering birding, and both median income and level of education are coming down. It isn't just white, college-educated, affluent Americans who are lifting binoculars these days—and more and more often, the sight of a dazzling spring warbler will elicit a whispered *"Hermosa."*

In taking on all these challenges, I think Kenn resembles no one so much as his childhood idol, Roger Tory Peterson. Peterson, too, tried to push a birding community more and more focused on lists and sophisticated ID to something more holistic—a greater focus on conservation, a greater commitment to preserving birds instead of just ticking them off on a list, and an attempt to make bird study as accessible as possible, to as many people as possible. He was, at best, only partially successful, but the fight isn't over. So as we sat, tired and dusty, in that border town diner, we raised our lemonades—*¡Salud!*—and toasted *Guía de campo a las aves de Norteamérica,* a book that was long overdue. I suspect that somewhere, in a place where you can still find passenger pigeons and great auks, Roger Peterson was toasting Kenn, too.

IN 1943 Joseph Hickey—a friend of Peterson's from their old Bronx County Bird Club days, a former student of Aldo Leopold's, and by then a professor of wildlife management at the University of Wisconsin—published a book called *A Guide to Bird Watching.* Old though it is, it remains one of my favorite bird books, not only for its elegant scratchboard drawings by Francis Lee Jaques, but for

Hickey's devotion to bird-watching in its original sense—the careful, awestruck study of the birds themselves.

Identification (by sight and sound) took up barely more than six pages of this thick volume. Instead, Hickey devoted the rest to instructing his readers on how to observe the ways in which birds live their lives—how to study their migration and habitat selection, their diets, the changes in local bird populations. He enumerated the many ways a bird student could become involved in research, through banding and color-marking, or through breeding-bird surveys; he even outlined a model life-history study that anyone could undertake in their own neighborhood. Over and over again, he showed how little we still knew about birds, and the contribution that any serious amateur could make.

It was a more ornithological approach than the competitive path on which his old mentor Ludlow Griscom and others had set the pastime, something Hickey acknowledged. "The art of bird watching has different meanings among different people," he wrote:

> To some it is the art of identifying birds in the field, or of recognizing their songs year after year. This is the Field Card School of Ornithology, which measures success in terms of the rarity, the first migrant, and the big list. At its best it is a sport, testing the eye, the ear, and one's legs. At its worst, it is a mad rush to the next oasis, with birds ticked off on the run, and a great reliance placed on both gasoline and brakes. Birds are *scanned*, but it can scarcely be said that they are *watched*—especially when one has an eye incessantly searching for a rarity in the next tree.

Bird watching is much more than this. It is the art of discovering how birds live. Through it the naturalist can cross the frontier of knowledge and explore an unknown world. His reward is more than a mere check on a field card; although personal and intimate, it can still be a contribution to science.

Hickey was pushing his boulder up a steep slope, and I think he knew it. Even then, "bird-watching" was morphing into "birding," and today, it's clear that the Field Card School has swept the field. As *Birding*'s former editor Paul Baicich pointed out more than a decade ago, Hickey's approach represents a road not taken, a path along which bird study *could* have evolved, into something more than a mere identification challenge and a numbers game. Today, though, there are a few tentative stirrings that suggest this missed opportunity in birding's past could eventually represent birding's future.

IT IS, AS I WRITE THIS, a frigid late-October night in the hills of eastern Pennsylvania. A cold front roared through yesterday, and this evening, there are snow flurries drifting down through the last rattling brown oak leaves.

I slip on a headlamp and, with two companions, walk through the chilly woods. The night air is pierced by a sound that resembles nothing so much as a garbage truck stuck in reverse—a monotonous, mechanical tooting loud enough to be heard half a mile away.

No truck, this is a recording of the territorial call of a male saw-whet owl, a small and mysterious species of the northern forests, which migrates south each autumn across much of North America, including along the ridges of the Appalachians where we are. Our station is one of about a hundred across Canada and the United States, mostly small, volunteer-run operations, that monitor the movements of saw-whets. Under the wan light of a half-moon, I can just make out a line of fine mist nets strung through the forest, each one gauzy as an old lady's hairnet, but forty feet long and eight feet high. The nets run for more than fifty yards in a giant L among the trees, with a small cooler sitting at the apex of the array, wires running from a battery-powered MP3 player and a juiced-up amplifier to two bullhorn speakers that broadcast the owl toots loudly enough to make my ears throb.

Painful as it may be for me, it is a siren song for migrating saw-whets. Hanging cradled in the nets are five of the small raptors, each the size of my fist, and weighing about as much as a robin. My companions and I quickly untangle the birds, pop each into a cloth holding bag and cinch the drawstring tight, then hike back down the hill to a cabin. There, I affix a lightweight numbered band to each owl's leg, take a series of measurements, and release all back into the dark forest.

Some autumns, we may catch as many as nine hundred owls at this and two other locations, showing how important the eastern ridges are as a migratory flyway—and showing how little we still know about the continent's birdlife, since this phenomenon was overlooked for centuries. Secretive and nocturnal, saw-whets were always considered rare, and no one even knew that they were migratory until about 1900, when they were reported crossing the Great Lakes in small numbers. In the 1930s, Bent's *Life Histories* account said only that the species "evidently migrates to some extent, or at least wanders widely." As late as 1993, when its regular and

On a cold autumn night, a newly banded northern saw-whet owl is measured before its release—the kind of "citizen science" project that is increasingly common and might offer a new avenue for birding, one fusing the science of birds with the joy of chasing them. *Photo by Scott Fraser*

widespread migration had at last been noted, the most authoritative account of the species identified just two routes in the East— through the Great Lakes region or down the Atlantic seaboard.

That's because those were the only two places anyone had bothered to look for them. The owls are so secretive by day that most birders go a lifetime without seeing a live saw-whet, but if you put up nets and play a recording of their call, you can find them almost anywhere during migration—on islands along the Pacific Northwest coast; in the Rockies; in shelterbelt woodlots in the Dakotas, surrounded by an eternity of prairie; in urban parks; and throughout the East. We now know that the Appalachian mountains alone carry vast numbers of saw-whets south each year. Far from being rare, this may be one of the most common raptors in North America—just one example of how little we still know, after four centuries of study, about most of our birds.

For a decade now, I've overseen this particular saw-whet banding project, under the auspices of the Ned Smith Center for Nature and Art in central Pennsylvania. It's a laborious undertaking; the three sites scattered over half the state are manned seven nights a week from the first of October through at least Thanksgiving, from dusk until well after midnight. To accomplish this, we have about a hundred volunteers, who annually contribute about five or six thousand person-hours to the effort.

You'd think that any project requiring people to stay up half the night in cold, unheated buildings would be hard to recruit for, but we have a waiting list of volunteers anxious to join. Part of that is due to the owls themselves—small, elfin, impossibly cute, they are an appealing species with which to work. But I suspect an even greater reason is the chance to connect directly with wild birds, using one of the most fascinating techniques in science.

Hickey devoted a chapter of his book to what he called "the romance of bird banding," and the charm hasn't waned in the more than six decades since he wrote it. To do as we do—catch a wild owl, put a numbered band on its leg, and let it go—is (as the naturalist Aldo Leopold once said), to hold a ticket in a great lottery. Each year, about thirty of our owls are recaptured by other banders, while we, in turn, catch a roughly equal number that already bear bands—birds whose travels we can begin to map when we learn where and when they were first marked.

There was, for example, 1353-43820, whom we captured on Halloween night in 2001; she had been banded in 1998 on the Bruce Peninsula of Lake Huron in Ontario, already at least three years

old. Or 844-23780, banded two years earlier by friends of mine
near Freeport, Maine. Or 614-59986, originally banded in late April
2003 as she crossed Bois Blanc Island in the wintry Straits of Mack-
inaw, and whom we caught heading south a year and a half later
and five hundred miles southeast.

Ours is an all-volunteer crew, and its makeup is, I think, in-
structive. Not surprisingly, there are a number of professional
wildlife biologists in the group—several who work for the state,
several more who work for conservation groups like the Nature
Conservancy and Audubon, and another who is a private consul-
tant specializing in endangered bog turtles. But the seventeen li-
censed banders who operate under my federal banding permit also
include a plumber, a retired soft-drink executive, two retired teachers, a sewage plant operator and two environmental educators. Of
the more than eighty others who volunteer weekly through the fall,
but who don't have a banding permit—well, they run the gamut
from teenaged homeschoolers to retirees, a university professor to
a massage therapist, a United Way executive to a state museum
specialist. A cross section, in other words.

Not only do we band owls, we also put tiny radio transmitters
on some of them so we can learn where they're roosting, what
habitats they're using, and (by collecting their regurgitated pellets
and examining the bones inside) what they're eating. We gently
pluck a few small body feathers from each one, so that DNA can be
teased from the skin cells that cling to the shaft, allowing us to compare them with the genetics of owls across the continent, building a map of regional saw-whet populations. (We've also assisted
many other researchers, from the Centers for Disease Control to
UCLA, by collecting samples of owl blood, feathers, and even
feces for their studies.)

We may be a bit odd, sitting in the woods listening to something that sounds like the alien mother-ship landing, but there are a lot of other people involved in similar projects that allow laymen to contribute to the science and study of birds. Some are home-made undertakings that grow out of one person's passion. Most, though, are a salubrious mix of academic and amateur—projects with professional guidance that harness the numbers and enthusiasm of average birders. Among the most famous is Project Feeder-Watch, a joint Canadian/American enterprise that began in Ontario in 1976 and is now jointly managed by the Cornell Lab of Ornithology and Bird Studies Canada. Every two weeks throughout the winter, more than sixteen thousand participants record the species and numbers of birds at their feeders—creating an unparalleled picture of bird populations.

FeederWatch tracked the progress of an epidemic eye disease that swept through house finches in the 1990s; it has traced the explosive northward push of formerly "southern" species like red-bellied woodpeckers into eastern Canada; and provides a glimpse of unexpected bird irruptions, like the 2005 invasion of varied thrushes into the East. It permits an annual snapshot of populations of birds like common redpolls and American tree sparrows, which nest in the Arctic—the only way to monitor species with such remote nesting grounds.

But there are thousands of such projects available to birders, from breeding-bird atlases to nesting-loon surveys, bluebird box trails to point counts assessing threatened warbler populations. Hawk migration counts (and now, a growing number of winter raptor surveys) are a common example, but there are now vulture counts, too—and surveys of owls, cranes, seabirds, shorebirds, nighthawks, hummingbirds, and herons, among others. The wildlife ecology unit at UC Davis has organized "Magpie Monitors" to keep tabs on the yellow-billed magpie found only in central California, a bird at significant risk from West Nile virus; the volunteers (many using bicycles) regularly count magpies along routes they devise themselves. Cornell has a suite of projects designed especially for urban students, focusing on city birds, like pigeons, crows, and gulls.

It isn't only birds; there are Fourth of July Butterfly Counts, sponsored by the North American Butterfly Association; a national amphibian network called FrogWatch USA; bat box surveys and moose monitoring, schemes to keep track of dragonflies, fish, marine mammals, and almost everything else in nature.

This trend has been given the catchy title "citizen-science," but in fact, this remerging of science and hobby brings ornithology back to its amateur roots in a way that is of immense and immediate benefit to the birds—an integration, all these centuries later, of the many threads that form the tapestry of American bird study: science, sport, and conservation.

The Christmas Bird Count, which started as pure fun, now provides vital data on winter bird populations—while still being a good excuse for some friendly competition. The Breeding Bird Survey, the 1960s brainchild of biologist and field guide author Chandler S. Robbins, has proven to be of immense value for conservation. Every spring, volunteers across the United States and Canada fan out at dawn along thousands of predetermined routes, listening for birdsong and counting what they hear; the BBS has been among the most important pieces of evidence tracing the decline of many groups of birds in the face of habitat loss and fragmentation. Science? Conservation? Yes, obviously; but for many who run those routes year after year, the BBS is also an excuse to enjoy the dawn chorus that makes the breeding season such a joy.

The late Fran Hamerstrom, a pioneer of wildlife research, coined the phrase "birding with a purpose" to describe her lifetime of work, but it neatly sums up most of these emerging citizen-science projects. Here in Pennsylvania, for example, we're in the midst of a five-year revision of the state's breeding-bird atlas—a mammoth undertaking that divides up the state into almost five thousand blocks, each of which are then surveyed by thousands of volunteer birders. It's a reason to explore new areas, hunt down rare species—motivation to get outside.

One reason I love to "atlas" is that it's more than simply ticking off species; the idea is to confirm whether or not a bird is nesting within that block, and so it becomes a treasure hunt, with behavior as the clues. Why is that female cardinal crouching in front of a male, wings quivering and bill agape while he passes her food? That's courtship behavior, one level of confirmation. Why is that red-eyed vireo carrying a beakful of caterpillars? Food for its chicks; another confirmed breeder. And that Baltimore oriole that just dropped a large white blob from its mouth? That was a fecal sac, extruded by a nestling and carried (for sanitary reasons) far from the nest by the parent. Bingo—another confirmed species. Atlasing is an excuse to harness the better angels of our listing nature, combine them with an ever-greater understanding of bird behavior, and employ them for the sake of the birds. The information that comes from such an atlas provides a level of detail regarding bird populations that was previously impossible, and absolutely critical if we're going to preserve vibrant bird populations into the future. And at the same time, participating birders can't help but learn a great deal about the lives of the birds they're chasing.

What I hope will happen—and this is far from a certain outcome—is that as more and more birders become involved in such citizen-science programs, they will develop a greater sense of obligation to the birds themselves. That may seem like an odd thing to worry about; after all, birders would seem to be natural conservationists, dependent upon the birds for their very pastime.

But the sorry truth is, birders as a community have been woefully neglectful of the conservation side of the birding equation. Not all of them, of course; there have always been prominent birders, from Peterson on down, who have lobbied loud and long for avian conservation. But for too many birders, that spirit of listing and competition has overshadowed the more elemental aspects of bird study and diluted what should be a strong and universal voice demanding better care of birds and the natural world on which they depend.

This was brought home to me forcefully several years ago at a birding festival in the Great Lakes. On the last day, I and the other speakers were taking part in a panel discussion and the subject arose of adding a small excise tax to the cost of birding gear like binoculars, feeders, field guides, and seed. It's an idea with a long and successful history; an 11 percent federal tax has been levied on sporting arms and ammunition since 1938, and 10 percent on fishing tackle since 1950; together, they raise hundreds of millions of dollars, mostly for game species conservation, every year.

Yet proposals for similar taxes on birding materials, with the proceeds targeted specifically for non-game-bird conservation programs, were dead in the water. Much of the resistance was coming from retailers, and the panelists were arguing about how to break the logjam. But in the midst of the discussion, my colleague Scott Shalaway asked a question that sliced to the core of the issue.

Addressing the three hundred or so birders in the audience, Scott said, "Let's see a show of hands—how many of you would be willing to pay 10 percent more for sunflower seed and binoculars if you knew the money would be going straight to bird conservation?"

At most, a quarter of the hands went up. "Okay," Scott asked, "how many of you would *not* want to pay any kind of tax, regardless of the amount, to fund bird conservation?" More than half the audience raised their hands. No wonder the funding idea was eventually killed—even the group of people who would most benefit from it wouldn't shoulder the responsibility.

There is among American birders today a residual sense of entitlement—pervasive though obviously not universal, and something that I think is often almost unconscious. Hunters and anglers have had it drummed into their heads for generations that conservation is expensive, and that if they want to enjoy the benefits of healthy wildlife populations, they have to pony up the money. Hunters (and I am one myself) are fiercely and justifiably proud of the money they've contributed over the years—the federal waterfowl stamp funds that buy national wildlife refuge lands, for instance, or the donations to organizations like Ducks Unlimited that have conserved millions of acres of habitat.

Birders, on the other hand, have long enjoyed a sport that is almost entirely free. You need buy no license, take no special training, buy no equipment beyond field glasses and a guide; it can be done anywhere, anytime, with whatever degree of intensity you wish to bring to it. It seems blissfully free of strings.

But, of course, there are strings—the ones that bind us to the birds upon which our joy and excitement depends. No habitat, no birds; it's as simple as that. There may not be 70 million birders in the country, but there are a lot of us—a huge and potentially effective bloc if we raised our voices (and our votes) in unison, demanding better of society and ourselves on behalf of birds.

It needn't be strident activism; you needn't wave placards or storm City Hall. But birders need to become far more vocal on behalf of the things they care about. Work with local conservation groups, and join national organizations like Audubon or the American Bird Conservancy that campaign hard for birds. Buy a federal (and if your state has them, a state) waterfowl stamp, since the money goes straight into land protection and habitat enhancement for many species. If you can, become involved in local land planning, to help steer development in ways that are less destructive to wildlife. Buy shade-grown coffee, to support winter habitat for neo-tropical migrants. Plant your yard with bird-friendly shrubs; eliminate pesticides and herbicides; and if you have a cat, keep it indoors. These are small changes with big impacts.

But most of all, make a conscious decision to work for the birds. One of the biggest steps we can make is to simply recognize that in a world of burgeoning population, diminishing natural habitat, changing climate, and shrinking resources, we cannot take birds for granted.

If you're a birder, I'm willing to bet you're reading those lines and shaking your head, *tsk-tsk*ing that anyone could be so shallow and self-centered as to ignore the wider issues of bird conservation. But ask yourself this question: Can you name a single, concrete action you've taken in the past week to better the world for birds? In the last month? The last year? If you had to think about it for more than a moment, then I gently suggest you rededicate yourself to doing more for the creatures on which our hobby is based.

Bird study has changed over the centuries, from the earliest days of a few eccentric visionaries tramping through the wilderness, to the rise of stuffy academicians smelling faintly of mothballs; it grew from amateur roots to become a profession, then split again into a vigorous hobby with an increasingly general appeal.

Now bird study is poised to enter what could be a fresh and, I hope, golden age. My hope for the future is a fusion of the science of birds with the love of chasing them, the best of the ornithologist and the lister, with a vehement commitment to avian well-being binding these approaches together.

Will that happen? I don't know. But I hope—and more on some nights than others. Like this one.

The temperature has dropped a few more degrees, but the clouds have rolled out, and with them the flurries. The electronic saw-whet still broadcasts its song to the night. We make another trip up the mountainside, walking among the newly leafless oaks. Four more owls in the nets, four more twitching cloth bags dangling from our wrists as we come back to the lodge.

We are not alone; a group of students from the local elementary school are waiting for us with their parents and teacher, third and fourth graders on a rare nighttime field trip. The kids are positively thrumming with excitement, like plucked wires; they jam around me as I pull the first owl out of the bag, a ripple of *ooh*s and *ahh*s as they take in the wide yellow eyes that can make the coldest heart melt. As I band the bird, I am peppered with questions: How does it feel to hold an owl? Can it hurt me? What does it eat? How long will it live? I spread open the wings and explain that it takes an owl several years to replace all its flight feathers; the molt pattern we see means this one is at least three years old. We talk about the dangers that face so small a hunter, the hurdles this female has overcome; the babies she's borne in a hollow tree in Quebec or Maine, the mice whose lives she's ended. The kids touch her reverently, their fingertips just brushing the downy feathers of her head. I finish the measurements, then process the next three birds as I answer a million more questions.

Then, mobbed by the kids, we walk outside, our breath streaming in white clouds. We stand beneath vivid stars, waiting for our eyes (and the owls') to adjust to the dark. At last, we reach into the bags one final time and place the owls on proffered arms and shoulders—where, instead of bolting in fear, they remain contentedly perched for long minutes, these small, winsome birds that seem to have little innate fear of humans.

The kids are breathless; those with owls clinging to their coats tremble with delight. No one speaks; I doubt they could. Then, one by one, the small birds look up at Cassiopeia and Orion wheeling overhead, and on soft, fluttering wings, launch themselves up into the night—and take a bit of us along with them.

I let out a long-held breath and look down; perhaps a seed has been planted, and I can only wonder if the next age of American bird study—one that unites the joy and science, the excitement and commitment, the majesty and responsibility—is reflected somewhere in the delighted faces I see around me in the moonlight.

Acknowledgments

I'M GRATEFUL FOR all the birders who have taken time to chat, reminisce, spin stories, and, most of all, go birding with me over the years, all of whom helped knit together the various strands of this story. Particular thanks go to Kenn Kaufman, David Sibley and Pete Dunne for their help and their leadership in this field, and for reviewing and correcting portions of the manuscript.

For additional help, including tracking down photos and illustrations, I'm grateful to Greg Budney at the Cornell Lab of Ornithology's Macaulay Library, to Ted Floyd and Bryan Patrick at the American Birding Association, Marlene Mudge at the Roger Tory Peterson Institute, Sally Ann Keith, Lisa White of Houghton Mifflin, and to the New York Historical Society, Independence National Historical Park, American Philosophical Society, Historical Society of Pennsylvania, Academy of Natural Sciences of Philadelphia,

Smith College Archives, the Smithsonian Institution Archives, and the Library of Congress.

I am once again obliged to Dr. Keith Bildstein and the staff of Hawk Mountain Sanctuary for the use of their fine ornithological library and archives. Thanks as well to the staff of the John James Audubon Center at Mill Grove, Pennsylvania, and to Seth Benz, director of the Hog Island Audubon Camp in Maine. Special thanks to Oliver James of El Cerrito, California, and to Peter Vickery and Don Mairs for introducing me to Mark Libby's story of pelagic birds on the coast of Maine.

Thanks as well to my longtime agent, Peter Matson, and to my editor at Harcourt, Rebecca Saletan, who first suggested this project and with whom it was a joy to work.

As always, I am most indebted to my wife, Amy, for her patience and support, and in this case, to my parents, Kay and the late Charles Weidensaul, for years ago putting up with a strange kid with a lot of strange passions, including an abiding one for birds. (Mom, I'm still sorry about that woodchuck pelt.)

Finally, thanks to the spiritual heirs of Wilson and Audubon, Griscom and Peterson, Hemenway and Grinnell (both of them), McCaskie and Stallcup—that is, to anyone who has ever caught their breath at the sight of a wild bird.

Notes and Bibliography

CHAPTER 1
Citations

5   "There may be birds": *Great Washington State Birding Trail Site Criteria* (April 2003), http://wa.audubon.org/PDFs/BT-SiteCriteria.pdf.

9   "faire meadows . . . full of Hernes": Quoted in "Jaques Le Moyne, First Zoological Artist in America," Elsa G. Allen, *Auk* 55 (Jan. 1938): 107.

10   "Having discharged our harquebuz-shot": Amadas and Barlowe et al., *The first voyage made to the coasts of America, with two barks, where in were Captaines M. Philip Amadas, and M. Arthur Barlowe, who discovered part of the Countrey now called Virginia, Anno 1584* (London, 1584), http://etext.lib.virginia.edu/etcbin/jamestown-browse?id=J1014.

11   "Squirels, Conies, Black Birds": George Percy, *Observations gathered out of a Discourse of the Plantation of the Southerne Colonie in Virginia by the English, 1606* (London, 1606), http://etext.lib.virginia.edu/etcbin/jamestown-browse?id=J1002.

12   "The Turkyes of that Countrie": Council of Virginia, *A True Declaration of the estate of the Colonie in Virginia, With a confutation of such scandalous reports as have tended to the disgrace of so worthy an enterprise* (London, 1610), 13, http://etext.lib.virginia.edu/etcbin/jamestown-browse?id=J1059.

12   "Fowls of the air": Rev. Francis Higginson, *New-Englands Plantation* (London, 1630; The Winthrop Society, 2003), http://www.winthropsociety.org/doc_higgin.php.

12   "Here are likewise": Ibid.

13   "They are of all colours": Ibid.

13   "Turkie cockes and Turkie hennes": Thomas Hariot, *A briefe and true report of the new found land of Virginia of the commodities and of the nature and manners of the naturall inhabitants* (London, 1588), http://etext.lib.virginia.edu/etcbin/jamestown-browse?id=J1009.

14   "Persons of the meaner Sort": John Lawson, *A New Voyage to Carolina* (London, 1709; University of North Carolina, 2001), iii, http://docsouth.unc.edu/nc/lawson/lawson.html.

14   "Birds in America": Ibid., 134.

14   "I never weigh'd": Ibid., 149.

14   "We all set out": Ibid., 44.

15   "they sing with the greatest Diversity": Ibid., 143.

15   "the Ground-Mocking-Bird": Ibid.

15   "makes a dismal Noise": Ibid., 147.

15   "about the Bigness of a Lark": Ibid., 151.

15   "of a green Colour": Ibid., 142.

15   "which were so numerous": Ibid., 44.

16   "The Humming-Bird is the Miracle": Ibid., 145.

16   "They are really better to us": Ibid., 235.

17   "too remote from *London*": Mark Catesby, *The Natural History of Carolina, Florida, and the Bahama Islands,* vols. 1 and 2 (London 1731–43; University of Wisconsin, 2003), 1: v, http://digital.library.wisc.edu/1711.dl/DLDecArts.CateNatHisV1.

17   "In the Seven Years": Ibid.

18   "which afforded": Ibid., viii.

19   "when they are brought": Ibid., 23.

20   "curious sketch of the natural dispositions": Ibid., 2:vii.

22   "As I was not bred a Painter": Ibid., 1:xi.

22   "I was induced chiefly": Ibid., ix.

23   "big as a middling goose": Lawson, *A New Voyage to Carolina,* 145.

23   "certain and speedy poison": Catesby, *The Natural History of Carolina, Florida, and the Bahama Islands,* 1:10.

24   "Notions so ill attested": Ibid., 2:xxxvi.

25   "The Place to which they retire": Ibid.

25   "most probably Brazil": Ibid.

26   "admitting the World:" Ibid., xxxv.

26   "To account therefore": Ibid.

27   "tall, meagre, hard-favoured": Elsa G. Allen, *The History of American Ornithology before Audubon*, vol. 41 of *Transactions of the American Philosophical Society*, 1951, 470.

32   "I want to put him to some business": Letter to Peter Collinson, Sept. 28, 1755, from William Darlington, *Memorials of John Bartram and Humphrey Marshall with Notices of Their Botanical Contemporaries* (Philadelphia: 1849), 198.

32   "No colouring can do justice": Henry Laurens to John Bartram, 1766, quoted in "Personal Character," *Bartram Heritage*, http://www.bartramtrail.org/pages/biography/bio6.html.

34   "the gay mock-bird": Ibid., 309.

34   "My progress was rendered delightful": Ibid., 49.

35   "the laughing coots": William Bartram, *Travels Through North & South Carolina, Georgia, East & West Florida* (Philadelphia: 1791), 118; Universitätsbibliothek Göttingen, GIF http://www-gdz.sub.uni-goettingen.de/cgi-bin/digbib.cgi? PPN245639845l.

35   "Behold him rushing forth": Ibid., 118.

35   "I was attacked on all sides": Ibid., 119.

36   "a mistake very injurious": Ibid., 299.

36   "we abound with all the fruits": Ibid., 301.

37   "In the spring of the year": Ibid., 288.

38   "disgustingly pompous": Quoted in Francis Harper, *The Travels of William Bartram: Naturalist's Edition* (New Haven: Yale University Press, 1958), xxiv.

38   "no other gratuity": Ibid., 130.

BIBLIOGRAPHY

Allen, Elsa G. "New Light on Mark Catesby." *Auk* 54 (Oct.–Dec. 1937): 349–363.

Banks, Richard C. "Evolution of a Citation." U.S. Geological Survey Patuxent Wildlife Research Center. Laurel, MD, Jan. 6, 2003. http://www.pwrc.usgs.gov/resshow/banks/banks1.htm.

Bartram Trail Conference. *Bartram Heritage*. Montgomery, AL, 1979. http://www.bartramtrail.org/pages/herit.html.

Cashin, Edward J. "William Bartram in Georgia." In *The New Georgia Encyclopedia*, June 28, 2004. http://www.newgeorgiaencyclopedia.org/nge/Article.jsp?id=h-2179.

Cordell, H. Ken, et al. "Outdoor Recreation Participation Trends." In *Outdoor Recreation in American Life*, H. Ken Cordell et al., eds. Champaign, IL: Sagamore Publishing, 1999.

de Vaca, Cabeza. *La relación*. 1555. Electronic edition of the 1851 T. Buckingham Smith translation. http://www.losttrails.com/pages/Tales/devaca_xx.html.

Feduccia, Alan. *Catesby's Birds of Colonial America*. Chapel Hill: University of North Carolina Press, 1985.

Grinnell, George Bird. *Blackfoot Indian Stories*. Old Saybrook, CT: Applewood Books/The Globe Pequot Press, 1993. Facsimile reprint of 1913 edition.

Hall, John C. "William Bartram: First Scientist of Alabama." *Alabama Heritage* 71 (Spring 2004).

Hoijer, Harry, and Morris E. Opler. *Chiricahua and Mescalero Apache Texts*. Chicago: University of Chicago Press, 1938. Electronic edition, University of Virginia, 2001. http://etext.lib.virginia.edu/apache/.

Houston, Lebame, and Wynne Dough. "John White." National Park Service, Manteo, NC. http://www.nps.gov/fora/jwhite.htm.

Jaeger, Edmund C. "Does the Poor-will Hibernate?" *Condor* 50 (Jan. 1948): 45–46.

———. "Further Observations on the Hibernation of the Poor-will." *Condor* 51 (May–June 1949): 105–109.

John Lawson Digital Exhibit. J. Y. Joyner Library, East Carolina State University, Aug. 30, 2004. http://digital.lib.ecu.edu/exhibits/lawson/index.html.

Phillips, Ralph W., et al. *Microlivestock*. Washington, DC: National Academy Press, 1991.

Schorger, A. W. *The Wild Turkey*. Norman, OK: University of Oklahoma Press, 1966.

Snyder, Noel. *The Carolina Parakeet*. Princeton, NJ: Princeton University Press, 2004.

Stone, Witmer, "Mark Catesby and the Nomenclature of North American Birds." *Auk* 46 (Oct.–Dec. 1929): 447–454.

U.S. Department of the Interior, U.S. Fish and Wildlife Service, U.S. Department of Commerce, and U.S. Census Bureau. *2001 National Survey of Fishing, Hunting, and Wildlife-Associated Recreation*. Washington, DC, Oct. 2002.

Williams, James J. "North America's Topflight Sewage Ponds." *Birding* 34 (June 2002): 228–235.

CHAPTER 2
Citations

44   "The enclosed poem": Quoted in Robert Cantwell, *Alexander Wilson: Naturalist and Pioneer*. (Philadelphia and New York: Lippincott, 1961), 267.

45   "the police and British agents": Ibid., 68.

46   "He looked like a bird": Charles Robert Leslie, quoted in "A Wilson Memorial," Bayard H. Christy, *Wilson Bulletin* 76 (Jan.–Mar. 1937): 19.

47   "good nature will excuse": Quoted in "Alexander Wilson: IV: The Making of the American Ornithology," Frank L. Burns, *Wilson Bulletin* 20 (Oct.–Dec. 1908): 167.

47   "I have now got": Ibid., 168.

48   "amusement and correction": Ibid.

48   "some beautiful native ochres": Quoted in Frank L. Burns, "Alexander Wilson IV: The Making of the American Ornithology," *Wilson Bulletin* 20 (Oct.–Dec. 1908): 170.

48   "so there should be no chance": Bayard H. Christy, *Wilson Bulletin* 76 (Jan.–Mar. 1937): 20.

50   "I would not give you": Quoted in Frank L. Burns, "Alexander Wilson IV: The Making of the American Ornithology," *Wilson Bulletin* 20 (Oct.–Dec. 1908): 173.

51   "would give two thousand two hundred and thirty millions": Alexander Wilson, *American Ornithology* (Philadelphia: Bradsford and Inskeep, 1812): 108.

52   "Science and literature": Quoted in Frank L. Burns, "Alexander Wilson I: The Audubon Controversy," *Wilson Bulletin* 20 (Jan.–Mar. 1908): 10.

53   "My days were happy": *Audubon and His Journals*, vols. 1 and 2, Maria R. Audubon (New York: Scribner, 1897; facsimile edition, Mineola, NY: Dover Books 1994), 1:28.

53   "I seldom passed": Ibid., 29.

53   "through the beautiful": Ibid., 30.

55   "graceful attitudes": Ibid., 2:523.

55   "grotesque figure": Ibid., 524.

57   "stamped his countenance": Ibid., 201.

57   "My dear Audubon": Ibid.

59   "surprise appeared to be great": Ibid.

61   "Nearly a full year": Cantwell, 240.

62   "there was no distinction": Ibid., 236.

62   "very much respected": Quoted in Frank L. Burns, "Miss Lawson's Recollections of Ornithologists," *Auk* 34 (July–Sept. 1917): 279.

62   "I have been extremely busy": Quoted in Frank L. Burns, "Alexander Wilson IV: the Making of the American Ornithology." *Wilson Bulletin* 20 (Oct.–Dec. 1908): 185.

66   "the most magnificent monument": Quoted in Alice Ford, *John James Audubon*, rev. ed. (New York: Abbeville Press, 1988), 487.

68   "The same sad heart to-day": *Audubon and His Journals*, 1:159.

68   "juicy venison": Ibid., 2:317.

70   "we may plant": William Bartram, *Travels Through North & South Carolina, Georgia, East & West Florida* (Philadelphia, 1791), 288. Universitätsbibliothek Göttingen, GIF http://www-gdz.sub.uni-goettingen.de/cgi-bin/digbib .cgi? PPN245639845l.

74   "a beautiful bird": Ibid., 151.

75   "purely mythical species": J. A. Allen, quoted in Francis Harper, "The *Vultur sacra* of William Bartram," *Auk* 53 (Oct.–Dec. 1936): 381–392.

BIBLIOGRAPHY

Anon. "Paisley History," 2006. http://www.paisley.org.uk/history/index.php.

Banks, Richard C. *Obsolete English Names of North American Birds and Their Modern Equivalents.* National Museum of Natural History, Washington, DC. Undated. http://www.pwrc.usgs.gov/research/pubs/banks/obsall.htm.

Burns, Frank L. "Alexander Wilson II: The Mystery of the Small-Headed Flycatcher." *Wilson Bulletin* 20 (Apr.–June 1908): 63–79.

———. "Alexander Wilson III: The Unsuccessful Lover." *Wilson Bulletin* 20 (July–Sept. 1908): 130–145.

———. "Alexander Wilson IV: The Making of 'The American Ornithology.'" *Wilson Bulletin* 20 (Oct.–Dec. 1908): 165–185.

———. "Alexander Wilson V: The Completion of 'The American Ornithology.'" *Wilson Bulletin* 21 (Jan.–Mar. 1909): 16–35.

———. "Alexander Wilson VI: His Nomenclature," *Wilson Bulletin* 21 (July–Sept. 1909): 132–151.

———. "Alexander Wilson VII: Biographies, Portraits and a Bibliography of the Various Editions of His Work." *Wilson Bulletin* 21 (Dec. 1909): 165–186.

———. "Alexander Wilson VIII: His Early Life and Writings." *Wilson Bulletin* 22 (Mar.–April 1910): 79–96.

———. "The Mechanical Execution of Wilson's 'American Ornithology.'" *Wilson Bulletin* (Jan.–Mar. 1929): 19–23.

Burtt, Edward H. Jr., and William E. Davis Jr. "Historic and Taxonomic Implications of Recently Found Artwork in Arithemic Books of Students of Alexander Wilson's." *Wilson Bulletin* 107 (June 1995): 193–213.

Burtt, Edward H. Jr., William E. Davis Jr., and Alan P. Peterson. "Alexander Wilson and the Founding of North American Ornithology." In *Contributions to the History of North American Ornithology,* ed. William E. Davis Jr. and Jerome A. Jackson. Cambridge, MA: Nuttall Ornithological Club, 1995.

Choate, Ernest A. *The Dictionary of American Bird Names,* rev. ed. Ed. Raymond A. Paynter Jr. Boston: Harvard Common Press, 1985.

Christy, Bayard H. "Alexander Lawson's Bird Engravings." *Auk* 43 (Jan. 1926): 47–61.

Davidson, Marshall B. *The Original Water-color Paintings by John James Audubon for 'The Birds of America.'* New York: American Heritage Publishing, 1966.

Deane, Ruthven. "Some Original Manuscript Relating to the History of Townsend's Bunting." *Auk* 27 (July 1909): 269–272.

Durant, Mary, and Michael Harwood. *On the Road with John James Audubon.* New York: Dodd, Mead, 1980.

Dwight, Edward H. *Audubon: Watercolors and Drawings.* Utica and New York, NY: Munson-Williams-Proctor Institute and Pierpont Morgan Library, 1965.

Ford, Alice. *John James Audubon.* Rev. ed. New York: Abbeville Press, 1988.

Gill, Frank B. "Philadelphia: 180 Years of Ornithology at the Academy of Natural Sciences." In *Contributions to the History of North American Ornithology*, ed. William E. Davis Jr. and Jerome A. Jackson. Cambridge, MA: Nuttall Ornithological Club, 1995.

Greenway, J. Jr. "A Jefferson Letter of Historical and Ornithological Interest." *Auk* 48 (Apr. 1931): 175–180.

Holt, Jeff. "Notes on Audubon's 'Mystery Birds.'" *Cassinia* 70 (2002–2003): 22–25.

Miller, Ashley. "Majesty Sublime: Alexander Wilson's Epic 1804 Walk from Philadelphia to Niagara Falls." Mann Library online exhibit, Cornell University 2004. http://exhibits.mannlib.cornell.edu/majestysublime/.

Rothstein, Edward. "A Rare Sighting of Audubon Prepares to Take Flight." *New York Times*, March 17, 2005.

Snyder, Noel, and Helen Snyder. *Birds of Prey*. Stillwater, MN: Voyageur Press, 1991.

Souder, William. *Under a Wild Sky*. New York: North Point Press, 2004.

Taylor, Mrs. H. J. "Alexander Wilson: A Sketch." *Wilson Bulletin* 35 (June 1928): 74–84.

Terres, John K. *Audubon Society Encyclopedia of North American Birds*. New York: Alfred A. Knopf, 1980.

CHAPTER 3
Citations

80   "wide and fertile vallies": Meriwether Lewis, quoted in *The Journals of Lewis and Clark*, ed. Bernard DeVoto. (New York: Houghton Mifflin, 1953), 99.

80   "The whol face of the country": Ibid.

82   "furious and formidable anamal" and "it is asstonishing": Ibid., 103.

82   "In the hands": Ibid.

87   "Heads of Lewis River": Quoted in "Selected Letters of Nathaniel J. Wyeth," Library of Western Fur Trade Historical Documents, http://www.xmission .com/~drudy/mtman/html/.

88   "I think I never before saw": John Townsend, May 28, 1834. *Narrative of a Journey across the Rocky Mountains to the Columbia River*, http://www .xmission.com/~drudy/mtman/html/townsend/chap4.html.

89   "It is noble": Ibid., Mar. 20, 1834.

89   "compelled all day": Ibid., June 22, 1834.

89   "a renewal": Ibid., July 4, 1834.

89   "I gave the men too much alcohol": Nathaniel J. Wyeth, July 4, 1832. *Journal of Captain Nathaniel J. Wyeth's Expeditions to the Oregon Country: First Expedition, 1832*. http://www.xmission.com/%7Edrudy/mtman/html/ wyeth1.html.

89   "From this time": Townsend, June 30, 1834.

90   "Already we have cast away": Ibid., May 25, 1834.

90   "The temptation was too great": Ibid., Sept. 2, 1834.

90   "appetite for ardent spirits": Ibid., July 4, 1835.

91   "an unhappy, bitter man": Frank B. Gill, "Philadelphia: 180 Years of Ornithology at the Academy of Natural Sciences," in *Contributions to the History of North American Ornithology,* ed. William E. Davis Jr. and Jerome A. Jackson (Cambridge, MA: Nuttall Ornithological Club, 1995), 10.

92   "How grand and impressive": John James Audubon, *Ornithological Biography,* 4:1.

93   "drunk, and many in that stupid mood": *Audubon and His Journals,* 1:455.

94   "Seeing a great number of Parrakeets": Ibid., 468.

94   "Killed a Cat-bird": Ibid., 470.

94   "I shot a Wild Pigeon": Ibid., 473.

95   "a new finch, and very curious": Ibid., 470.

98   "the finest sight of all": Ibid., 2:28.

98   "What a terrible destruction of life": Ibid., 107.

98   "Handsome, and really courteous": Ibid., 111.

99   "with little or no effect": Ibid., 95.

101   "that I have no doubt": Ibid., 163–164.

102   "Had he merely stuck to painting birds": Quoted in Alice Ford, *John James Audubon,* rev. ed. (New York: Abbeville Press, 1988), 427.

102   "most kindly, gentle, benignant woman": George Bird Grinnell, "Recollections of Audubon Park," *Auk* 37 (July–Sept. 1920): 373.

103   "In the hall were antlers": Ibid., 374.

103   "Boylike, I treasured this memory": Ibid., 379.

104   "Dear young friend": Ibid., 377.

104   "with all the care": Ibid.

BIBLIOGRAPHY

Cassin, John. *Illustrations of the Birds of California, Texas, Oregon, British and Russian America.* Facsimile ed. with intro. by Robert McCracken Peck. Austin, TX: Texas State Historical Society, 1991.

Davis, William B., and James Stevenson. "Type Localities of Three Birds Collected by Lewis and Clark in 1806." *Condor* 36 (July 1934): 161–163.

Evans, Howard Ensign. *The Natural History of the Long Expedition to the Rocky Mountains.* New York: Oxford University Press, 1997.

Fisher, Albert K. "In Memorium: George Bird Grinnell." *Auk* 56 (Jan. 1939): 1–12.

Goode, George Brown. *The Smithsonian Institution 1846–1895: The History of its First Half-Century.* Washington, DC, 1897. National Oceanic and Atmospheric Administration, 2004. http://www.history.noaa.gov/giants/baird3.html.

Hall, George. "Ornithological Literature." *Wilson Bulletin* 85 (Dec. 1973): 521–522.

Harwood, Michael. "Mr. Audubon's Last Hurrah." *Audubon* 87 (Nov. 1985): 80–117.

Holt, Jeff. "Wilson, Audubon, Ord and a Flycatcher." *Cassinia* 70 (2002–2003): 11–21.

"J.G." "Notes and News" (discussion of William Gambel's death). *Condor* 41 (May 1939): 128.

Muhly, Frank. "Firm Foundations in Philadelphia: The Lewis and Clark Expedition's Ties to Pennsylvania." *Pennsylvania Heritage* (Summer 2001), 14.

National Park Service. "Fort Union Trading Post" http://www.nps.gov/fous/.

Nuttall, Thomas. *A Manual of Ornithology of the United States.* Vol. 1, 2nd ed. Boston: Hillard, Gray and Co., 1840.

Powell, Nancy. "Provenance of Audubon's oil painting 'The Eagle and the Lamb.'" Pers. comm., May 12, 2006.

Stevens, O.A. "The First Descriptions of North American Birds." *Wilson Bulletin* (Sept. 1936), 203–215.

Taylor, J. Golden, and Thomas J. Lyon, eds. *A Literary History of the American West.* Fort Worth, TX: Texas Christian University Press, 1987.

Townsend, John K. *Narrative of a Journey across the Rocky Mountains to the Columbia River.* Introduction by George A. Jobanek. Corvallis, OR: Oregon State University Press, 1999.

Walton, Richard K. "At the Feet of the Eagle." *Birding* 22, no. 5 (October 1990): 217–221.

Wyeth, Nathaniel. "Selected Letters of Nathaniel J. Wyeth." http://www.xmission .com/~drudy/mtman/html/wyethltr.html#3.

CHAPTER 4
Citations

109   "able-bodied men": Recruiting advertisement, Indianapolis *Journal,* Feb. 8, 1847, quoted in "First Dragoons," March 21, 2005, http://www.musketoon .com/.

112   "but a single": Charles E. Bendire, *Life Histories of North American Birds,* vol. 1 (New York: Arno Press, 1974, facsimile edition of Smithsonian Institution Special Bulletin 1, 1892), 231–232.

113   "Climbing to the nest": Ibid.

113   "and a rather uncomfortably large": Ibid.

113   "I returned to that place": Ibid.

116   "the most unreliable man ever": Quoted in Gordon M. Meade, "Surgeons, Birds and the U.S. Army: Part II," *Birding* 19 (June 1987): 14.

116   "The inflection of the Prairie Warbler's notes": Elliott Coues, *Birds of the Northwest* (Washington, DC: U.S. Geological Survey of the Territories, 1874), 64.

118   "To those who would charge": Paul Russell Cutright and Michael J. Brodhead, *Elliott Coues: Naturalist and Frontier Historian* (Urbana, IL: University of Illinois Press, 1981), 429.

119   "slender, pale-faced": Ibid., 52.

121   "thousands of miles": *Ibis* (Oct. 1865), 536.

124   "a kind of academy": Quoted in Maxine Benson, *Martha Maxwell: Rocky Mountain Naturalist* (Lincoln, NE: University of Nebraska Press, 1986), 97.

128   "seemed a bit too cocksure": Quoted in Wendell Taber, "In Memorium: Charles Foster Batchelder," *Auk* 75 (Jan.–Mar. 1958): 19.

129   "overmodest young gentlemen": Quoted in Charles F. Batchelder, "An Account of the Nuttall Ornithological Club," in *Contributions to the History of American Ornithology.* Ed. Keir B. Sterling (New York: Arno Press, 1974): 39.

130   "did not 'know a hawk from a handsaw',": Quoted in Harry Harris, "Robert Ridgway," *Condor* 30 (Jan.–Feb. 1928): 16.

133   "that most abhorred and abhorrable occupation": Quoted in Paul H. Oehser, "In Memorium: Florence Merriam Bailey," *Auk* 69 (Jan.–Mar. 1952): 20.

134   "Focus your glass on the meadow": Florence Merriam, *Birds Through an Opera-Glass* (Cleveland, OH: Chautauqua Press, 1889), 40–41.

137   Every town of any considerable size: John Burroughs, *Signs and Seasons,* reprint of the 1886 original (New York: Harper Colophon, 1981), 225–230.

138   "wanton destruction": Quoted in "A.C. Bent's application for a collecting permit (1887), with outline of his plan for ornithological research," Ralph W. Dexter, *Bird Banding* 35 (Apr. 1964): 121–122.

138   "small collection": Ibid.

142   *"All you can get"*: Elliott Coues, *Key to North American Birds,* vol. 1, 5th ed. (Boston: Dana Estes and Co., 1903), 12–15.

142   "Say fifty or a hundred": Ibid.

143   "Birdskins are a medium of exchange": Coues, *Key to North American Birds,* 1:13.

143   "There are too many inspired idiots": Quoted in "Dr. Elliott Coues—A Sketch," Mrs. J. H. Taylor, *Wilson Bulletin* 41 (Oct.–Dec. 1929): 223.

143   "The shotgun people": Quoted in "Dr. Elliott Coues—A Sketch," Mrs. H.J. Taylor, *Wilson Bulletin* 41 (Oct.–Dec. 1929): 223.

144   "I do not protect birds": Quoted in Mark V. Barrow Jr., *A Passion for Birds* (Princeton, NJ: Princeton University Press, 1998), 141.

BIBLIOGRAPHY

Anon. "Spencer Baird's Vision for a National Museum." Smithsonian Institution. http://siarchives.si.edu/history/exhibits/baird/bairdhm.htm.

Arcese, P., M. K. Sogge, A. B. Marr, and M. A. Patten. "Song Sparrow (*Melospiza melodia*)." In *The Birds of North America,* no. 704. Ed. A. Poole and F. Gill. Philadelphia: Birds of North America, 2002.

Banks, Richard C., et al. "Forty-seventh Supplement to the American Ornithologists' Union *Check-List of North American Birds.*" *Auk* 123 (July–Sept. 2006): 926–936.

Banks, Richard C. "Ornithology at the U.S. National Museum of Natural History." In *Contributions to the History of North American Ornithology.* Ed. William E. Davis Jr. and Jerome A. Jackson. Cambridge, MA: Nuttall Ornithological Club, 1995.

Barrow, Mark V. Jr. *A Passion for Birds.* Princeton, NJ: Princeton University Press, 1998.

Batchelder, Charles F. "An Account of the Nuttall Ornithological Club, 1873–1919." In *Contributions to the History of American Ornithology.* Ed. Keir B. Sterling. New York: Arno Press, 1974 reprint.

Bonta, Marcia M. *American Women Afield.* College Station, TX: Texas A&M Press, 1995.

Brandt, Herbert. *Arizona and its Bird Life.* Cleveland, OH: Bird Research Foundation, 1951.

Coues, Elliott. *Birds of the Colorado Valley.* Washington, DC: U.S. Geological Survey of the Territories, 1878.

Gehlbach, Frederick R. *Mountain Islands and Desert Seas.* College Station, TX: Texas A&M Press, 1993.

Grinnell, Joseph. "Old Fort Tejon." *Condor* 7 (Jan. 1905): 9–13.

Harris, Harry. "Robert Ridgway." *Condor* 30 (Jan.–Feb. 1928): 5–118.

Henshaw, Henry W. "In Memorium: William Brewster." *Auk* 37 (Jan.–Mar. 1920): 1–23.

Hoose, Phil. *The Race to Save the Lord God Bird.* New York: Farrar, Straus & Giroux, 2004.

Johnson, S. R., and R. W. Campbell. "Crested Myna (*Acridotheres cristatellus*)." In *The Birds of North America,* no. 157. Ed. A. Poole and F. Gill. Philadelphia: The Academy of Natural Sciences, and Washington, DC: American Ornithologists' Union, 1995.

Lowther, P. E., and C. L. Cink. "House Sparrow (*Passer domesticus*)." In *The Birds of North America,* no. 12. Ed. A. Poole, P. Stettenheim, and F. Gill. Philadelphia: The Academy of Natural Sciences, and Washington, DC: American Ornithologists' Union, 1992.

McAtee, W. L. "Economic Ornithology." In *Contributions to the History of American Ornithology.* Ed. Keir B. Sterling. New York: Arno Press, 1974 reprint.

Mindell, David P. "Harlan's Hawk (*Buteo jamaicensis harlani*): A Valid Subspecies." *Auk* 100 (Jan. 1983): 161–169.

Palmer, T. S. "A Brief History of the American Ornithologists' Union." American Ornithologists' Union, 1933. Reprinted in *Contributions to the History of American Ornithology.* Ed. Keir B. Sterling. New York: Arno Press, 1974.

————. "Notes on Persons Whose Names Appear in the Nomenclature of California Birds." *Condor* 30 (Sept.–Oct. 1928): 261–307.

Phillips, Allan, Joe Marshall, and Gale Monson. *The Birds of Arizona.* Tucson, AZ: University of Arizona Press, 1978.

Preston, C. R., and R. D. Beane. "Red-tailed Hawk (*Buteo jamaicensis*)." In *The Birds of North America,* no. 52. Ed. A. Poole and F. Gill. Philadelphia: The Academy of Natural Sciences, and Washington, DC: American Ornithologists' Union, 1993.

Snyder, Noel. *The Carolina Parakeet.* Princeton, NJ: Princeton University Press, 2004.

Sprot, G. D. "Notes on the Introduced Skylark in the Victoria District of Vancouver Island." *Condor* 39 (Jan. 1937): 24–31.

Stone, Witmer. "Philadelphia to the Coast in Early Days, and the Development of Western Ornithology Prior to 1850." *Condor* 18 (Jan.–Feb. 1916): 3–14.

Tanner, James T. *The Ivory-billed Woodpecker.* New York: National Audubon Society, 1942.

Taverner, P. A. "Taxonomic Comments on Red-tailed Hawks." *Condor* 38 (Mar. 1936): 66–71.

Taylor, Mrs. H. J. "Pioneers in Economic Ornithology." *Wilson Bulletin* 43 (July–Sept. 1931): 177–189.

Wood, Norman. "Harlan's Hawk." *Wilson Bulletin* 44 (June 1932): 78–87.

CHAPTER 5
Citations

150   "an Association for the protection of wild birds": George Bird Grinnell, *Forest and Stream,* Feb. 11, 1886, 41.

151   There, strewn on the floating water weed: A. E. H. Mattingley, quoted in Arthur Cleveland Bent, *Life Histories of North American Marsh Birds* (Washington, DC: Smithsonian Institution, 1926), 153.

152   "There, notebook in hand": Frank M. Chapman, *Autobiography of a Bird-Lover* (New York: D. Appleton-Century, 1933), 38.

154   "Fashion decrees feathers": George Bird Grinnell, *Forest and Stream,* Nov. 15, 1888, 321.

157   "We marked the ladies": Quoted in Frank Graham Jr., *The Audubon Ark* (Austin, TX: Un. of Texas Press, 1992): 15.

157   "Although Harriet Hemenway": Ibid.

157   "She was aware": Ibid.

159   "this increasingly popular branch of nature study": Florence Merriam, *Birds of Village and Field* (Boston: Houghton Mifflin, 1898), iv.

159   In a shrubby back yard: Ibid., iii–iv.

160   "Where he should have received encouragement": William Dutcher, "Results of Special Protection to Gulls and Terns Obtaned Through the Thayer Fund," *Auk* 18 (Jan.–Mar. 1901): 76.

162   "I do not understand": Theodore Roosevelt to Frank Chapman, printed in "Letter from Governor Roosevelt," *Bird-Lore* 1 (April 1899): 65.

162   "as if he were a sentient being": Olive Thorne Miller, "On the Ethics of Caging Birds," *Bird-Lore* 1 (June 1899): 90.

162   "toying with ornithology": Elliott Coues, quoted in Paul Russell Cutright and Michael J. Brodhead, *Elliott Coues: Naturalist and Frontier Historian* (Urbana, IL: University of Illinois Press, 1981), 399.

163   "Too proud to accept help": Marcia Bonta, *American Women Afield* (College Station, TX: Texas A&M, 1995), 115.

164   "How or why Wright learned so much about birds": Deborah Strom, *Birdwatching with American Women* (New York: W. W. Norton, 1986), 145.

166   "Every time you children": Mabel Osgood Wright and Elliott Coues, *Citizen Bird* (New York: MacMillan, 1907), 61.

166   "earning his living": Ibid., 243.

166   "a good friend to horses and cattle": Ibid., 286.

166   "An analysis of the food": T. Gilbert Pearson, *Birds of America* (Garden City, NY: Garden City Publishing, 1936), 139.

167   "Porter, a quintessential Victorian": Felton Gibbons and Deborah Strom, *Neighbors to the Birds* (New York: W. W. Norton, 1988), 186–187.

167   "really bad cannibals": Wright and Coues, *Citizen Bird* (New York: MacMillan, 1907), 341.

167   "From the economic standpoint": George Miksch Sutton, *Birds of Pennsylvania* (Harrisburg, PA: J. Horace McFarland Co., 1928), 6.

168   "a felon . . . on trial for high crimes and misdemeanors": Althea R. Sherman, "Down with the House Wren Boxes," *Wilson Bulletin* 37 (Mar. 1925): 4.

168   "criminal character": Ibid., 6.

168   "Capital punishment has not been demanded": Ibid., 12.

169   "The main question right now": T. C. Stephens, "Editorial," *Wilson Bulletin* 37 (June 1925): 90.

169   "additional evidence of the viciousness of this species": Althea R. Sherman, "Additional Evidence Against the House Wren," *Wilson Bulletin* 37 (Sept. 1925): 130.

169   "the contemptuous leering of incredulity," Ibid.

169   "The Wren's methods are no worse": Witmer Stone, "Miss Sherman on the House Wren," *Auk* 42 (July 1925): 461.

171   "At last a miracle": Quoted in Peter Edge, "A Most Determined Lady," Hawk Mountain Sanctuary Association, http://www.hawkmountain.org/default/rosalie_edge.htm.

172   "Rosalie Edge sailed almost without warning": Frank Graham Jr., *Audubon Ark* (New York: Knopf, 1990), 112.

175   "More than twenty years ago": Mabel Osgood Wright, *Birdcraft*, 9th ed. (New York: Macmillan and Co., 1936), iii.

178   "It is to be hoped": Anon., *Bulletin of the Nuttall Ornithological Club* 8 (1883): 236.
178   "is the element of competition": Witmer Stone, "Griscom on problems of Field Identification," *Auk* 53 (Apr. 1936): 239.
179   "The present day arguments": Ibid., 238.
181   "It will be my life work": Arthur Cleveland Bent, quoted in Wendell Taber, "In Memorium: Arthur Cleveland Bent," *Auk* 72 (Oct. 1955): 338.
183   "The resultant storm of criticism": Ludlow Griscom, "Problems of Field Identification," *Auk* 39 (Jan. 1932): 31.
185   "With the great growth in recent years": Ludlow Griscom, "Role of the Amateur," *Bulletin of Northeastern Bird-Banding Association* 5 (Jan. 1929): 19.

BIBLIOGRAPHY

No finer history of the founding and growth pains of the National Audubon Society exists than Frank Graham Jr.'s marvelous book *The Audubon Ark* (New York: Knopf, 1990), on which I leaned heavily for this chapter.

Allen, J. A. "Bendire's 'Life Histories of North American Birds.'" *Auk* 9 (Oct.–Dec. 1892): 375–376.
Anon. "Christmas Bird Count: History & Objectives." National Audubon Society, 2005. http://www.audubon.org/bird/cbc/history.html.
Babcock, Charles A. *Bird Day: How to Prepare for it*. New York: Silver, Burdett and Co., 1901.
Brett, James. "American Conservation's 'Glorious Joan of Arc.'" *Hawk Mountain News* 62 (Sept. 1984): 4–14.
Broun, Maurice. *Hawks Aloft*. Kutztown, PA: Kutztown Publishing Co., 1948.
Gibbons, Felton, and Deborah Strom. *Neighbors to the Birds*. New York: W. W. Norton, 1988.
Fisher, Albert Kenrick. "In Memorium: George Bird Grinnell." *Auk* 56 (Jan.–Mar. 1939): 1–12.
Harwood, Michael. *The View from Hawk Mountain*. New York: Scribner's, 1973.
LeBaron, Geoffrey S. "The 105th Christmas Bird Count." *American Birds* 59 (2004–2005): 2–7.
Manson, Kathy S. "Out of Fashion: Harriet Hemenway and the Audubon Society, 1896–1905." *Historian* 65 (Fall 2002): 1–14.
McIver, Stuart B. *Death in the Everglades*. Gainesville, FL: University Press of Florida, 2003.
Palmer, T. S. "In Memorium: William Dutcher." *Auk* 38 (Oct.–Dec. 1921): 501–513.
Pearson, T. Gilbert. "Fifty Years of Bird Protection in the United States." In *Contributions to the History of American Ornithology*. Ed. Keir B. Sterling. New York: Arno Press, 1974 reprint.

Price, Jennifer. "Hats Off to Audubon." *Audubon* 106 (Nov.–Dec. 2004): 44–50.

Stinson, John D. "National Audubon Society Records, 1883–1991." New York Public Library, March 1994. http://www.nypl.org/research/chss/spe/rbk/faids/nas.pdf.

Trefethen, James B. *Crusade for Wildlife*. Harrisburg, PA: Stackpole, 1961.

Vuilleumier, François. "Dean of American Ornithologists: The Multiple Legacies of Frank M. Chapman of the American Museum of Natural History." *Auk* 122 (Apr. 2005): 389–402.

Wright, Mabel Osgood. *Birdcraft*. 9th ed. New York, 1936, Macmillan and Co.

CHAPTER 6
Citations

194   "For the first time": Frank M. Chapman, *Autobiography of a Bird-Lover* (New York: D. Appleton-Century Co., 1933), 32.

194   "The day of the bird collector": Ibid., 190.

195   "His sentiment is the wholesome every-day sort": Florence Merriam, *Birds Through an Opera-Glass* (Cleveland, OH: Chautauqua Press, 1889), 5.

196   "the identification of the bird in the bush": Frank M. Chapman, *Color Key to North American Birds* (New York: Doubleday, 1903), vii.

196   "perfect reproductions of every shade": Ibid., x.

198   "Dealer in Instruments": Charles K. Reed, *Illustrated Price-List of Naturalists' Supplies and Books* (Worcester, MA: 1890), cover.

199   "Prowling the fields and thickets": Alan Devoe, quoted in *The Bird Watcher's Anthology*, ed. Roger Tory Peterson. (New York: Bonanza Books, 1957), 46.

204   "By and by he got a book": Ernest Thompson Seton, *Two Little Savages* (New York: Manhattan Press, 1903), 385–386.

204   "These he afterward carefully finished": Ibid., 393.

204   "Gadwall or Gray Duck (*Anas strepera*)": Ibid., 386.

205   "Griscom was our god": Roger Tory Peterson, in *Birds of Massachusetts*, ed. Richard R. Veit and Wayne R. Petersen, (Lincoln, MA: Massachusetts Audubon Society, 1993), xi.

205   "Had it not been for Ludlow Griscom": Ibid.

206   "wherein live birds": Roger Tory Peterson, *A Field Guide to the Birds*, rev. ed. (Boston: Houghton Mifflin, 1939), v.

207   "No attempt has been made": John B. May, "Recent Literature," *Bird-Banding* 5 (July–Sept. 1934): 146.

209   "Birds have their love-and-mating song": E. B. White, "The Listener's Guide to Birds."

209   "In this century": Paul Ehrlich, David Dobkin, and Darryl Wheye, *The Birder's Handbook* (New York: Fireside, 1988), 563.

210   "It could be argued": Pete Dunne, "Roger Tory Peterson, 1908–1996," *Birding* 28 (Sept. 1996): 357.

222 "It was clear the book wanted to be born": Joan Walsh, quoted in "Zaaaaaa zoooo!" Jeff Klinkenberg, *St. Petersburg Times,* Oct. 5, 2000, http://www.sptimes.com/News/100500/news_pf/Floridian/zaaaaaa_zooooooo.shtml.

BIBLIOGRAPHY

Armistead, Henry, Ron Naveen, Claudia Wilds, Will Russell, Lawrence Balch, and Roger Tory Peterson. "Bird Book Wars." *Birding* 13 (Aug. 1981): 116–128.

Bull, John, and John Farrand Jr. *National Audubon Society Field Guide to North American Birds.* New York: Knopf, 1977.

Carlson, Douglas. "Peterson, the *Guide,* and the Times." *Birding* 37 (Sept.–Oct. 2005): 524–527.

Cruickshank, Allan D. *Cruickshank's Pocket Guide to the Birds.* New York: Dodd, Mead & Co., 1953.

Devlin, John C., and Grace Naismith. *The World of Roger Tory Peterson.* New York: Times Books, 1977.

Drennan, Susan Roney. "In Memoriam: Roger Tory Peterson, 1908–1996," *Auk* 115 (Apr. 1998): 465–469.

Farrand, John Jr., ed. *Audubon Society Master Birding Guide.* New York: Knopf, 1983.

Harrison, Peter. *Seabirds.* Boston: Houghton Mifflin, 1983.

Hayman, Peter, John Marchant, and Tony Prater. *Shorebirds.* Boston: Houghton Mifflin, 1986.

Hess, Paul. "Sixty Visionary Years" (Chandler S. Robbins). *Birding* XX (July–Aug. 2006): 26–27.

Hoffmann, Ralph. *A Guide to the Birds of New England and Eastern New York.* Boston: Houghton Mifflin, 1904.

Jonsson, Lars. *Birds of Europe.* Princeton, NJ: Princeton University Press, 1993.

Parkes, Kenneth C. "Reviews." *Auk* 84 (Apr. 1967): 282–283.

Reed, Chester A. *Bird Guide: Land Birds East of the Rockies* and *Water Birds, Game Birds, and Birds of Prey.* Garden City, NY: Doubleday, 1906.

Robbins, Chandler S., Bertel Bruun, and Herbert S. Zim. *Birds of North America.* Racine, WI: Golden Press, 1966.

Schaffner, Spencer. "Birding with the First American Field Guides to Birds." *Birding* 37 (Jan.–Feb. 2005): 90–93.

Seigel, Steven. "Century-old Books that Set Birding Free." *Birding* 36 (June 2003): 294–298.

Sibley, David Allen. *The Sibley Guide to Birds.* New York: Knopf, 2000.

Siebenheller, Norma. "Nuttall's Manual." *Bird Watcher's Digest* (Sept.–Oct. 2006): 62–66.

CHAPTER 7
Citations

231   "Bird watching is old enough": Joseph J. Hickey, *A Guide to Bird Watching* (New York: Oxford Un. Press, 1943), 3.

231   "Bird watching today": Ibid., 4.

235   "Collecting has proven": Roger Tory Peterson, *A Field Guide to Western Birds,* 2nd ed. (Boston: Houghton Mifflin, 1961), 153.

237   "not whistled reproductions": Witmer Stone, "Recent Literature," *Auk* 51 (July 1934): 409.

237   "Here are the bird song recordings": J. Van Tyne, "Ornithological Literature," *Wilson Bulletin* 54 (June 1942): 148.

238   "Voice descriptions vary": Roger Tory Peterson, *A Field Guide to the Birds,* 2nd ed. (Boston: Houghton Mifflin, 1947), 152.

241   "Our field-records": Joseph Grinnell, quoted in "Grinnellian Methodology," Museum of Vertebrate Zoology, July 2001, http://www.mip.berkeley.edu/mvz/history/GrinnellianMethodology.html.

241   "There were trap lines to be visited": Hilda Wood Grinnell, "Joseph Grinnell: 1877–1939," *Condor* 42 (Jan. 1940), 10.

244   "It has been the privilege": W. B. Alexander, *Birds of the Ocean* (New York: G.P. Putnam's Sons, 1928), iii.

244   "It is hoped": Ibid.

244   "unless it should be a species still unknown to science": Ibid.

250   "Mentor is not the right word": Rich Stallcup, quoted in Oliver James, unpublished oral history (pers. comm.).

251   "So we did a lot of sneaking": Ibid.

252   "I thought it would be great": Ibid.

252   "There were almost no visitors": Ibid.

255   "The way it was before": Ibid.

255   "No one can see": Susan Roney Drennan, "McCaskie as Mentor," *American Birds* vol. 46 (1992): 204.

258   "It would be nice": James A. Tucker, "*Birding* and Conservation," *Birding* 2 (Jan. 1970): 3.

258   "Sooner or later": Ibid.

258   "It has been obvious": Ibid.

260   "insist that our brand of birdwatching": Roger Tory Peterson, speech transcript, "Roger Tory Peterson Reminisces," *Birding* 7 (Mar. 1975): 63.

262   "this may well be": James A. Tucker, "*Birding* and Conservation," *Birding* 2 (Jan. 1970): 3.

270   "One of your friends": Eirik A. T. Blom, "North American Birding: The Next Twenty-five Years," *Birding* (Feb. 1994): 27.

BIBLIOGRAPHY

Adams, Majorie Valentine. *Bird-witched!* Austin, TX: University of Texas Press, 2005.

American Birding Association. "Articles of the Constitution." *Birding* 2 (July 1970), unnumbered insert.

Anon. "Annie Montague Alexander." University of California Museum of Paleontology. http://www.ucmp.berkeley.edu/history/alexander.html.

————. "Annie Montague Alexander." Museum of Vertebrate Zoology. http://www.mip.berkeley.edu/mvz/history/Alexander.html.

Balch, Larry. "A Report from the President." *Birding* 19 (Jan. 1987): 2–4.

Bent, A. C. *Life Histories of North American Flycatchers, Larks, Swallows and Their Allies.* Washington, DC: Smithsonian Institution, 1942.

Bousman, William G. *Local [Santa Clara Co., CA] Ornithology in the 19th and Early 20th Centuries.* Santa Clara Valley Audubon Society. http://www.scvas.org/pdf/localornithology.pdf.

Broun, Maurice. *Hawks Aloft.* Kutztown, PA: Kutztown Publishing Co., 1948.

Cornell Lab of Ornithology. "History of the Macaulay Library." http://www.birds.cornell.edu/MacaulayLibrary/About/mlHistory.html.

Drennan, Susan. "McCaskie as Mentor." *American Birds* 46 (Spring 1992): 204–213.

Floyd, Ted. "The History of *Birding*, Pt. I, 1968–1974," *Birding* 38 (Jan. 2006): 20–21.

————. "The History of *Birding*, Pt. II, 1975–1980," *Birding* 38 (Mar. 2006): 20–21.

————. "The History of *Birding*, Pt. III, 1981–1987." *Birding* 38 (May 2006): 18–19.

————. "The History of *Birding*, Pt. IV, 1988–1993." *Birding* 38 (July 2006): 18–19.

Hawn, Amanda T. "In California, Ecologists Retrace a Pioneer's Footsteps." *New York Times*, Nov. 7, 2006.

Jarmamillo, Alvaro. "Tales from the Cryptic Species." *Birding* 38 (May 2006): 30–38.

Keith, G. Stuart. "ABA's First Convention." *Birding* 5 (Sept. 1973): 125–134.

Lowther, Peter E. "Alder Flycatcher, *Empidonax alnorum.*" In *The Birds of North America.* No. 446. Ed. A. Poole and F. Gill. Philadelphia: Birds of North America, 1999.

Lukas, David. "Pacific-slope Flycatcher, *Empidonax difficilis* and Cordilleran Flycatcher, *Empidonax occidentalis.*" In *The Birds of North America.* No. 556. Ed. A. Poole and F. Gill. Philadelphia: Birds of North America, 2000.

————. "Point Reyes Bird Observatory Profile." *Birding* 31 (Dec. 1999): 532–535.

Pettingill, Olin Sewall. *A Guide to Bird Finding East of the Mississippi.* New York: Oxford University Press, 1951.

————. *A Guide to Bird Finding West of the Mississippi.* New York: Oxford University Press, 1953.

PRBO Conservation Science homepage, 2006. http://www.prbo.org/cms/index.php.

Roberson, Don. "A Birding Milestone" (Guy McCaskie). *Birding* 38 (July 2006): 16.
———. "California and Stallcup—the Best of Both in '74." *Birding* 7 (May 1975): 172–178.
———. "Who was Who in California Birding, 1965–1989." April 2005. http://montereybay.com/creagrus/CAwhoswhointro.html.
Rutkowski, Sandy. "The Reel Thing" (history of Borror Lab of Bioacoustics). *Ohio State Synergy* 17 (1997–98 Academic Year). http://researchnews.osu.edu/synergy/borror.htm.
Ryan, Richard. "Birding in the New York Area: Looking Back." *Birding* 30 (Oct. 1998): 384–389.
Sedgwick, James A. "Willow Flycatcher, *Empidonax traillii*." In *The Birds of North America*. No. 533. Ed. A. Poole and F. Gill. Philadelphia: Birds of North America, 2000.
Shearwater, Debra Love. "A Brief History of Pelagic Birding in North America." *Birding* 36 (Dec. 2004): 634–638.
———. "I Thought it Was Magic." *Birding* 36 (Dec. 2004): 582–585.
Small, Arnold. "Birding in California: Looking Back." *Birding* 30 (Oct. 1998): 388–391.
Smyrl, Vivian Elizabeth. "Edgar Bryan Kincaid Jr." *Handbook of Texas Online*. Texas State Historical Society, June 6, 2001. http://www.tsha.utexas.edu/handbook/online/articles/KK/fki52.html.
Wolfe, Roger. "Interview with Rollo Beck biographer Matt James." *Surfbirds.com*. April 11, 2006. http://www.surfbirds.com/blog/seawolfe/1298/Interview+with+Rollo+Beck+biographer+Matt+James.html.

CHAPTER 8

Elements of this chapter were adapted from "A Bird in the Hand," first published in *Nature Conservancy* 55 (Winter 2005): 20–27.

Citations

283   "This all-out May-day tournament": Roger Tory Peterson, *Birds Over America* (Cornwall, NY: Cornwall Press, 1948), 26–27.
284   The really unfortunate feature of the "Christmas Lists": Witmer Stone, *Auk* 53 (Apr. 1936): 239.
284   "Are you a bird watcher": Roger Tory Peterson, *Bird Watcher's Digest* (Mar.–Apr. 1984), reprinted in *All Things Reconsidered,* ed. Roger Tory Peterson and Bill Thompson III, (Boston: Houghton Mifflin, 2006), 10.
288   "I never doubted I would die": Phoebe Snetsinger, "Birding on Borrowed Time," *Birding* 22 (Feb. 1990): 29.
289   "It occurred to me": Roger Tory Peterson, *Wild America* (Boston: Houghton Mifflin, 1955), 15.

293 "The Big Year had been a great excuse": Kenn Kaufman, *The Kingbird Highway* (Boston: Houghton Mifflin, 1997), 305.

293 "I didn't need anybody to like my project": Jim Vardaman, quoted in "Jim Vardaman," *Birding* 12 (Feb. 1980): 39.

294 "I decided": Kenn Kaufman, quoted in "A Man of His Bird," *Grist*, May 9, 2005, http://www.grist.org/comments/interactivist/2005/05/09/kaufman/.

298 "race-obsessed, guilt-ridden, high priests of liberalism": Letter to editor, *Birding* 31 (Aug. 1999): 407.

298 "white Americans writing about white American topics": Ibid., 407–408.

301 "The art of bird watching": Joseph J. Hickey, *A Guide to Bird Watching* (New York: Oxford University Press, 1943), 147.

303 "evidently migrates to some extent": Arthur Cleveland Bent, *Life Histories of North American Birds of Prey*, vol. 2 (Washington, DC: Smithsonian Institution, 1938), 237.

BIBLIOGRAPHY

Baicich, Paul J. "A Road Not Taken." *Birding* 26 (Feb. 1994): 18.

Cannings, Richard J. "Northern Saw-whet Owl (*Aegolius acadicus*)." In *The Birds of North America*. No. 42. Ed. A. Poole and F. Gill. Philadelphia: Birds of North America, 1993.

Cordell, H. Ken, and Nancy G. Herbert. "The Popularity of Birding is Still Growing." *Birding* 34 (Feb. 2002): 54–61.

Davis, William E. Jr. *Dean of the Birdwatchers: A Biography of Ludlow Griscom*. Washington, DC: Smithsonian Institution Press, 1994.

Eisenmann, Eugene, et al. "Thirty-second supplement to the American Ornithologists' Union Check-list of North American Birds." *Auk* 90 (Apr. 1973): 411–419.

Green, Paul. "Stuart Keith, 1931–2003." *Birding* 35 (June 2003): 230–231.

———. "Thirty-third supplement to the American Ornithologists' Union Check-list of North American Birds." *Auk* 93 (Oct. 1976): 875–879.

Haas, Franklin C. "70 Million Birders?" *Birding* 34 (Aug. 2002): 314–320.

Hartley, David. "Birding Festivals." *Birding* 37 (Jan. 2005): 34–37.

Hickey, Joseph J. *A Guide to Bird Watching*. New York and London: Oxford University Press, 1943.

Kaufman, Kenn. *Advanced Birding*. Boston: Houghton Mifflin, 1990.

———. *Birds of North America*. Boston: Houghton Mifflin, 2000.

———. *Guía de campo a las aves de Norteamérica*. Boston: Houghton Mifflin, 2005.

———. "Perspectives in Birding." *Birding* 26 (Feb. 1994): 13–25.

Keith, Stuart. "700 in North America." *Birding* 4 (Mar. 1972): 114–116.

Magpie Monitor homepage, Oct. 26, 2006. http://www.magpiemonitor.org/index
.html.

Moss, Stephen. *A Bird in the Bush*. London: Aurum Press, 2004.

Obmascik, Mark. *The Big Year*. New York: Free Press, 2004.

Parker, Ted III. "626 Species in One Year: A New North American Record." *Birding*
4 (Jan. 1972): 6–10.

Reid, Martin. "Why are we so white?" *Birding* 31 (Feb. 1999): 12–13.

Semo, Larry, ed. *2005 ABA List and Big Day Reports*. Colorado Springs, CO:
American Birding Association, 2006.

Shin, Hyon B., and Rosalind Bruno. *Language Use and English-Speaking Ability*.
Washington, DC: U.S. Census Bureau, October 2003. http://www.census.gov/
prod/2003pubs/c2kbr-29.pdf.

Snetsinger, Phoebe. *Birding on Borrowed Time*. Colorado Springs, CO: American
Birding Association, 2003.

Taylor, Joe. "Is 700 Possible?" *Birding* 2 (July 1970): 10–11.

Weidensaul, Scott. "Close Focus: Joe Taylor." *Bird Watcher's Digest* (July 1992),
110–117.

Index